Poor Bloody
Infantry
1939–1945

The only way you get out of the Infantry
is on a stretcher or six feet under.

Traditional Infantry gripe

POOR BLOODY INFANTRY

1939–1945

by

Charles Whiting

SPELLMOUNT

First published in 1987 by Stanley Paul & Co. Ltd

Copyright © Charles Whiting 1987, 2007
Map copyright © Charles Whiting 1987, 2007

10-ISBN 1-86227-377-4
13-ISBN 978-1-86227-377-1

This edition published in Great Britain in 2007 by
SPELLMOUNT (PUBLISHERS) LTD.
The Mill, Brimscombe Port, Stroud
Gloucestershire GL5 2QG

Tel: 0044 (0) 1453 883300
Fax: 0044 (0) 1453 883233
www.spellmount.com

1 3 5 7 9 8 6 4 2

British Library Cataloguing in Publication Data:
A catalogue record for this book is available
from the British Library

The right of Charles Whiting to be identified
as the author of this work has been asserted by him
in accordance with the Copyright, Designs
and Patents Act 1988

Printed in Great Britain by
Oaklands Book Services
Stonehouse, Gloucestershire GL10 3RQ

Contents

BOOK THREE, 1942–1943

BOOK FOUR, 1944–1945

To David Oakley Whiting, my grandson,
born the day this book was completed.
Let us hope he never has to fight
with the Poor Bloody Infantry.

Author's note

This book is not a history.

It has nothing to do with politics, strategy, national interest, the grand design. If anyone reads an indictment into it of the men and the policies which led to the mistakes for which the infantry paid the price – in their own blood – let them. It is simply the story of a gravely neglected, unglamorous breed – the infantryman of World War Two.

It tells the story of young men of various nationalities – in their own words – who had to learn the old, old lessons yet once again; had to learn anew what their fathers had learned twenty-odd years before – about cowardice and courage, cruelty and comradeship, sudden, violent death.

Nobody in World War Two paid a higher price for the failure of the politicians and the generals, whatever their nationality, than the infantry. Most battalions engaged in the fighting, whatever the front, had a 100 per cent turnover, due to battle casualties; some went as high as 200 per cent.

The US 3rd Infantry Division, for example, which fought in Africa, Italy, and southern France lost a staggering 30,000 casualties in its three-year combat career – a loss the size of the population of a small town. In a mere 11 months of battle in north-west Europe, the British 43rd Infantry Division suffered 12,482 battle casualties. This meant that the rifle companies had a 150 per cent loss rate, for nearly one-third of the Division was engaged in administrative duties and never entered combat.

Yet in spite of the terrible casualties, with a young subaltern's life expectancy limited to 30 days in 1944–5 and that of the ordinary footslogger to perhaps twice that, there was a great, fine side to the infantryman's existence. In spite of the fear, the hardship, the tiredness, the hunger and cold, there was also the comradeship and that wonderful feeling of security which, in the darkest moments, they drew from the close proximity of staunch and reliable comrades. This feeling alone seemed to make their lives bearable. It was that comradeship of the times when they had been young and in constant danger that would remain with them always – those who survived.

They were condemned men from the start, and they knew it. Going up the line for the first time, young Private Wingfield of the Queen's Royal Regiment was lectured thus by his section corporal: 'Now consider our case. We're in trouble 24 hours a day. We get used to the idea of danger until even Death is the normal thing, so we build up a way of life, a state of mind, at first a resistance to Death, a fight for life, but that finally becomes a submission and resignation to constant danger. You've heard the old gag, "Any change in Infantry is bound to be for the worse". If you accept that, you've conquered Fear. Death doesn't worry you any more ... We have little hope of survival. We accept that and spin it out as best we can. We don't have any distractions like comfort. Our life goes along smoothly at a permanent level of tension. We're as good as dead. A slit trench, after all, is the nearest thing to a grave we'll be in while we're alive. It *is* a grave!'*

Before the campaign in north-west Europe was over, that corporal would be dead and Lance-Corporal Wingfield would be lying under shellfire with two tracer bullets in his hips in no-man's land nearly dead. They had 'spun out' their few remaining months of life. But Death had come for them in the end, as it always did for those brave young men in field-grey, olive drab, khaki. What else could their fate be? For they were the 'P.B.I.', as they called themselves in wry resignation – THE POOR BLOODY INFANTRY ...

For their great help in the preparation of this book, I should like to thank the officials of the British Army's Correction Centre at Colchester (the once-feared 'glasshouse'), the West German Military Research Office in Freiburg; and naturally Messrs Tom Dickinson (the New York Central Library), Hy Schorr, Tom Stubbs (Bitburg Air Base) and Eric Taylor (my fellow author) – all of whom once belonged in another time to that select band – the P.B.I.

---

* R.W. Wingfield: *The Only Way Out.* (Hutchinson)

BOOK ONE
1939–1940

No great dependence is to be placed on the
eagerness of young soldiers for action, for the
prospect of fighting is agreeable to those who are
strangers to it.

Vegetius, Roman military writer,
4th century AD

I

'Farley, My Lad. There's bloody big news. The War's on!'

Now they waited.

Almost a year before they had waited like this, too. In their barracks, their tented camps, their drill halls, church halls and the like. It had poured down for almost the two weeks that the emergency had lasted. In the end, however, the old man had come back from Munich, waving his scrap of worthless paper, promising 'peace in our time' and the reservists and territorials had been sent home again, five pounds the richer. Would it be the same this time?

For the Regulars there was the usual compulsory church parade. But the reservists and the territorials, many of them locked in their temporary accommodation in case they deserted, were glued to the wireless, just like the civilians outside. For at ten o'clock this Sunday morning, the BBC had announced that the Prime Minister would speak to the nation at 11.15. And they all knew why. Three days before, Germany had invaded Poland. So far no reply had been received from 'Herr Hitler', as they were still calling him in the BBC news bulletin, to Britain's demand that he withdraw his troops from Poland.

So they waited, smoking their Woodbines, listening to Parry Jones singing *The Passionate Shepherd*, followed by a recorded talk on 'Making the Most of Tinned Foods', until the tired, old man who governed the destinies of the British Empire began to speak. He was now 70 and his voice was infinitely weary. His news was bad.

'I am speaking to you from the Cabinet Room at No. 10 Downing Street,' he told the tense young men in khaki crowded round their pear-shaped radio sets, hands on each other's shoulders, even their 'coffin nails' forgotten now. 'This morning, the British Ambassador in Berlin handed the German government a final note, stating that unless the British government heard from them by 11 o'clock that they were prepared at once to withdraw their troops from Poland, a state of war would exist between us. I have to tell you now that no such undertaking has been received, and that consequently this country is at war with Germany ... May God bless you all. May he defend the right, for it is evil things that we shall be fighting against – brute force, bad faith, injustice, oppression and persecution; and against them I am certain that the right will prevail.'

Hurriedly the young soldiers, who would now be doing that fighting, sprang to attention as the first strains of the national anthem followed Premier Chamberlain's speech. He would be dead before that right prevailed – *in bed*! Many of his listeners in khaki would be, too. But they would die violently in remote places, thousands of miles away from their homes: places whose very names they did not know as yet, or ones which were not even marked on the maps. These young men, mostly in their early twenties, would die on the bathing beaches of northern France, the parched hills of Greece and Crete, the arid wastes of the Western Desert, the steaming, rotting jungles of South-East Asia, the fetid coal mines of Upper Silesia, the concentration camps of southern Germany. They would die in their hundreds, thousands, in great battles. They would die slowly of tropical diseases, broken men, abandoned to their fate in the Jap slave camps. They would die alone, hunted with every man's hand against them, their graves never found.

For the next six years they would live, love, fight – and die – on three continents, undergoing experiences of a kind which were – on this Sunday – beyond their wildest dreams. Of every hundred young men already 'with the colours' and of those who would continue to be called up over the years to come, perhaps only 15 of them would ever see the front line. But these young men would all right. They'd see fighting enough!

These callow young men, projected from their narrow materialistic world of pay day, pub, *palais de danse* and 'pictures', would grow in stature month by month. An immense change would take place in these ordinary young men. For many of them this new world into which they had now entered would be sordid, violent, but also, at times, heroic. Their own lives often would be short, brutal, desperate. But for some of them this new violent existence would allow them to realize that confused adolescent dream of self-sacrifice, true, loyal comradeship; perhaps even greatness. For these young men would, from now on, be at the 'sharp end'. They were the infantry, the ones who, in the last resort, went in with the bayonet and fought hand-to-hand, just as their primitive ancestors had done. One day, after they had been 'blooded', they would begin to call themselves, wearily and cynically, 'the P.B.I.' – *the poor bloody infantry*! But in the end, that cynical label would become a badge of honour. For those who survived. …

They had been mobilizing for over a week now, the regulars, the reservists, the territorials, the few keen volunteers (for unlike 1914, there was no great outburst of patriotic fervour and a flood of volunteers at the recruiting offices – two decades of anti-war propaganda had seen to that). For most of the reservists and territorials, the call to mobilize on 24 August,

1939, came as a shock. H.F. Ellis was in his office when he received 'the summons' by phone. 'I remember laying down the receiver and looking slowly round the office. It seemed much the same. The sun still streamed through the window onto the papers on my desk, the half-written letter, the note to ring up So-and-so at four, the memo about tomorrow's meeting. On the window sill lay the brown-paper parcel containing the new pullover to which I had treated myself during the lunch hour. Across the street a man suspended in a cradle of ropes and planks was busily cleaning the windows of the building opposite. It was incredible that I should have been concerned, a few short moments ago, with the phrasing of a letter that seemed to belong to so remote a point in time, to have been written by so dim and irrecoverable a personality. This sense of being suddenly cut off from one's own past and future is the strongest recollection of this peculiar day.'[1]

'Old sweat' Spike Mays felt not only shock, but anger, too, when he received his 'call-up', which was 'short and to the point'. It read, 'Report Balham HQ 0900 Hours Field Service Marching Order'. But when he reached Paddington Station, where he was to take the train, he found all was chaos. 'Droves of worried women and multitudes of children filled almost every inch of the station, waiting for the evacuation specials. ... One woman committed suicide near a barrier; others were weeping and shrieking out the names of children who had been separated from them'.[2]

Finally he made it, to listen to Chamberlain's announcement that Sunday, followed eight minutes later by the first dread wail of the air-raid sirens, which were sounding now all over southern England. 'We all looked skywards and I could see the apprehension in the faces of our married lads.' 'It can't last,' he thought, 'it'll be all over by Christmas.'[3]

Some had been mobilized with the greatest of difficulty, especially the territorials of the ill-fated 51st Highland Division, which, within the year, would suffer the ignominy of mass surrender to the Germans. For they were recruited in the remote highlands, in some cases, where sheep outnumbered men. Here commanding officers had to allow several days to travel round the various collecting points for their companies, using not only motor transport, but horses and boats as well to cross to the Outer Hebrides. Many of these men, who were finally assembled (as the official forms ran out, mobilization orders were issued on pieces of toilet roll), would not see another Christmas at home until 1945. Some would never see another Christmas at all. ...

A few responded to the call with alacrity, even enthusiasm. Archaeologist and future brigadier Mortimer Wheeler, when he heard the news of impending war, hurriedly left 'the archaeological destinies of Normandy', where he had been leading a dig, to his partners and took the next boat-train for London. By lunchtime he was in Enfield, looking for a house

5

where he could recruit what he dubbed 'Enfield's Own'.

He found one and swiftly drafted an appeal to the patriotic citizens of the borough to come forward for 'King and Country'.

The next day his appeal, 'decked out prettily in red, white and blue', was printed and adorned every shop window in Enfield. Now he needed his 'staff'. They turned out to be the future MO of the 'Enfield's Own', his son, another colleague in the field of archaeology, and a regular sergeant, who was the only one who wore uniform. And so the five of them waited for the flood of recruits.

The start was very slow. Their first recruit was an immense man, who 'surveyed with mild surprise the threadbare scene in front of him' and announced his name with a suspicion of hesitation, almost apology, as A. Goodman. 'Enfield's Own' had its first 'other rank' – in the shape of the future Lord Goodman.[4]

Another volunteer that September was Thomas Firbank, the Canadian novelist, whose book on Welsh sheep farming, *I Bought A Mountain*, was a best-seller. He, too, hurried from France, eager to join the Guards. His aspirations were no higher than becoming an ordinary guardsman. To his surprise, however, he found himself being ushered in to the regimental adjutant of the Coldstream Guards, who told him in a matter-of-fact way, 'I don't know if we can get you a commission right away. Hang on for a minute.'

Ten minutes later the dazed novelist found himself outside the barracks once more, in possession of a 'chit' from the regimental colonel stating that he was accepted as a potential officer in the Guards provided he passed the medical. Flushed with his good fortune, the future Guardee dined off lobster and a great deal of beer before presenting himself to the recruiting officer's MO for his medical. Everything went well until he was told, 'We wish to take a sample. Hurry please.'

'My exertions among the medical men without had taken effect on a bladder distended by quantities of the best City ale. I was much relieved to oblige the acolyte, but it was immediately apparent that my beaker was a paltry receptacle. Once the flood of my incontinence was loosed, there was no withholding.

'"Another beaker!" I cried in anguish, as I snatched the chalice in the nick of time from a startled fellow-disciple.

'"Again", I cried. "And again! And again!"

'The shrouded novices ran to my bidding. The high priests deserted their tables to watch this monstrous ceremonial. The chain of examination was broken up as all beakers diverted to my purpose.'[5] Then it was over and he could breathe a sigh of relief. He was passed A1. ...

If in Britain there was no great rush to volunteer that September, it was different in the Empire. On the very same day that Chamberlain had declared war on Germany, the dominions began immediately to follow suit. New Zealand was one of the first, though the skeleton military force which did exist was poorly prepared for the intake of volunteers. As Brigadier Howard Kippenberger, who was to see much action in the Middle East and Italy later, recalled: 'We had a week before the men came in. The huts were barely finished and ablution stands not completed ... as the drafts came in by special trains. ... All were in civilian clothes and many were far from sober. As I watched some of my men trudge in, I remarked to Gordon Washbourn, "This is going to be the best infantry in the world."[6] And one day the Brigadier would be proved right.'

It was no different in Australia and Canada. In the latter country young Farley Mowat, one day to be famous for his nature books, was painting the porch of his clapboard house in Richmond Hill, Ontario, on that Sunday when his father drove up. He looked as if he might have had a drink or two. 'Farley, my lad,' he cried excitedly, 'there's bloody big news. *The war is on!* ... I'm to go back in with the rank of major, bum arm and all. There'll be a place for you, too. You'll have to sweat a bit for it, of course, but if you keep your nose clean and work like hell, there'll be a King's Commission.'[7]

His son thought the old man spoke 'as if he was offering me a knighthood'; but he 'kept his nose clean' and in due course was rewarded by being offered a commission in the Hastings and Prince Edward Infantry Regiment, known familiarly if inelegantly, as 'The Hasty Pees'. Three years later in Italy, the teenage volunteer would find himself looking down at the dead and wounded faces of his once so confident friends of that September and crying uncontrollably.

But for the time being these young volunteers for Canada's infantry regiments, eager for some desperate glory, had to be content, just like the Australians and New Zealanders, with training with the meagre resources available to them. The Royal Regiment of Canada would learn the British Army's centuries-old drill in civilian clothes and shoes, till the latter fell apart. The drill sergeants of the Les Fusiliers Mont Royal would instruct, clad in civilian suits, too, but with their stripes pinned to their sleeves. As one of them, Sergeant Dumais, recalled after the war: 'We had no equipment, apart from a rifle for every fourth or fifth man and about 10 old worn-out machine guns left over from the 1914 war ... When I was commanding the anti-tank platoon, we not only had no trucks to tow the guns – we had no guns! We learned the mechanics from a handbook and carried out sham drill in front of a picture of a gun. Nobody in the platoon had ever seen a real one. It was difficult to keep up the men's interest with this sort of thing; they tried hard though and took up position around the picture imagining things as best they could. The loading of ammunition was an easy job since we had none.'[8] Two years later nearly half the men of that same 2nd Canadian Infantry Division would be lost in their first action in Dieppe, dead, wounded or captured.

Regulars and volunteers alike, they came not just from the free dominions, but from the colonies, too. The million-strong infantry of the British Empire was made up of men of every colour and creed. There was the Gold Coast Regiment, the King's Own African Rifles, the Sudan Regiment, the Burma Rifles, the Hong Kong Regiment, etc. etc. One day West African parachutists would drop in Burma – 'Do we really get a parachute?' one was reported as asking. Gurkhas would slice off the heads of surprised Germans in Italy. Indians would fight our erstwhile allies the French in Syria.

Of course, India supplied the largest force of infantry for the 'King Emperor'. In spite of the Congress Party and its status as 'an oppressed country' (at least in the eyes of many native politicians), there was no shortage of men coming forward to fight. Young men of every race and religious creed flocked to the recruiting centres in their thousands and hundreds of thousands. There would, in the end, be infantry of the Indian Army fighting on every front over three continents.

And they would fight, not only for the 'King Emperor'. In due course, several thousand would change sides. An Indian National Army would be formed from former prisoners by the Japanese, and the 'Gandhi Brigade' would fight against their fellow countrymen and the Gurkhas, who refused to let them surrender until they were ordered to do so by their officers.

Although Hitler thought little of soldiers whose religion forbade them 'to crush a fly', he, too, formed an 'Indian Legion' of renegade Indians, Sikhs, and Muslims.* Under the command of a German colonel they, too, would fight against British, Canadian and American soldiers, though admittedly not very effectively.

But all this was in the future. Now, as this eventful 3 September, which would change the face of the world, came to an end, a violent electrical storm broke out in the north. Lightning flashed over the North Sea, as the blackout was enforced for the first time. A heavy drizzle began to fall, as if Nature itself was joining in the general mood of apprehension and uncertainty.

On guard on the Lincolnshire coast near Immingham, two 20-year-old territorials, armed with nothing more lethal than bayonets welded on to steel poles, watched as barrage balloon after barrage balloon suddenly 'fizzed up' and came fluttering down in flames. They had been told seven days before, as soon as they had been called up, that England could expect a German invasion almost immediately. Now they wondered if this were 'it' and they were fated to defend this desolate stretch of the Lincolnshire coast all by themselves.

---

* Depending on your point of view, they could also be regarded as patriots. Both groups are still honoured in India today.

Already they had suffered their first 'casualty on active service' in the shape of 'Egg-and-Bacon Dicko' (nicknamed thus due to his fondness for that particular breakfast dish). Private Dickinson had been fooling around, putting his finger in one of the holes of a gun-trail, when the piece had fallen and neatly sliced off the digit. Were they now fated to be the next active service casualties? For directly to their front in the flickering gloom the two apprehensive territorials could see a score of dark, bent shapes slowly advancing upon them.

'It's no good, Coupie,' Private Buckley whispered to his friend Private Coupe, 'We've got to do something.'

'But what can we do, Bucko?' the other territorial hissed apprehensively, gripping his pike more tightly in hands which were suddenly sticky with sweat.

'We've got to charge 'em!' the other young man replied with sudden determination. 'Come on!'

So the two of them charged, yelling their heads off wildly, determined to sacrifice themselves, if necessary, against the German invaders, bodies tensed, waiting for the first burst of German fire. But no enemy bullets came their way. Instead the young men charging across the rough, wet cliff-top were met by a series of frightened baas. They were attacking, as ex-Sergeant-Major Coates put it wryly 40-odd years later, *a bunch of bloody frightened sheep!*[9]

It was midnight on 3 September, 1939. The phoney war had commenced!

II

'Are you a credit to your Unit?'

Now the regular and territorial divisions had gone to France to form the BEF (the British Expeditionary Force). They had departed secretly. No music, no song on their lips, laden like mules, ammunition boots crunching on the gravel, gone by night, using several ports, some 150,000 of them. Under the command of Lord Gort, VC, they were to be placed at the disposal of the French, who would fit them into the line in due course. What they would be asked to do, or what the huge French Army would do, was anyone's guess. For while Poland, on whose account Britain and France had gone to war, bled and died, the Western Allies sat behind the Maginot Line – and did absolutely nothing!

One British officer, commanding the 3rd Infantry Division ('The Iron Division'), a somewhat abrasive, pushy little fellow called Montgomery was glad of the respite, for he considered that 'the British Army was totally unfit to fight a first-class war on the continent of Europe … In the years preceding the outbreak of war no large-scale exercises with troops had been held in England for some time. Indeed, the Regular Army was unfit to take part in a realistic exercise. The Field Army had an inadequate signals system, no administrative backing and no organization for high command; all these had to be improvised on mobilization. The transport was inadequate and was completed on mobilization by vehicles requisitioned from civilian firms. Much of the transport of my division consisted of civilian vans and lorries from the towns of England; they were in bad repair and when my division moved from the ports up to its concentration area near the French frontier, the countryside of France was strewn with broken-down vehicles.'[1]

Now while the regulars and territorials began to settle in France, the cadres in the depots up and down the United Kingdom started to train the thousands of young men being 'called up' under the National Service (Armed Forces) Act, which had been passed within a few hours of the war having been declared. It made all fit men between the ages of 18 and 41 liable for military service.

Unlike 1914 there was no rush of volunteers. 'When they need me, they'll send for me,' seemed to have been the prevailing attitude. Some men heaved a heartfelt sigh of relief when doctors told them that they were unfit for service. One Edinburgh medical student was so overjoyed when he was told by the examining doctor, 'Laddie, ye'r in a tairrable state!' that he went out and got drunk yet once again.[2] But most went willingly enough, even though the pay for a private was only a paltry two shillings a day; and from this miserable sum a married man was forced to 'allot' (this was the official term) part to his wife.

For most of the young men called up in 1939, it all started in some grim 18th-century barracks or some remote camp in Yorkshire or on Salisbury Plain. Here they were shorn of their hair, the Army's 'short back and sides', often known as the 'tuppeny all-off'. Kit was issued next. 'If it touches, it fits,' the quartermaster – or 'quarter bloke', as they would soon come to call him – would say at their protests that this or that was not their size. Thereupon they were ordered to pack up their civilian clothes and send them home. For most of them this seemed to break the last link with their former civilian life.

In their stiff new khaki uniforms, which smelled of the anti-gas chemical with which they were impregnated, and their cumbersome 'unbroken-in' boots they would be marched to their squad hut. This was long and narrow usually, bare of any furniture save a coal bin for the gleaming stove, a long, scrubbed wooden table, and beds lining each wall. All the windows would be opened exactly and uniformly half-way, even if there were a freezing gale blowing outside. As a result, the hut would be often very cold, but the fire remained unlit. For in those hard days young infantry soldiers did not feel the cold until after '1600 hours' on working days and '1400 hours' on Sundays.

The beds would now be 'allotted' and would become the recruit's 'home' for the period of his training. Sometimes they were double-deckers made of wood, but mostly they were iron cots with, at the foot, a square wooden box and, at the head, two shelves, on which in due course would be displayed all the personal articles, such as shaving kit, boot brushes, 'button stick' (used for cleaning brass buttons), for the daily morning inspection. On the bed itself there were the three regulation 'biscuits' which could be made up into a mattress at night. Now, however, they rested one upon another, beneath four blankets. Soon the recruit's name, number, etc., would be sewn on each blanket, and he would be taught the daily task of making them up.

This entailed folding three blankets into precise squares, with the labels directly underneath each other; the fourth blanket would then be wrapped round the other three to form a rigid, 'squared-off' pack. But the daily morning ritual of making up the bed did not end there. For now each bed, with its biscuits, blankets and the rest of the 'laid-out' kit had to be lined up in an exact line. Otherwise the squad sergeant might well work himself up into one of those artificial rages which were fearful to behold and go down the line slashing at the laboriously laid-out kits with his swagger cane, knocking them on the floor so that the whole procedure had to be done all over again.

The squad sergeants, with the 'lance-jacks' (lance-corporals) who assisted them, were formidable men, feared more by the recruit than any general. Red of face, endowed with tremendous voices, often wearing a small trim moustache, they came basically in two kinds. There were shouters, who possessed a tremendous vocabulary of phrases and words unknown to the recruits up to now. 'I'm going to make soldiers out of you bunch of pregnant penguins whether you like it or not!' they'd bellow at the quaking recruits. 'You might have broken yer mothers' hearts, but yer won't bleeding break mine. Now get fell in!' Then there was the other kind, the deceptively quiet type whom Guardsman Firbank encountered on his first day in the Coldstream Guards. Sergeant Smartly impressed the recruits 'with an air of infallibility, with self-confidence without cock-suredness and, above all, with inherent decency. Here's a nice man we thought. He'll check our faults but he'll do it in the right way.'

But Guardsman Firbank and his fellow would-be officers were in for a surprise. Just as the former had made his assessment of their new squad commander, another recruit strayed into their room absent-mindedly, and seeing it wasn't his, exclaimed, 'Sorry, Sarge. Wrong room.'

'Lance-Sergeant Smartly whipped round on him like a viper. His moustache quivered with emotion and his hands clenched until the knuckles showed white. He took on greater stature and then let out a bellow that frightened all of us. The recruit reeled back and put a hand on the door-post to steady himself. This was my first experience of the power of the human voice.

'"Don't call me 'sarge', you horrible, idle, dozy man, you! Come here. Double! Double! I said! Turn your wrists in when you stand to attention! Now what do you call me? Sergeant, yes! What are you doing in here? Come in without thinking? Well think. Or I'll put you in the Guard Room. Now, get out. *Double!*"'[3]

He doubled away, as if the Devil himself were after him. ...

'If it moves,' they learned to quip, 'salute it. If it doesn't *paint it!*' For now bull (short for 'bullshit') reigned supreme. They soon learnt how to scrub a floor with a toothbrush, dust the holly leaves of the bushes around their huts, give their dull ammunition boots the look of patent leather through hours of patient spitting, polishing and buffing with a toothbrush handle. The buttons of their collarless shirts were metal and they were polished, too, even though the shirts were hidden beneath tunics. The insteps of their boots were polished, just as the insides of their badges were. Night after night, these young recruits to the infantry would spend hours, sitting on their hard beds, shining and polishing and blancoing their webbing equipment until the squad hut smelled permanently of Brasso and blanco powder.

Of course, being the British Army, drill was paramount. As Brigadier Sir John Smyth, VC, wrote at the time: 'it has been found from experience that units which are good at drill and which are well turned out rarely fail in battle. At the head of the Army ... men like Lord Gort and General Dill ... were both great believers in drill and many of the senior officers were apt to judge a unit entirely by its appearance on parade.'[4] So many hours were spent preparing for total war, when the enemy himself was gradually dispensing with drill (by 1943 the SS had virtually given up drill altogether), by learning the intricate 300-year-old drill movements of the Regular Army. How to present arms for a general officer; how to salute the dead by a reversal of arms; how to salute an officer below the rank of lieutenant-colonel; how to salute while riding on a bicycle with a package under one arm, even!

But as the weeks passed and they began to fill out with the good solid Army fare, their cheeks reddened by hours spent in the open in one of the worst winters within living memory, they started to look and feel like soldiers. They had started to develop an ease of movement, a perceptible arrogance in the posture of the head and shoulders as they marched and marched, even to church to the compulsory Sunday church parades. 'C of Es over here, Roman Candles over there, odds and sods and 'ebrews *stand fast!*'

Three times a day they would march to the cookhouse, swinging their metal plates at one side. Here they would sit 12 to a trestle table, elbows to ribs, as the big 'dixies' of 'M & V'* stew, spotted dick, and prunes and custard were brought to be polished off in double quick time.

As always the Orderly Officer, followed by a grim-faced sergeant, clipboard at the ready, would make his appearance and ask, as the sergeant bellowed 'Sit to attention', 'Any complaints?'

But however bad the food was, nobody complained, for the cooks' revenge could be terrible. 'So yer told 'is nibs ye'r not getting enough grub, eh?' Thereupon the offending soldier's plate would be heaped with mountains of mashed potatoes, chunks of half-cooked cheap mutton, seas of greasy gravy and he would be ordered to eat 'the lot'. He would, too. For the penalty for the 'criminal waste of Government property, i.e. food' could be a month's 'jankers', which meant that every evening would be spent painting, cleaning, scraping huge bathtubs of potatoes in cold water until the 'criminal's' hands were as grey and wrinkled as those of an old charwoman.

---

* Meat and vegetable stew out of tins.

But in spite of the incessant drill and the constant 'bull', they were also learning their future craft: the lethal business of being an infantryman. They practised bayonet training with the stilted formality of the pre-war drillbook. But the end run did approach the exhilarating thrill of the real thing. '*Get in there!*' the drill instructors would yell, '*Give him the frigging point! … Rip his bleeding guts open man, willyer!*' And they would savage the straw dummies, slicing in the long bayonet, ripping it out and then following with a savage blow from the cruel, brass-shod butt.

They learned how to throw live grenades. At first most of them were a little scared. The British Army's standard grenade was the Mills bomb, designed to fit snugly into the right hand, while the detonator, which would set off the explosive charge, was held in place by a lever, secured by a split pin. Once the pin was pulled out and the lever was released, the hand grenade would explode within four or five seconds.

The first time the nervous recruits would be led into the throwing pit by a sergeant, often by an officer, and then detailed to throw the grenades individually. Each man in turn aimed at the target some 20 yards beyond the pit, withdrawing the split pin with one hand and lobbing the bomb like bowling with a cricket ball with the other. Then came the sharp command '*duck!*'. If he was smart and not too nervous, the recruit would do so. Others were mesmerized by the whole business and would remain standing to receive a smart slap across the face like a blow from a hot, open palm. But that was the first time. In years to come in the jungle, at Anzio beach with Germans only yards away, 'mouseholing' through the smoking ruins at Cassino, they'd be tossing grenades at the enemy as if they *were* really only harmless cricket balls.

Now after their first six weeks in the Army, they were let loose on the civilian world once more, but only after they had been inspected by the guard commander at the gate to the camp, with its full-size mirror, bearing the legend: 'ARE YOU A CREDIT TO YOUR UNIT?'

But on the streets at least there was no relaxing of their military smartness. For the civilian world had been transformed. There were hard-eyed, suspicious military police – 'the redcaps' – patrolling in pairs everywhere. Officers and NCOs, too. Indeed the streets, where a couple of months before a soldiers had been an unwelcome rarity, had now developed a rash of khaki. So they took care to keep their hands out of their pockets, walk in step with one another, not to lounge or lean anywhere and, above all, salute anything or everything which looked like an officer. Cinema commissionaires were saluted and more than one of the rookies swore he had saluted the uniformed dummy in the window of a multiple tailor!

As we have seen pay was low, but with a pint of beer costing sixpence the ten shillings or so which most of them received on pay day, paid to them by an officer who had to be saluted twice for his 'generosity', were enough for them to wash away the indignities and hardships of the week.

In the crowded pubs, secure from interference by officers and NCOs, red-faced and flushed with 'gnat's piss', as beer had now become known, they would rip open their tunics, shove their forage caps to the backs of their cropped heads and let rip with a defiant chorus of '*Fuck 'em all, the long and the short and the tall! Fuck all the sergeants and WO1s. Fuck all the corporals and their bleeding sons. For we're saying good-bye to them all. ...* 'Not just yet, but it wouldn't be long now.

After the pubs, there would be the local dance-halls, heavy with the smell of cheap tobacco and even cheaper scent. Emboldened by the 'gnat's piss', they would pit themselves against the 'Brylcreem boys' (RAF men), other soldiers, even NCOs ('civvies' didn't count) for the favours of the local girls in their floral dresses and high heels, doing their level best not to slide about on the dance floor in their clumsy hob-nailed ammunition boots.

Those who were lucky would take the 'tart' (for all girls were 'tarts' now) down the local lovers' lane, trying to feel a nipple or 'just yer knee, I promise, I won't go higher than yer stocking-top, *honest!*' until the sudden recollection of the time shattered the idyll and they would be flying back to the camp to report in at the guardroom before the witching hour of one minute before midnight.

Others, who hadn't the patience to attempt to seduce one of the local factory girls, would recourse to illegal 'knocking shops', amateur brothels or the local 'goodtime girls', who for 30 shillings – three weeks' pay – would satisfy the soldier's lust, which contrary to rumour had not been depressed by the bromide allegedly slipped into the tea by the Army authorities.

On the very day war had been declared, a Ministry of Health circular had alerted local health authorities that 'It is well known that a state of war favours the spread of VD in the population'. But little was done, save in London, where the police tried to curb the numbers of 'Piccadilly Warriors', as the whores roaming the squares of blacked-out Central London were called. For although 'disorderly houses', as brothels were called quaintly, were forbidden by law, no action could be taken against street-walking prostitutes unless they were actually caught soliciting.

As a result the national VD statistics were rising alarmingly. In places like Liverpool there was a frightening fourfold increase in syphilis cases, and by mid-1941 the figures for the whole of the United Kingdom had increased by 70 per cent since 3 September, 1939. So it was the case that many an unfortunate discovered at one of the frequent 'short-arm inspections', where he would exhibit his 'John Thomas' (as Army MOs called the penis) to the medical orderlies, that his lady friend had left behind a little 'souvenir'. Perhaps a 'dose of the clap', or if he were exceedingly unlucky it would be what the cynical old sweats called 'a full house' – *both!*

Soon the Army would be forced to institute a system by which a soldier seeking intercourse would sign for a 'french letter' in the condom book, adding his regimental number for good measure. If he later contracted VD, but could prove that he had 'drawn' a condom and used it, he would be all right. If he hadn't, he risked 30 days in the dreaded 'glasshouse' in Aldershot. Much later, when the infantry were suffering dreadful casualties in north-west Europe and Italy, some commanders declared that a soldier who contracted VD had deliberately attempted to avoid front-line service and that the sickness was a 'self-inflicted wound'. This was a court-martial offence which carried a sentence of up to seven years' hard labour!

But that was later, much later. Many of those presently being prepared for battle, diseased or otherwise, would never survive to fight at Monte Cassino or in the *Reichswald*. Those battles, in which the infantry died in their thousands, would be fought by teenagers, who in this winter of 1939–40 were still schoolboys in short pants, being bored by their lessons in the senior schools.

But now as 1939 gave way to 1940, time was beginning to run out for the men called up in September, and territorial formations such as the 51st Highland Division, which had remained behind in England. Lord Gort, the commander of the BEF (which had still seen no action save some minor patrolling activity in the French sector along the Saar), was building up his force to 12 divisions, and he needed more infantry, however partially trained or raw. France wanted 'bodies'.

In January 1940, the 51st Division, stationed in the Aldershot area, was alerted for the move to France. Since September the Division had been able to rid itself of much of its World War One equipment, though the Black Watch, for instance, were still using cattle floats and furniture vans for transport. Some of the older territorial officers had been sacked, too, and as one hard-bitten reservist who had had nine years with the colours noted: 'Well, at least the new ones didn't allow the men to call them by their first names, which the others had done. In the beginning those terrier battalions were a real Fred Karno's!'[5]

But still the old ways died hard in the 51st. Some battalions were in favour of retaining the kilt, such as the Black Watch and the Cameronians. Others thought the kilt an unsuitable garment for the needs of total war. What would happen to the Jock's naked rump and other important appendages (no undergarments were allowed to be worn under the kilt and regularly inspecting officers checked with a flick of their cane whether some miserable soldier had dared to wear the offending garment) in case of a mustard gas attack, for instance? The traditionalists gave serious consideration to the provision of 'Drawers, Highland, Anti-Gas for the use of'. These were to be rolled down from under the kilt or to be hitched over one's nose on the warning 'Gas!'

In the end, both factions – for and against – prevailed. The Black Watch handed in their kilts before embarking; the Cameronians kept theirs, as did the Gordon Highlanders. One young subaltern of the latter regiment, who was an Englishman who didn't favour the kilt, the future Brigadier Charles N. Barker, was later wounded and thus escaped the débâcle that overtook the 51st Highland Division. Yet in spite of his opposition to 'an unsuitable garment for modern warfare, I can remember, just before embarking at St Nazaire, being ordered to leave my valise behind and stripping off my battledress trousers and pants and proudly donning my kilt, much to the amusement of many men and women on the quay-side'.[6]

The future brigadier would be one of the few who would serve with the Division from October 1939 to May 1945. Infantry officers didn't last long in combat. He was lucky, for most of his comrades would not see Scotland again, including the Division's commander General Victor Fortune, who had served in the Black Watch for four years in the trenches in the Great War without a scratch, the only officer in the whole regiment to do so. This time, however, General Fortune's luck would run out. He would die in German captivity.

So these half-trained young infantrymen sailed to France, perhaps expecting a heroes' welcome. As one of them wrote at the time, 'I'm afraid we all found it something in the nature of an anti-climax. We had expected cheers and smiles and perhaps kisses. ... We were sure that the French would be overjoyed to see our faces and our new battle-dress.

'Perhaps we were foolish to expect all this. Perhaps times had changed. Perhaps this is a war in which nobody feels inclined to cheer. Or perhaps we were just unlucky.

'Still the fact remains we landed at Cherbourg at 8 a.m. on a dreary and depressing morning. The crowds assembled to welcome us consisted of a French naval sentry, some old market women, a fisherman and two or three gendarmes. As a reception committee they were a decided failure. They vouchsafed us a disinterested glance or two, and then went about their business.

'And some of us had actually expected kisses!'[7]*

---

* This officer was fortunate. The officers of General Montgomery's 3rd Division all had their kits stolen by Cherbourg dockers.

III

'The General was worried and ill at ease. He was haunted by the subject of venereal disease!'

In France, they dug.

All that winter of the 'phoney war', the British infantry of the BEF had been located on the French frontier with neutral Belgium, digging, digging, digging. Their aim was to prepare an extension to the French Maginot Line, which ended in that region, the so-called 'Gort Line'. In the event of the Germans attacking through Belgium and attempting to turn the French flank, Gort's 12 divisions would stop the enemy on the Line named after him. As it turned out, both lines, the Maginot and the Gort, would never be used.

Thus it was that Gort's divisions, which had never once exercised as whole divisions, not to mention corps, remained without the vital training the period of the 'phoney war' could have afforded them. Lieutenant Anthony Irwin, who was going to be the first officer in his infantry battalion to win the Military Cross in World War Two (just as his father had been the first to do so in the same regiment 25 years before), recalled just after the débâcle: 'There's little to be said about the months of the "phoney war", which preceded the German invasion. So much of the time was spent in digging or drinking that there was little left for training. During those eight months, I don't think I took part in one field exercise, though I did construct a railway-yard station, built a road and turned a stream into an anti-tank obstacle. No, I'm wrong; not a complete obstacle. When it was finished we left it to build the road. Again I'm wrong; we half-finished the road and left it to construct the railway yard. That we did finish, but a late frost almost immediately undid our work. You shouldn't make railways of asphalt when there's frost about ...'[1]

The conditions under which the infantrymen turned builders were dreadful. The men dug in mud up to their knees for five or six hours a day, their main tools picks and shovels, for the BEF had little mechanical equipment. Feet were never dry by day and boots were still damp the next day. Gumboots were in short supply and men paid out of their own pockets to buy gumboots from the French shops.

Every morning at reveille they were roused from the barns, the farms and the tumbledown cottages in which they were billeted after a fitful night's sleep in the straw under one blanket, given breakfast, and at 8 a.m. marched to the day's digging. Bully beef and jam sandwiches made up their midday meal. Their day ended at 4 o'clock and they were fed for the last time at 4.30; thereafter there would be 16 hours without food or a hot drink.

Naturally they could spend their own pay on buying egg and chips, their favourite meal, at the suddenly inflated prices charged at the local *estaminets*. But they knew they were not particularly liked by the northern French. The dour locals of that impoverished area, which had hardly recovered from World War One, had not been pleased by the abrupt dumping of thousands of these khaki-clad foreigners in their midst back in the autumn, and they showed it – in that typically French way: the care- less shrug of the shoulders when questioned; the constant complaining to the liaison officers about the destruction wrought by the 'Tommies' and demands for money; the eagerness and cunning with which they tried to part the foreigners from their money, little that it was.

Sometimes they were openly hostile, too. 'The people of northern France hated the Boche,' Lieutenant Irwin recalled a year later. 'But our reception was not, on the whole, cordial. One day, for instance a Hun aircraft came over on its usual reconnaissance beat. A piece of ack-ack shell (British) fell through the roof of a small farmhouse, making a hole about two inches square in the tiles, but otherwise causing no damage. I went along to ask the old woman of the house if we could mend it for her. All the thanks I got was a hysterical tirade on England's responsibility for the war – and a pewter mug hurled at my head.'[2]

To most of the BEF it seemed that the French were totally unconcerned by this *'drôle de guerre'*, as they called the 'phoney war'. When the 51st Highland Division arrived at its sector in the snowbound January of 1940, they found the defences there 'grossly inadequate and nobody appeared to be too concerned. There seemed to be no great urgency to get things done. A general easygoing spirit pervaded the whole country and when French soldiers or civilians were asked if the Germans would invade France this time, the answer was always, "*Jamais, jamais*"'.[3]

In due course, those frontier people would find out just how wrong they were. But for the time being, the Germans stayed behind their own Siegfried Line, on which the infantry boasted in their marching song they would soon hang out their washing – 'have yer any dirty washing, mother dear?' – and the BEF continued to dig and dig.

Visiting a working party of the East Yorkshire Regiment that winter, war correspondent James Hodson, who had fought over the same area as an infantry officer in the 'Old War', watched how the infantrymen got 'stuck in', recording for the public the kind of dialogue that they seemed to like. 'Why, it's money for jam is this,' he reported one of them saying in a broad Yorkshire voice. 'Ere tha art, seein' t'Continent and knowin' Maddymoselle at first hand – all for nowt.' He turned to his comrade resting on his mud-encrusted shovel, breathing heavily, 'Th'art a regular Christopher Columbus, if tha only knew it.'

'Christopher Columbus am I?' the other soldier snorted. 'Tha'd better tell t'company officer. 'E seems to think I'm McAlpine's mechanical excavator. I'st soon ha' dug o'er every bit o' France my brother didn't dig last time!'

'Aw reet, Len,' his mate attempted to appease him, 'We know what's wrong wi' thee. She hasn't written this week.'[4]

It was all a bit bogus, a bit like Bruce Bairnsfather and his cockneys of the Great War. 'Our boys over there', as they were invariably called, 'were obviously in good spirits, in spite of the terrible conditions and the lack of amenities.' 'They were seeing it through', as the slogan of the time had it. Even the correspondent of *The Times*, an experienced journalist who had been through the Spanish Civil War, a deceptively mild man with a bad stutter, named Kim Philby, thought the troops were in 'good spirits'.

In fact, most of the territorials were bewildered and sometimes a little angry by now. They had been plucked from their comfortable civilian jobs, presumably to fight Hitler and bring the war to a speedy close, the previous September. Instead they were still doing nothing but dig and dig and dig. Back in Britain, on what was now called the 'Home Front', the 'civvies' seemed to have forgotten them stuck out here, 'Somewhere in France', while they earned good money in the booming war factories. As they marched to yet another day of digging on the 'Gort Line', they no longer sang *'We're Gonna Hang Our Washing on the Siegfried Line'*. Now they sang, *'We're soldiers of the BEF … Working for the war … Soldiers of the BEF … frozen to the bloody core …'*

By February 1940, Commander-in-Chief Gort, located in a great sprawling HQ which stretched to a radius of 25 miles around Arras, decided that with no German attack imminent it was safe to let a certain number of the men go on local leave to break the hardship and monotony of their lives at 'the front'; officers would even be allowed to go to Paris. General Montgomery, the commander of the 3rd Infantry Division, had already made his own arrangements for leave in his area. Here he gave his infantrymen of the 'Iron Division' permission to enjoy whatever fleshpots the northern industrial town of Lille could offer. Selected parties began to go on weekend leaves to the town, where the French brothels were clean and regularly inspected.

In spite of that, however, the number of reported cases of VD in his division began to rise alarmingly. Montgomery didn't like that. He knew from his experiences in the First World War that divisions with a high rate of men taken prisoner and a high rate of VD were suspect at GHQ. It was generally thought that commanders of divisions like this were lax. He made urgent enquiries and found that the VD had not been contracted in Lille's brothels. His men had been subsidizing the local country girls for sexual favours in the 'beetroot fields', infected girls passing on the scourge from man to man.

This was something that the cocky birdlike commander simply could not tolerate. He sat down and drafted a Divisional Order, which would become one of the major issues within the BEF that winter and nearly ruined his career. 'My view is,' he wrote, 'that if a man wants to have a woman, let him do so by all means; but he must use his common sense and take the necessary precautions against infection – otherwise he becomes a casualty by his own neglect and this is helping the enemy.'[5]

Montgomery's solution was simple and to the point. The NAAFI should sell condoms, troops should be advised to go to the clean brothels of Lille if they wanted a woman, and everyone should be taught the French for 'french letter' so that they could buy one in the local shops when needed.

Montgomery later confessed he was rather proud of his effort. But he little realized what a storm it would bring about his ears when the Divisional Order was brought to the attention of the Commander-in-Chief, Gort. As Montgomery, who detested Gort, wrote later: 'There was a father-and-mother of a row. They were all after my blood at GHQ. But my Corps Commander (Brooke) saved me by insisting on being allowed to handle the matter himself.'[6]

'I did not know about the storm which was blowing up,' Montgomery stated later, 'and when I received a message that the Corps Commander was coming to see me and I was to remain in until he arrived, I thought in my innocence that some urgent tactical problem was to be discussed. I was mistaken! He arrived, and I could tell by the look on his face and his abrupt manner that I was for it.'[7]

He was. Brooke told him, 'that I had a very high opinion of his military capabilities and an equally low one of his literary ones'.[8] Brooke, the bird-watching commander who would lead Britain to victory in World War Two, informed Montgomery, who would become his principal commander, that he had narrowly escaped being sacked; he must never again do anything so shocking. Montgomery agreed tamely, for as he wrote himself later, 'it achieved what I wanted, since venereal disease ceased.'[9] Thereafter, the 'General of Love', as some wits within the Third Infantry Division now called the really puritanical Montgomery, kept his nose out of the brothels of Lille, clean or otherwise. ...

An anonymous ditty, 1940 on Montgomery's famous 'VD Order'

MARS AMATORIA

The General was worried and was very ill at ease,
He was haunted by the subject of venereal disease.

For four and forty soldiers was the tale he had to tell
Had lain among the beets and loved not wisely but too well.
It was plain that copulation was a tonic for the bored,
But the gallant British Soldier was an Innocent Abroad;
So ere he takes his pleasure with amateur or whore
He must learn the way from officers who've trod that path before.
No kind of doubt existed in the Major-General's head
That the men who really knew the game of Love from A to Z
Were his Colonels and his Adjutants and those above the ruck,
For the higher up an officer the better he can f—k.
The Colonels and the Major were not a bit dismayed
They gave the orders for the holding of a Unit Love Parade,
And the Adjutants by numbers showed exactly how it's done,
How not to be a casualty and still have lots of fun.
The Adjutants explained that 'capote' did not mean a cup,
That refreshment horizontal must be taken standing up,
They told the troops to work at Love according to the rules
And after digging in to take precautions with their tools.
Now the General is happy and perfectly at ease
No longer is he troubled with venereal disease.
His problems solved, his soldiers clean (their badge is now a dove)
He has earned the cross of Venus, our General of Love.

Cupid (Royal Corps of Signals)

Journalist Skene Catling was the first pressman 'to see the first man wounded by a British bullet on the Western Front,' as he wrote tongue in cheek that winter. 'He is a Frenchman!'

'I saw him in a French military hospital. He was lying on a hospital trolley on his way from the X-ray theatre to the operating table. His left arm had been ripped open by a shot from a rifle. Four doctors and three nurses were in attendance.

'A simple peasant, he had been pushing a barrow across a field after dark and approached a position guarded by a British sentry.

'The sentry challenged him. He made no reply; but went slowly on his way.

'The sentry fired. The countryman dropped.

'Later, the sentry discovered the cause of the man's failure to answer his challenge.

'*The peasant is stone deaf!*'[10]

But by now the BEF were beginning to have their first skirmishes with the real enemy, the Germans. A sector of the French line in the Maginot Line had been allotted to the British so that they could be 'blooded' in the sporadic patrol actions and artillery duels which were taking place there as the Germans probed for weaknesses in the defences. East of Metz, the great frontier fortress city, was the area called by the German-speaking people on *both* sides of the front, *das Dreilaendereck*, the 'three countries' corner', because it formed the boundary between France, Germany and neutral Luxembourg.*

It was a rugged, lonely area of deep valleys and steep wooded hills, an ideal place for patrols of both sides to slip back and forth unobserved and one where, in 1944–5, it would take hundreds of thousands of American and French soldiers months to overcome German resistance.

The new boys were not impressed by the quality of the French troops from whom they took over the sector. They were, as one officer of the British division reported, 'a disunited collection of unshaven, ill-clad, dirty-looking individuals. On close inspection we found that things were even worse than they had appeared at first sight ... Finally when they marched away their discipline was non-existent. In fact, there was no attempt made to keep proper marching discipline. They looked and acted like a disorderly rabble.'[11]

Back in December 1939, the war correspondent James Hodson had come across a major of the Duke of Wellington's Regiment – 'big square face, twinkling grey eyes and strong teeth' – who claimed to have led the first British action against the German Army in World War Two. What he said was historic. It was this: 'We fired the first shots – if you call a grenade a shot. We heard 'em outside our wire fiddling about. A Mills bomb was thrown – we had a few with us.'[12]

But the unknown major of the Duke of Wellington's had been only on temporary attachment to the French. This time the British had come to stay. But first, being the British Army, the area had to be 'bulled' up before they could do battle. Colonel Mike Ansell, the CO of a Yeomanry Regiment who had gone up with the infantry, found his billet, the village of Waldweistrof, as filthy as the rest of the places abandoned by the French. He ordered it cleaned up at once and 'within a few days muck heaps were squared up'** gardens quite tidy and the houses whitewashed'. There were even cows to provide milk for his tea, and as he wrote much later, 'we always had lovely flowers in the mews and my bedroom.'[13]

Now that the amenities had been taken care of in true British Army fashion, the tall handsome Colonel, who before the war had been a celebrated horseman, prepared to do battle with the enemy just on the other side of the wooded ridge. But just like all the other units in the area, his had been warned not to 'provoke' the Germans. Action had to be limited

---

* In French Lorraine, nearby Luxembourg, most of the border people spoke a German dialect as their first language.

** In that area the small farmer keeps his heap underneath his kitchen window. Thus passers-by will know the larger the heap, the more prosperous the farmer.

to offensive patrols. Then the French philosophy was to let sleeping dogs lie. Up to now the only action had been limited to loudspeaker duels, with the German propaganda company soldiers yelling to the French a hundred yards or so away, that while they were languishing in the front line, the 'Tommies' were living it up to the rear, bedding their wives and girlfriends. The French wanted no all-out battle.

So Colonel Ansell prepared for his first 'fighting patrol'. 'This was an intensely exciting game: faces and hands blacked, armed with Tommy guns, revolvers, Very light pistols and strung with hand grenades, we'd move silently for three or four hundred yards then lie down to listen. One night, crossing a bridge over a deserted branch railway line, we heard rustling in the undergrowth below; crouching, my heart banged as we waited to fire, for we feared an ambush.' He need not have feared. For suddenly 'an unmistakeable grunt told us there were pigs in the area. And that was the nearest we ever got to any Germans.'[14]

Soon Colonel Ansell would see his fill of Germans. Trying to escape in the débâcle to come, he would be riddled with bullets by a German Tommy-gunner and blinded.

But for the time being British activity on the 'Western Front' was limited solely to patrols. Now more civilians were being killed at home in the new blackout than in the whole of the British Army in France – some 33 a week.

Just before he, too, returned home, war correspondent James Hodson made his last visit to the 'front'. To him it seemed strangely reminiscent of the trenches of the 'Old War' without the fighting. 'It is eerie in the outposts at night … German Very lights soar into the air … German Alsatian dogs bark – you can hear four or five. An occasional train far off. In the woods the hard frost is causing twigs to snap … Or snow falls off a branch with a light thud. It is very dark for some hours till the moon comes up. Sentries are doubled. Out in front is the patrol creeping about. For long periods everything is quiet. The men stand there, softly treading their feet to keep the circulation going.

'Inside the dug-out, the men off duty lie close together to keep warm. Ground-sheets are pegged over the door. The stove can't be used at night. A candle burns there. They try to sleep, but it's too cold – feet are numbed. They talk of the match between Celtic and Rangers. Cigarettes glow. Somebody brings out a pack of cards and they try to play, but there's little room. Prospects of leave are discussed; leave and football – those are the great topics – and the Germans are within rifle distance, at times within bombing distance. One night the German patrol throws a stick grenade, but it falls short, doesn't reach the trench'.[15]

It was hard and rugged in the coldest winter in Europe within living memory, but it wasn't war. Hodson, the former infantry officer, knew it. Just like his international journalist colleagues of the war correspondents' team, who had departed 'to Finland, Romania and elsewhere in search of war', he decided, too, that there was nothing really worth reporting with the BEF 'on the Western Front'. He left for England.

There, the war was just as remote as in France. In London, where 43 theatres were open again and doing land-office business, the American naval attaché noted the 'undercurrent of distaste and apathy for the whole war'.[16] Admittedly people were now rationed to four ounces of bacon, four of butter and twelve of sugar a week, but most of them either forgot the war or hoped, as did Neville Chamberlain, the Prime Minister, not for a military victory but for 'a collapse of the German home front'. The Ministry of Information's secret investigators estimated that four million Britons would settle for peace at *any* price; while the members of the Communist Party and fellow- travellers actively opposed the war and declared it 'a capitalist struggle'*.

Back in September the nation had been geared up for an Armageddon.

What had happened had been a total anti-climax, the 'phoney war'. Now the man in the street wanted to forget it. Even at the top no one was prepared to launch the first blow which might precipitate a real conflict. Urged by his RAF advisers to bomb the Black Forest, just over the French border, and savage Germany's timber supplies, the undersized Secretary of State for Air, Sir Kingsley Wood, declared in outrage: 'Are you aware it is private property? *Why, you'll be asking me to bomb Essen next!*'[17]

Back in England, Hodson, the war correspondent, noted the apathy everywhere that icy winter. 'I run into a good many people who appear to think the war or fighting the war is hardly their concern. They're rubbing along as close to their old life as possible, quite ready to let the Regular Army, and the lads young enough to be conscripted or those who chanced to be in the Territorials, do the fighting, pretty complacent about the way things are going, harbouring a sneaking belief that it will be all over by the end of March. It's extremely unlikely it will. Perhaps not by the end of the following March either.'[18]

Neither Hodson nor the Great British Public could have visualized that winter just how many bitter Marches would pass and how many of those 'lads' would die in action before it was all over. It would end eventually, but by then their world would have been transformed for ever ...

---

* At this time Russia and Germany were still allies. The British CP was acting on orders from Moscow. In this devious, tortured manner of thinking, Stalin, the Soviet dictator, thought Britain's war with Germany was a threat to Soviet security.

IV

'It sure looks like the end of the phoney war'

Thursday, 9 May, 1940, was a beautiful day. Everywhere the young infantrymen of the BEF enjoyed the warm spring sunshine after the rigours of the hard, icy winter. Most of them looked forward to the weekend. They'd knock off at 12 o'clock on Saturday afternoon and then it would be 'in bed or out of barracks' for most of them. Some of them had finally got their 'feet under the table', as they phrased it, visiting local families, and if they were very lucky, they might even be getting their 'oats' as well. The less fortunate ones would have to be content with a soccer match, a spelling bee, or perhaps a visit to a camp concert, ending in a sing-song. *'There was jam, jam, mixed up with the ham in the stores … in the stores … My eyes are dim, I cannot see … I have not got my specs with me. …'*

Since April, there had been a slight increase in enemy activity over the British front. As Lieutenant Irwin, whose father commanded the 2nd Infantry Division, noted: 'Hun reconnaissance aircraft, which throughout the winter had paid us only occasional visits, now came over every day. They flew at great heights and were seldom hit. No word came for us to expect trouble. We just continued on our boring way.'[1]

Up in the Saar the 51st Highland Division, which was in position in front of the Maginot Line, had noted a certain *decrease* in German patrol activity. This unsettled some of the Great War veterans, for they knew that when patrolling ceased, it *could* mean that the enemy knew everything they wanted to know; or they didn't want any of their men captured, just in case they gave something away about impending operations during interrogation.

But what could any potential prisoner give away? Germany's war with Poland had been over for months now. Since October 1939 the Germans could have launched their attack in the West with impunity, knowing that their rear in the East was covered. Why start anything now after six months of inactivity? The Germans, too, had their phoney war – *der Sitzkrieg.**

---

* Literally 'the sitting war'.

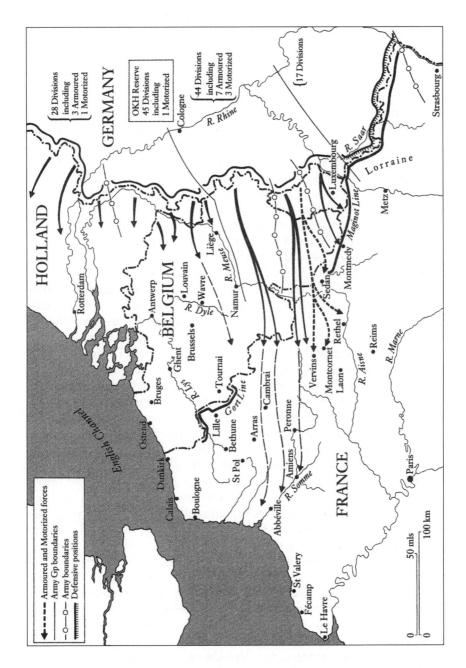

The final plan 'yellow' for the German invasion of Holland and Belgium.

Thus that sunny Thursday, before the world changed so irrevocably, passed away without a shot being fired throughout the BEF area of the front. The troops worked and exercised a little, enjoying the sun, telling themselves confidently, 'roll on Saturday!'

Behind the lines, however, things *were* moving. The 3rd Infantry Division, to be followed by the 50th and 4th Infantry Divisions, was alerted to prepare to move into Belgium, once the Germans had violated that country's neutrality. The Second Corps, to which these divisions belonged, would seize the line of the River Dyle from Wavre to Louvain, as planned.

That night troops lying awake in their billets could hear more and more German planes droning overhead. As the 51st Division in the Saar stood down at the end of another long gruelling night of doing nothing, the infantry were surprised to see 'whole flotillas of German aircraft' flying eastwards. Unknown to the Jocks these were the German bombers returning from dropping their loads of death on the French lines of communication. Three-quarters of an hour after the 51st stood down at five that morning, the French GHQ issued 'Alerts 1, 2, and 3', and as the startled troops began to tumble out of their billets, they could already hear the snarl and whine of German bombers attacking the airfields to the rear of the Gort Line. One hour later, Montgomery's 3rd Division was ordered to move into Belgium. After nearly eight months digging and setting up the Gort Line, they were to abandon it, now that the balloon had finally 'gone up'. The whole winter had been wasted digging a completely useless line of fortifications!

As the black and olive camouflaged fifteen hundredweights and the Bedford trucks, named 'Doc', 'Sneezy', 'Snow White' and the like, started to roll towards the Belgian frontier, a strange air of unreality prevailed. No one – general or private – seemed to realize that this sunny May Friday, which Hitler had declared would 'decide the fate of the German nation for the next 1,000 years', marked a significant changing point in the history of Europe. After this day nothing would ever be the same again. But things went on completely normally. As Lieutenant Irwin recorded, '10 May, 1940, was just like the 9th as far as I could see. I don't recollect any tension in the air, or any dark clouds in the sky ... To say we were caught with our pants down would not be a mis-statement.'[2]

As one column of the 3rd Division reached the Belgian frontier, for example, they found the familiar red-and-white striped pole of the *douane* down and barring their way. The Belgian official on duty there, in his tall, old-fashioned shako, stepped forward and demanded a *'permit'*. Without it, the new allies would not be able to enter. The driver of the first fifteen hundredweight did not waste words. He reversed and went at the pole at full speed. It splintered into a dozen pieces and the column moved on into a Belgium that seemingly didn't want them as allies.

Up to now the three most common complaints of this cheerful khaki army, rolling northwards to do battle with 'old Jerry' at last, had been 'gippo'

28

tummy, scabies and VD: the result of strange food, strange beds – and stranger women. Now it was going to be death and mutilation that would afflict them. For they were totally unprepared for the realities of modern warfare.

Only seven months before the Secretary of State for War, Hore-Belisha (now remembered only for his 'belisha crossings'), had declared that the BEF was 'as well if not better equipped than any similar army'. It was 'equipped in the finest possible manner that could not be excelled'.[3]

But it wasn't true. The years of public neglect up to 1938, when the Munich Crisis spurred the authorities into doing something, could not be made up in a matter of months. The BEF's heavy machine guns and, to a certain extent, other guns were of World War One vintage. The infantry's sole anti-tank weapon, the cumbersome Boyes rifle, had no penetrating power at all, while their two-inch mortars didn't even have a range finder; it had to be fired on a hit-or-miss basis. The 44th Infantry Division, for instance, might well have six mobile cinemas, but it lacked its full complement of anti-tank rifles, hopeless as they were.

Now while Montgomery's 3rd Infantry Division rolled into Belgium by truck, the 5th Infantry Division, which was following it up, simply didn't have enough trucks to convey its men north. Instead the infantry of the Northamptons and the King's Own Yorkshire Light Infantry marched to battle, as their forefathers had done a quarter of a century before. For four long days they would be slogging their way north along the endless, dead-straight *pavé*, under a burning sun – 12 miles, 14 miles, 25 miles a day – until they arrived, *exhausted*!

But already the illusions of the months of phoney war were beginning to die this Friday. Moving up ahead of the troops with his officer on a reconnaissance, young Sergeant Gordon Instone entered the border town of Tournai, just after it had been bombed by the Germans. Everywhere there were scenes of death and destruction, with dead shopkeepers sprawled in the ruins of their shops. But it was the sight of a bombed *bistro* which most affected the young sergeant, whose life was going to be dramatically transformed this terrible May.

There, the demolished front revealed 'the extraordinary sight of seven or eight tables neatly laid for dinner on red-and-white checked tablecloths, the food half-eaten and the wine still in the glasses; a woman in a green frock lay slumped across a table, a fork clutched in her hand; a coat of dust had settled on her and she didn't look real. The body of a child lay bleeding on the floor nearby.'

Bemused and shocked, Sergeant Instone went over to speak to an old man, who leaned against a doorway, seemingly shocked into immobility by the horror. 'His eyes stared and he didn't answer me. I touched him and he fell forward. He was dead!'

Instone and the officer pushed on through the smoking, burning ruins of Tournai. 'Further up the street we came upon a nun kneeling in prayer beside a dying woman. Screaming mothers were searching for their children among the ruins and I heard one woman cry, "Oh God, poor Belgium again!"'

It was just then that a powerful car drew up and some American war correspondents got out to view the scene. One of them began to make charcoal drawings of the burning ruins* and Instone heard him say, as if to himself, 'It sure looks like the end of the phoney war'...[4]

The Germans attacked on 14 May.

For three days now the infantry had waited for the enemy to attack Louvain, the furthest point in the BEF's line. On the 11th, the day of the 3rd Division's arrival, they had been fired upon by the Belgian infantry division which was already there. But that had soon been sorted out and the Belgian 10th Infantry Division, which had declared hotly that it would defend Louvain, had thought better of it and had departed hastily, la gloire and similar heroics forgotten as the Germans approached.

Now, as all the bridges across the River Dyle were blown, the German artillery started to shell the British positions, as their patrols began to probe Montgomery's perimeter looking for weak spots. The infantrymen in their pits tensed, hands gripping their rifles damp with sweat, jerking with every fresh explosion, wishing they could open their flies and 'take a leak', but not daring to take their eyes off their front for a moment.

The German bombardment began to intensify. The enemy threw in the Stukas. Like evil black hawks they hovered over the 3rd's positions, while the leading German elements fired smoke and Very flares towards the British to indicate exactly where they were dug in. Suddenly, startlingly, their leader peeled off. Sirens howling, engine snarling all out, the German seemed to drop out of the May sky as if bent on self-destruction, hurtling down at a tremendous rate, heading straight for the earth. But at the very last moment, he levelled out. A scatter of black eggs fell from the Stuka's belly and then all hell was let loose as more and more bombs came raining down on the terrified men under attack for the first time. The very earth seemed to reel and quiver, as they huddled in their slit trenches, hands clasped over their ears like frightened children trying to blot out some terrifying sound.

One observer of the attack, a veteran of the 'Old War', noted: 'No one spoke. Words were beyond their power. The only sounds they could have uttered were inarticulate sounds of their gripping fears and these were choked back, for they were still ashamed to show the terror that had momentarily overcome them. They were suffering from the illusion that afflicts all men, however brave, when subjected to their first dive-bombing

---

* This could have been John Groth, who often made sketches to accompany his reports from the front.

attack – the terrible, ineradicable belief that you yourself had been singled out specifically for destruction, that the diving plane has seen you personally and is coming straight for you, and that nothing on God's earth can stop it!'[5]

Here and there men couldn't take it. A Colonel Horrocks, one day to become one of Montgomery's most celebrated corps commanders and a TV 'personality', arriving to take over the Middlesex Regiment, spotted a handful of men from the Ulster Rifles running back from Louvain to the rear. They didn't get far. Their CO, Colonel Knox, soon stopped them. He spoke to them quietly and they began to trot back to the front, 'looking rather ashamed of themselves'. 'Wait a minute,' Knox said, 'let's have a cigarette.' In spite of the heavy shelling, he made them finish their smoke. Then he said, 'Now *walk* back to your positions!'[6] Later Horrocks recalled, 'this was my first lesson in practical command'. But before this war was over, Horrocks would see many more British soldiers breaking and running away.

It was the Ulster Rifles who bore the brunt of the first German attack. They were dug in around the main railway station, as the German artillery reduced the lines and the rolling stock to a shambles of blazing smashed wagons and grotesquely twisted metal. Now the enemy infantry started to infiltrate, creeping in through the wreckage, lobbing their stick grenades from the far platform at the Ulstermen's sandbagged positions, giving and taking casualties.

The pressure mounted. The British bren-guns, which could fire a mere 30 rounds at one go, were no match for the German MG32, which reportedly could loose off 1,000 rounds per minute. The Ulsters started to fall back. Now they occupied a trench, dug in cinders by the Belgians, who had been there before them, on a high embankment. The top could be reached only by a vertical builder's ladder. When anyone was hit, he had to be lowered by ropes. But most of the men hit were dead when they reached the bottom of the pit, for the Germans had captured the three-storey administrative building which dominated the trench.

Lieutenant 'Digger' Tighe-Wood, who would one day become a brigadier, remembered many years later what it was like that day in the cinder pit. 'The enemy now got a spandau across the line between the Rifles and the 1st Grenadiers on the left. This opened up on the platoon from the rear, the bullets striking the wall at the top of the ladder. ... About the same time they worked a heavy 20-mm machine gun forward and this opened up on the position from about 100 yards range, the heavy armour-piercing bullets knocking the parapet back into the trench and filling the air with cinders and earth. ... The shouts of the German NCOs, accompanied by the blowing of whistles, could be heard above the din as they formed up to rush the position. A line of railway trucks on their side of the embankment gave them some shelter. Corporal Gibbons had now taken over a bren and he got a better aim at them through the wheels of the trucks. He laid across the parapet firing until he was hit and knocked back into the trench. He heaved himself and his bren back into the open again and kept his gun hammering away until he was killed.

'Opposite the supporting trench, now occupied by the Company HQ details, was a tunnel under the main embankment. A German in a shiny helmet which had obviously known applications of black boot polish stuck his head round to see if the way was clear. It wasn't, and that was the last corner *he* looked round!'

But now the Ulster Rifles' position was becoming desperate. One platoon of the defenders had been cut down and the Germans were infiltrating again between the Ulstermen and the Grenadiers. The young second-lieutenant prepared for the inevitable, as the enemy NCOs shrilled their whistles urgently and bellowed at their men to form up for the final assault. 'Suddenly above the din I heard Bala's* voice shout *"Fix swords!"* and above the top of the trench a line of bayonets appeared as they were clamped on to the rifles. It was a wonderful moment and I knew if the enemy came they were going to be met half-way in the open' ...[7]

The Ulster Rifles and their comrades of the Grenadier and Coldstream Guards would hold Louvain, with the Battalion HQ of the former receiving a bold message from one of its hard-pressed companies stating: 'All positions intact and unless the Germans send over two army corps they will remain so.'[8]

But as the French Army to the BEF's right and the Belgian Army to its left started to crumble and break down under the intense German pressure, the situation of Brooke's Corps, to which the 3rd, 50th and 5th Infantry Divisions belonged, began to look very serious. 'I wouldn't trust the Belgians a yard,' he confided to his diary on 15 May.

But Brooke's allies were not the only problem. To the rear, Gort's system of command, which he had not rehearsed in all the months before the great attack, began to break down. He started to lose contact with his forward formations, such as Montgomery in Louvain. Now he was swayed back and forth by the needs of various corps commanders urging him to make decisions. Already he was like a helpless captain whose ship was sinking fast and didn't know what to do. Again all those years of waste and apathy before the war were making themselves felt. The chickens were coming home to roost. Soon Gort would cable Eden in London, 'I must not conceal from you that a great part of the BEF and its equipment will invariably be lost in the best of circumstances. You know the day I joined up, I never thought I'd lead the British army to its biggest defeat in history.'[9]

As yet, however, the unshaven, dirty British infantryman at the front doing the fighting didn't *know* he was beaten. Lieutenant Irwin and his

---

* Lieutenant Bala Bredin, who had been taking a few minutes' 'shuteye'.

platoon were holding a bridge in Belgium, ready to blow it as soon as the first German appeared. They had not eaten for two days, but there was plenty of beer and an 'extraordinary' girl in the pub who, to use her own words, 'gave her body to the brave British Tommies who were fighting for her land'. As Lieutenant Irwin commented wryly, 'How much of that was true, God knows. But she took three of my blokes into a back room, whether it was for Belgium or for five francs I didn't ask'.[10]

Now the bridge was blown. The Germans appeared on the heights. Lieutenant Irwin's infantrymen started to dig in in earnest, the beer and the 'patriotic' Belgian girl forgotten now. A pompous major from another unit came up to watch them. A French soldier, dirty and unshaven, one of the many stragglers from both the French and Belgian armies who had already passed through their positions, appeared on the other side of the canal. He tore off his equipment in rage and started to curse the English with Gallic fluency. In the end Irwin had enough of his '*salauds*' and '*sales cons*'! He shouted across to the enraged French straggler to shut up, or he'd shoot.

Still the Frenchman continued to curse. Irwin nodded to his sergeant. The latter aimed, grunted, and shot the fellow dead. The strange major blew his top, and 'put the sergeant, myself, and anyone else in sight under close arrest.'[11] Thereupon he disappeared quickly, as the Germans came ever closer. Irwin never saw him again, but from now onwards he and his platoon would fight the 'Battle of France' under close arrest.

Now it was clear that the BEF would have to retreat from Belgium. The whole front was breaking up and the infantry were gripped by a Fifth Column psychosis. They saw spies and German agents everywhere. The hard-pressed Black Watch were told by the regiment they were relieving that 100 Germans had crossed a bridge in threes, dressed in battle-dress and singing 'Tipperary'. Later on, however, the Black Watch were struck by the persistent tolling of the bell in the village they held. They became suspicious and smashed open the door of the switch-room on the railway station to stop it. It was a level-crossing bell and all the lights were on along the railway. Rightly or wrongly the tired Jocks thought it was the work of spies signalling to the advancing Germans. They arrested 'two spies', who they felt were responsible. Their fate was not recorded.

The notes of one of their company commanders that week throw a sharp light on the life the infantry led as the great retreat south got underway. 'Milking cows, making our own butter, gathering eggs ... slept in borrowed civvy trousers and next morning promptly arrested as a German parachutist ... arranged whistles for air raids and bugles for alarms ... sent our party for rations and they brought back two pigs and loads of provisions [by now looting by the half-starved infantrymen, who were receiving few rations, was becoming widespread], had a head-on crash with a motor-cycle in dark lane ... saw hordes of Belgians with white flags on rifles … enemy observation balloon up and saw every movement we made. … We look like a holiday football crowd.'[12]

Thus they moved back, fighting and marching, battling their way through the crowds of frightened refugees who filled the roads everywhere, abandoning their heavier equipment as they went, regiments and units mixed together inextricably, trying to drag their wounded with them. One captain of the Ulster Rifles, marching down a road littered with dead and dying British soldiers, came across a badly wounded man, who called out, 'Is that the Second Grenadiers, Sir?' 'No,' he replied, 'I'm afraid they've gone. I'll try to find you a stretcher-bearer.' But the Grenadier was too far gone for that. Yet on the point of death as he was, he remained a guardsman to the very end. He said weakly, 'Permission to fall out, Sir, please?'[13] And then he died.

A Black Watch doctor amputated a wounded man's leg in a farmhouse with a razor. For a while their colonel marched with his stick handle in a goat's collar, while the sergeant-major led a calf by the ear for miles. 'It was grand, man, because when we halted, I could lean on the calf.' An infantryman dressed his French girl friend up in battledress obtained from his pals. Now she marched along with the rest. Three weary foot-sloggers unhitched the horses from an abandoned Belgian gun limber and gently jogged south. One of them had never been on a horse before and was unable to stop it when it decided to join a column of French cavalry going in the *opposite* direction. Another lugged with him his pet canary in a cage. An officer was observed carefully and savagely shredding the strings of his tennis racquet with a bayonet. It was part of his own private scorched earth policy.

But in the midst of this retreat, with their world falling apart visibly by the hour, the exhausted soldiers still kept their sense of humour. Colonel Horrocks, slogging south with what was left of the Middlesex Regiment, chanced upon one of his company commanders, who had just had a sharp brush with the Germans. He asked the tired, dirty officer how he was getting on. The latter replied, 'Don't look round, sir. I think we're being followed.'[14]

And they were!

V

'What a bloody way to die!'

The SS started shooting their British prisoners on the afternoon of 28 May, 1940. All that long day the odds-and-sods from the Royal Warwickshire Regiment, the Cheshire Regiment and the Royal Artillery had fought the élite of the *Wehrmacht*, Hitler's own bodyguard regiment, *Die Leibstandarte Adolf Hitler*. For a while they had even managed to pin down its commander, Sepp Dietrich, an old Party bully boy, in a ditch just outside the small French town of Wormhout, which they were defending. But all they had to defend themselves against the tanks of the SS were the useless Boyes rifles. Their 'armour-piercing' bullets had bounced off the German Mk IIIs like glowing ping-pong balls. In the end there had been nothing for it but to break out of the shattered, burning town, leaving Wormhout to the dead and those who would now fall into German hands.

Four years before, Sir Stafford Cripps, a prominent figure in the Labour Party had told his working-class audience in Stockport that he disagreed with his party's reluctant decision to agree to re-arm. It would not be a bad thing, he told them, if Germany defeated Britain in any future conflict, particularly for the working class. 'It would be disaster to profit makers,' the tall, skinny politico, whose veins, Churchill felt, were 'filled with lemonade', intoned, 'and the capitalists, but not necessarily to the working class.'[1] Now those representatives of the working class in khaki, whose plight, in part, was due to the pre-war anti-rearmament stance of 'Major' Attlee's party, were going to see the true face of National Socialism. The prisoners from the 48th Infantry Division and the 44th Infantry Division, which had gone to war two weeks before so well equipped with mobile cinemas, now were to be at the receiving end of the '1,000 Year Reich's' naked brutality.

The prisoners, many of them wounded, were herded into a barn. A Captain Lynn-Allen protested. He approached the nearest SS man and said, 'I wish to complain that there are wounded men inside and there is not enough room for them to lie down.'

The SS soldier, in his camouflaged tunic, answered cryptically in American-English, 'Yellow Englishmen, there will be plenty of room where you are going.'

The British officer shook his head and said, 'I am not satisfied.'

The SS man's face flushed with anger. He reached for the stick grenade stuck down the side of his jackboot. Ripping out the pin, he lobbed it overarm!

As men went down everywhere, Private Evans, standing next to the officer, felt a sharp bang against his right arm. He had been hit, as had many of the others. Lynn-Allen grabbed him and yelled 'Quick! Run for it!'

Together, with Lynn-Allen urging Evans 'to keep going and keep low', they staggered to a stagnant pond some 200 yards away from the barn. Both went into it up to their chests. 'Get down,' the officer hissed, 'and keep your arm out of the water!'

But it was no use, the Germans had spotted them. Suddenly a German loomed up at the edge of the pond. He didn't hesitate. He fired twice. Evans could hear the whack of the slugs as they hit the captain in the head. 'Oh, my God,' he cried and disappeared below the surface. Now the German turned his attention to the private. Again he fired two shots. But Evans was lucky, for the bullets ricocheted off a nearby tree and hit him in the neck. But as he fell full-length in the pond, the SS man was satisfied and moved off leaving the teenage infantryman for dead.

Now as he lay there, wanting to run away but knowing it would be fatal, he could hear the rattle of gunfire and the screams of his comrades as they were slaughtered in cold blood. It was too much for the 19-year-old boy, wounded and all alone. He broke down and wept.

But Evans, who would be saved later by some kind Germans of another unit, was not the only one to survive. A Private John Lavelle, who had been wounded in the foot, was outside the barn, peering in through a crack, when the SS started to toss in grenades. He saw CSM Jennings and Sergeant Moore throw themselves on one to protect the screaming, panicking men. But the others kept hitting their targets, filling the place with dead and dying men and the few who had been saved from injury by the bodies of the others.

Suddenly there was a loud echoing silence and Lavelle heard a hoarse German voice command, 'raus!' The men inside didn't understand the meaning of the word, but the tone sufficed. Someone said, 'Come on, if we've got to go, we've got to go.'

Five men went outside to be faced with a rough and ready firing squad. One asked for a last cigarette before he was shot. The request was refused. A moment later they were mown down. Now the SS demanded another five. But this time the men inside weren't coming. Pandemonium broke out as the Germans began to fire their machine pistols into the barn, trampling over writhing, screaming men as they entered to ensure nobody would escape. The few who would survive were deep beneath the bodies of their comrades and they were witnesses to the horror that took place in the barn that evening. 'Shoot me, shoot me!' someone yelled in agony. Another cried, 'What a bloody way to die!' A third stammered out the Lord's Prayer as he breathed his last.[2]

In the end some five men survived, with over 90 being massacred in the barn at Wormhout. At last the BEF, which had gone to France so light heartedly, boasting about the washing they were going to hang on the Siegfried Line – 'if the Siegfried Line's still there' – had been confronted with the harsh, brutal realities of total war. ...

Two days before that massacre had taken place, General Alan Brooke, Commander of the 2nd Corps, had noted in his diary, 'Nothing but a miracle can save the BEF now and the end cannot be far off. We carried out a withdrawal successfully last night back to the old frontier defences ... But where the danger lies is on our right rear. The German armoured divisions have penetrated to the coast; Abbeville, Boulogne and Calais have been rendered useless. We are, therefore, cut off from our sea communications, beginning to be short of ammunition. ...

'Armentières has been very heavily bombed and we are well out of it; half the town is demolished, including the madhouse, and its inmates are now wandering about the country.

'These lunatics let loose ... were the last straw. With catastrophe on all sides, bombarded by rumours of every description, flooded by refugees and a demoralized French Army, bombed from a low altitude, and now on top of it all lunatics in brown corduroy suits standing at the side of the road grinning at one with an inane smile, a flow of saliva running from the corners of their mouths and dripping noses! Had it not been that by then one's senses were numbed with the magnitude of the catastrophe that surrounded one, the situation would have been unbearable.'[3]

Soon Colonel Horrocks, as a newly appointed brigadier who had lost his brigade, would be trudging miserably along the wet sands of Dunkirk, as lost as everyone else, to come across 'General Brooke and my divisional commander General Montgomery. The former was under a considerable emotional strain. His shoulders were bowed and it looked as though he were weeping. Monty was patting him on the back.'[4]

But Brooke wasn't the only one of the senior generals finding it difficult to bear the almost impossible strain. General Michael Barker, the commander of the 1st Corps, had begun to suffer from hallucinations from lack of sleep, and the commander of his 2nd Division was heading for a nervous breakdown and had to be relieved. Even Commander-in-Chief Gort, the winner of the Victoria Cross in World War One, seemed to have given up. Later Montgomery would write of his meeting with him on the beach at La Panne, 'I don't think I have ever seen a more pathetic sight: the great and supposedly famous C-in-C of the British Army on the Continent alone; the staff of GHQ scattered to the four winds; he had in La Panne two staff officers, one was first class; the other was useless.

'Gort, in my opinion, was finished. He was incapable of grasping the military situation firmly and issuing clear orders. He was incapable of instilling confidence or morale. He had "had it".'[5]

Montgomery, with his overweening vanity and almost pathological self-confidence, might have been prejudiced. But it was obvious that the military authorities agreed with him. Gort never again held an active military command afterwards and most of his divisional and corps commanders were 'kicked upstairs'. They would never lead British soldiers into battle again.

But in spite of the chaos and confusion, and the breakdown of communications at the top, the better infantry formations kept their cohesion as fighting formations, making their way to the beaches in an orderly fashion. The 50th Infantry Division, a territorial unit, made sure that none of its men ran away during attacks or bombardments by the expedient of placing a senior staff officer, once even the divisional commander himself, at spots where the men were likely to break. These experienced officers knew that there would always be some who would run. So they would stop them and say, as if shocked, 'Do you mean that you – men of the 50th Division – are leaving your posts?' The ploy seemed to work. For while other divisions lost up to half their strength in the great retreat, even though they did not see as much fighting as the 50th Division, the latter kept up its numbers with practically no men missing right up to the last day.

But good generals or bad, superior infantry divisions or poor ones, it didn't really matter any more. Nothing could stop the victorious Germans. They pressed home their attacks relentlessly, breaking through one 'last ditch' defensive position after another. With their tanks and feared dive-bombers in the van, they pressed the 300,000 weary, hungry men of the BEF ever tighter against the Channel coast and that one remaining port of any value – Dunkirk.

'Mile after mile down the road the column grew and grew and crawled and crawled,' one of those who was saved remembered afterwards. 'Everyone was worn out for want of sleep. Drivers kept going mechanically, the movement just sufficient to keep them awake and no more. If an enforced halt occurred, however brief, they dropped sound asleep in their seats immediately. When we moved on a bit many of the drivers remained asleep. The column proceeded, leaving them behind, blocking the road. Traffic control of the Divisional Staff and the CMP then chased up and down the road in the darkness, waking up the delinquents in no gentle fashion.

'"Wake up, blast you!"

'"Get moving, you bastard!"

'"You're holding the whole bloody column up, curse you!"

'Officers and men, they all got it alike. A blinding torch flashed in the sleeper's face, then – salvo!'[6]

And all the while there was the constant aerial attack, which killed soldiers and civilians indiscriminately. Passing through the recently bombed French township of Carvin the same observer spotted something 'transcending even the normal imagined horrors of war'.

'Behind some railings in the main street stood a redbrick convent school that had been badly bombed. And spread out on the wide white pavement in front were the bodies of 60 victims, all girls between the ages of fifteen and sixteen. The corpses had been arranged in four regular rows, one behind the other on the broad flags. There they lay, rigid and motionless in the moonlight, staring up at the sky, exactly like a company that had formed fours and then fallen down flat on their backs. The mathematical precision of the arrangement added to the terror of the scene. You could fancy yourself looking upon the finale of some marionette show – 'Death's Drill' or 'Death by Numbers'. To heighten the horrible, inhuman aspect of this pavement mortuary, the faces, bare arms and legs were discoloured by a ghastly mauve tint, the result, probably, of shock or blast from the bomb. Perhaps the bodies had been laid out in this pattern for identification and collection by relatives. But there was little chance of this. All the living inhabitants of the village had fled. Not a soul dared remain to watch over and guard the mauve-faced dead. Alone, deserted, there they lay on their backs. Alone with their wide-eyed appeal to the heavens.'[7] But this terrible May the heavens were deaf and God seemed to have abandoned His creatures. ...

'Defence of Calais to the utmost is of the highest importance to our country as symbolizing our continental co-operation with France. The eyes of the Empire are upon the defence of Calais and HM Government are confident you and your gallant regiments will perform an exploit worthy of the British name.'[8] Thus wrote Anthony Eden, a former officer of the 60th Rifles, to Brigadier Nicholson, a 42-year-old regular officer, who had just arrived in the French Channel port. Under his command he had the 1st Battalion the Queen's Victoria Rifles, the Rifle Brigade and the 3rd Tank Regiment, some of the finest troops still left in the Army's reserve. Indeed as the Rifle Brigade had marched to the boats which were to convey them to Calais, passing by civilians calmly playing cricket as if this was still peacetime, one rifleman was heard to declare: 'The only crack regiment left in England will be the ATS!'[9] *

---

* The female auxiliary of the British Army.

Why they had been brought to Calais, no one really knew. Some thought it was to bolster up the French. Others believed they were there to ensure that supplies could reach the retreating BEF through the port. A few, the optimists, were of the opinion that from here the British Army would launch a counter-attack into the flank of the German Army, which had now reached nearby Boulogne – with what, however, not even the optimists were prepared to hazard a guess. But in the end, the reasons why they were there did not matter. Within five days the 4,000-odd men who landed in Calais on that cold morning in May 1940 would be either dead, wounded or prisoner.

The first riflemen of the Queen Victoria's Rifles to be shot in the battle for the port were the victims of the snipers of the French Fifth Column. They had just approached a deserted building near the *Gare Maritime*, where in peacetime thousands of British tourists had descended upon the boat-train, when a crackle of ragged firing broke out. Men went down here and there. A company sergeant-major bellowed 'fix bayonets!' But by the time the territorial riflemen were ready to charge, the Frenchmen had disappeared and they were able to push on into the crowd of stragglers and 'useless mouths', the supply people who were soon to be evacuated, coming to meet them, crying their tales of woe. They had no water, no food, and little ammunition. The Fifth Column was everywhere in the docks and the canals which criss-crossed the area. No British soldier by himself was safe in the area. The French seemed to be co-operating totally with the Germans already bearing down on the port. Thus while some French soldiers fought bravely side by side with Nicholson's men, anyone else not wearing British uniform was to be treated as a potential enemy.

As it began to darken and the first German mortar bombs started to fall on the port itself, a British destroyer slid into the harbour, its guns blazing. Hurriedly the stragglers and 'useless mouths' began to move towards the lean grey shape. It had come to take them off. But, surprisingly enough. no one seemed to be in a hurry to embark the riflemen, although by now they had already guessed the port was doomed; the Germans had surrounded it completely.

Adrian Vincent, who was one of the riflemen present that shell-racked night, asked his NCO, 'What's happening, Sarge?' Others followed with similar anxious questions.

The sergeant looked around him. 'No one's going on board,' he said quietly. 'The ship's brought us more ammunition to keep us going, that's all.'

The men sank to the debris-littered quay in stunned silence. But there was worse to come, as an officer bustled up to them and the NCO barked, 'On your feet, men!'

'Are we going aboard now, Sir?' someone asked, thinking the authorities might have changed their mind.

'No, we're not,' the officer said grimly. '*Not now or tomorrow – or ever*! We're staying here to the end. Now get yourselves sorted out into your platoons. We're making a counter-attack!'[10]

Now the Germans of a whole armoured division, the 10th Panzer, started to increase the pressure on the defenders, while the artillery thundered and massed groups of Stukas, 30, 40, 50 of them at a time came howling down to plaster Calais with bombs. Everyone was pressed into service now, even the remaining stragglers and 'useless mouths'. One of the latter, Sergeant Instone, found himself in the firing line with a trapped German only a hundred yards away, easy meat for a trained soldier. But he simply could not press the trigger and kill the German; a lifetime of civilian inhibitions about killing is hard to overcome.

Instead he took the German prisoner, wondering who was more scared, the prisoner or himself. The German 'was a boy of not more than 17, with a fair down on his cheeks and upper lip, and large frightened blue eyes. He was shaking all over.' In sign language Sergeant Instone signalled him to come along, and was just handing him over to the French when a shell scored a direct hit on a French truck nearby. 'The driver had been leaning against it a second or two before and I saw him decapitated, his crushed head scattered round his crumpled torso.'[11]

Now it was Instone's turn to get the shakes. But after downing several bottles of beer he felt better and began to withdraw yet once again with the ad hoc infantry platoon that had been formed from the odds-and-sods. It was now that he came across the strangest, most bizarre sight of the five-day battle. 'From the direction of the docks appeared 10 or 12 young females in tight satin skirts and cheap furs, their platinum and auburn hair bobbing on their shoulders, mincing along the sand dunes in their high heels and shining silk stockings, their carefully painted faces quite expressionless, as they were shepherded along our front by Madame, middle-aged and all in black.'[12] These were the last of the civilians to leave Calais. They had bravely serviced the troops to the very last. Now the danger was too great. But undoubtedly they would return to service the Germans in due course. To the victor – the spoils!

On the morning of 25 May the desperate commander of the 10th Panzer Division, General Schaal, with the High Command breathing down his neck, prepared for a last all-out assault on what was left of the British defenders holding out in the ruins of Calais-Nord. But first he decided to attempt to talk them into surrender.

Under a white flag he sent the mayor of Calais, André Gershell, who was Jewish and would die in a concentration camp, to talk with Brigadier Nicholson. But the Brigadier, who himself would die in a German POW camp before the war ended, would hear no talk of surrender. Brusquely he told Gershell, whom he would soon arrest, '*Surrender*? If the Germans want Calais, they will have to fight for it.'

So the one-sided fight went on with the Germans throwing in the full weight of their artillery and dive-bombers. But still their tanks and infantry made little progress, though the defenders were forced to shorten their lines yet once again, moving back under cover of darkness. As the diary of the 10th Panzer Division recorded for that day: 'The attack on the Old Town has been held up. The enemy fights with hitherto unheard of obstinacy. They are English, extremely brave and tenacious.'[12]

Once again the Germans sent parliamentaires to Nicholson asking him to surrender. He sent his answer in writing. It read: 'The answer is no, as it is the British Army's duty to fight as well as it is the German's'.[14] Of course the Brigadier knew that his decision to continue the hopeless struggle would mean further loss of life. But he was motivated by Eden's message. The former Greenjacket officer surely would not order him to waste the lives of the men of his old Regiment unnecessarily. Being the firm-principled man that he was, Brigadier Nicholson obeyed that command to the letter, believing that every further day that Calais was held was vitally important for the British Empire.

On Sunday, 26 May, the Germans launched an all-out attack on that part of Calais still held by the British. The *Gare Maritime* had to be abandoned. The survivors were pressed ever closer to the harbour. A small group of riflemen under Lieutenant Rolt, who had won the Military Cross the day before, made a last desperate assault on the Germans, who were only 10 yards away. Most of his men fell writhing and dying on the littered cobbles, but he managed to drive them off, firing at them like a western gun-slinger with a revolver in both hands. *Click* ... first one, then the other. *Click*. He was out of ammunition. Sadly the young officer surrendered.

It was the same everywhere now, as the ammunition started to give out. Even the destroyers of the Royal Navy that had supported the hard-pressed defenders off-shore for so long had vanished. There was no hope left. Lying wounded and immobilized in one of the underground chambers near the *Gare Maritime*, Captain Airey Neave listened miserably to 'the hoarse shouts of German under-officers and the noise of rifles being flung on the floor', as the riflemen up above surrendered.[15] 'Through the doorway came field-grey figures waving revolvers. It was a sad ending.'

It was for Brigadier Nicholson, too. Later that same day, as the guns began to go quiet, a white flag was hoisted over the Citadel, which was the Brigadier's headquarters. With a German NCO, drawn revolver in his hand, Nicholson was led out and one observer recorded the 'bitter agony of defeat (which) lay unmistakably written on his face'.[16]

Calais was in German hands. Now the road to Dunkirk from the south was open to the Germans at last.

VI

'We will not hear much more of the British in this war'

The face of the countryside had changed. Before the weary, hungry men lay mile after mile of low-lying marshland. Everywhere it was criss-crossed by canals, waterways and roads. Each field was below the level of the canals so that they all had diminutive dykes running round them. Trees were few and far between so to the eyes of the men pouring towards Dunkirk, the land in front of them looked like a green and blue draught-board.

But most of those who had fought their way from Belgium had no time for poetic images. They were eager to seize the last chance to escape from this doomed country. For every road was packed with lorries, mobile search lights, bren-gun carriers, fifteen hundredweights, ambulances, breakdown lorries, anything on wheels. This then was a modern army in retreat: a defeated army, in its greyish camouflage paint, looking from a distance like a lava of mud crawling slowly towards the sea from a far-off eruption.

Everywhere white flags fluttered. The little brick-house villages through which they crawled were hung with the tokens of surrender – sheets, tow-els, tablecloths, even handkerchiefs. It would be five long years before some of them would once again see this kind of abject, total surrender – that would be Germany, March 1945. Most of the houses were barricaded behind their wooden shutters, though the anxious soldiers could sense the tense expectant life going on behind those shutters. Here and there, however, little groups of women stood, arms crossed over their aproned bosoms, watching the defeated army go without any feeling, as if it were no concern of theirs; as if these beaten young men in khaki might be aliens from some other and remote world.

Tempers were taut. Anyone trying to jump the mile-long queue for the beaches risked serious trouble. Not that the *poilus* cared for what the English thought or did any more. The war was lost. They were heading for home. Let the English, who had got them into this mess, do what they liked. Time and time again they jumped the columns, cursed and threatened by the Tommies.

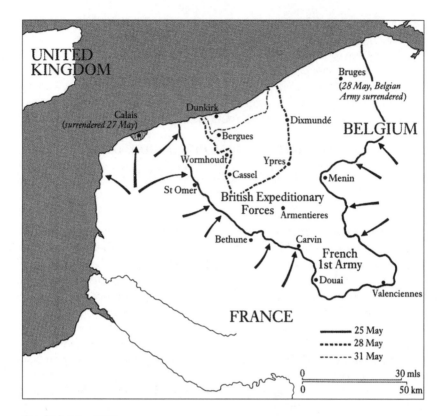

Dunkirk, May 1940

A survivor remembered how when coming to a part of the road where it narrowed, 'a truck full of *poilus*, who seemed to be in a panic to get away, insisted on trying to pass all the other vehicles on the road. They were blocking up the whole procession and causing dangerous delays, as aeroplanes could be heard overhead. Shouts of "*pull-in … pull-in …* wait your turn … what's your hurry?" came from the angry British troops, mingled with oaths and curses. But the *poilus* took no heed. They insisted on forcing a passage through. At last they endeavoured to pass my truck. I didn't waste any words. I leaped out, drew my revolver and told the driver that if he did not get back in line instantly, I'd shoot him. He pulled in.'[1]

Indeed, the troops were wasting no words or time on those who attempted to delay them. Many were trigger-happy, for they had marched and fought for over two weeks now with little food and less rest. They tended to shoot first and ask questions later. Fifth columnists, real or imagined, men or women, were shot out of hand. Vehicles that barred their way were ruthlessly shoved into the ditch. Redcaps, other ranks or officers who tried to delay them had weapons levelled at their chests and the looks in those red-rimmed, half-crazed eyes left no doubt of their intentions if they were halted any longer.

For they were looting and drinking now. The 'frogs' had let them down. Like the 'Belgies' they had gone and 'jacked it in', leaving them 'to carry the frigging can'. So why should they respect the civvies' property? If they couldn't fight for their own frigging country, why should they care? Shop windows were smashed in, estaminets were looted, cellars pillaged. The *vin rouge* disappeared, together with the fizzy northern French beer, down parched throats, and on empty stomachs the result was predictable.

But now, as the motor convoys came ever closer to the beaches, they saw for the first time regiments and battalions doing something totally unthinkable only a couple of weeks before. They were deliberately wrecking War Department property! Before it had all started, the loss of even a penny rifle pull-through had meant a 'charge'. Now the men who had arrived before them were wrecking thousands of pounds' worth of equipment before marching on foot the rest of the way.

As one officer reported, 'It was now that I saw ... regiments in the doleful process of wrecking their equipment. New wireless sets, costing perhaps £20 apiece, were placed in rows in the fields, 20 in a row sometimes, while a soldier with a pick-axe proceeded up and down knocking them to pieces. Trucks were being dealt with just as drastically. Radiators and engines were smashed with sledgehammers; tyres slashed and sawn after they had been deflated. Vehicles that were near the canals were finally pushed in. Some of the canals were choked with the wrecks, all piled on top of each other. There was more wreck than water.'[2] The victorious *Wehrmacht* would, in the end, accumulate so much abandoned British equipment and weapons that they would be using them still as late as 1944!

Meanwhile as the soldiers, now on foot, trudged towards Dunkirk – 'just head towards the smoke' – the wildest rumours flourished. '*Some o' the poor buggers have been on the beaches for three days waiting for a bleeding boat ... Cor luck a frigging duck, there's hundreds of our lads dead and dying on the beaches! ... Ain't got a chance agen them ruddy Stukas. Even when yer get a boat, old Jerry goes and sends the sod to the bottom of the drink ... Course, the officers and gents, they get taken off first ... They ain't gonna stay behind like us poor sods and go into the bleeding bag. Officers – I'VE SHAT 'EM! ..."*

In truth, as discipline began to break down on the beaches themselves and the men went wild, drinking themselves into insensibility with looted drink, some men did think their officers had failed them, had abandoned them to their fate. Officers broke down, too. Private Sidney Grainger saw a senior officer, paralysed with fear, explaining he couldn't venture out of his hole because he was guarding his precious eggs. But there were no eggs. Another major panicked and, breaking the long queue, thrashed into the water towards the waiting boat only to be shot and killed by a naval officer armed with a revolver. Lieutenant Irwin, already on a boat with what was left of his infantry platoon, saw 'one fool of an officer' who panicked and ordered all those who had been rescued to move to the port side, thus threatening the craft. 'The men, already wetting themselves, lost all semblance of control!'[3] At pistol point, they forced the panicked men to stay where they were, while 'the army chaplain, a hell of a good type, leapt in and panned the nutty officer over the head with a leaded stick, which kept him quiet.'[4]

It was typical of the mood of some of the men that one of them broke away from the throng on the mole waiting to be evacuated and approached that imperturbable, debonair guardee General Alexander, who would claim later that he was last off the beaches. 'Hey, you look like a big brass hat,' the private snapped to the major-general. 'Perhaps *you* can tell me where we get a boat for England?' Though his handful of staff officers bristled with anger at this dreadful insubordination, unthinkable in the British Army up to now, Alexander kept calm. 'Follow that lot there, son,' he answered quietly. 'Thanks a lot – you're the best pal I've had in 100 kilometres,' the private said, appeased.[5]

But if there was looting, drunkenness and some lack of discipline on the beaches, there was still plenty of courage and spirit in those last-ditch defenders of the infantry who were desperately trying to hold the Germans back. One such group were the three battalions of Alexander's First Division – the 3rd Grenadier Guards, the Black Watch and the North Staffordshires. They had been marching, fighting – and starving – just like the rest of the retreating army. Now they were ordered to halt and make a stand.

But in the case of the Grenadiers they were already running out of ammunition rapidly, as the German infantry closed in over piles of their own dead. A Lieutenant Edward Ford offered to make a run for it and try to bring back ammunition to the front. He piled his carrier full of wounded guardsmen and set off with German bullets pattering off the sides of the bren-carrier like heavy tropical rain on a tin roof. Just short of the Grenadiers' farmhouse HQ the carrier took a burst of armour-piercing bullets. Ford skidded to a stop and the wounded baled out hurriedly as the little vehicle burst into flames.

Inside the farmhouse Ford found his CO, Major Adair, one day to become the commander of a whole division of guards regiments, the Guards Armoured Division. Now, unshaven and unwashed, he was bandaging a wounded corporal. Courteous as ever, he turned and spotting Ford said, 'My dear chap, how *nice* to see you! … Have you time for tea?'[6]

But Ford was too pressed 'to take tea'. Instead he asked for two more carriers full of ammunition; the men at the front (who were so hungry that they had stuffed themselves with raw suet, the only foodstuff they could find an hour before) were now down to one round per man. In a flash, the carriers were loaded with the needed supplies and Ford set off for Captain Starkey's company, who were holding that section of the line.

He was received with whoops of joy. But they were short-lived. In his frantic haste, Ford had loaded mainly Very light cartirdges! What were the Grenadiers going to do now?

Captain Starkey, a professional officer, had noted one thing about the German tactics. Their assault so far had conformed to a strict pattern. The infantry would advance, then when they got close to the Grenadiers' positions, they called for a mortar barrage to keep the guards' heads down. They did this by signalling with Very lights in the order of red – white – red. Once the attackers were ready to close in, they called the mortars off by flares in the reverse order, white – red – white. Thereafter they would make their final rush, shrilling their whistles, cursing obscenely, yelling 'Heil Hitler!' So far the Grenadiers had managed to hold off their repeated attacks, but what now when they were virtually out of ammunition? Starkey decided to attempt one last desperate ruse.

Again the Germans prepared to attack. Across the field, the tense, expectant Grenadiers could hear the usual whistles, the hoarse cries of the NCOs rallying their men, the rattle and clatter of equipment. They were coming. Now the defenders could see them. They plodded across the shell- pocked field slowly, almost thoughtfully, well spread out, rifles held at the high port, like weary farm labourers returning home after a hard day's work.

Starkey waited till they came closer, as to left and right his men in their pits, bent over their rifles, then he raised his pistol and pressed the trigger. A soft hush. Effortlessly the flares soared into the lowering sky; red – white – red, and hung there, colouring the startled, upturned faces of the advancing Germans an unreal, glowing hue. *What was going on?*

The Germans didn't have long to wait. Their mortars reacted almost instantly. An obscene howl followed by a soft thump. Deadly black shapes started to fall from the heavens. Abruptly great brown smoking pits were appearing in the field to their front like the work of giant moles, as red-hot gleaming shards of silver steel scythed through the air, cutting down the startled enemy by the score, their bodies galvanized into frenetic, crazed action as they were hit.

To the rear of the surprised German infantry, an officer tried to call off that terrible barrage. He fired his flares into the air. Starkey was just as quick off the mark. He countered with his own 'fire' signal. A war of flares broke out as the German infantry died at the hands of their own fellow countrymen. In the end the Germans gave up and the survivors fled back the way they had come, leaving the bodies of their comrades sprawled out in the wild, extravagant postures of those done violently to death.

As quiet settled on Starkey's front once more, though in the background the sound of the 'heavies' shelling Dunkirk rumbled on and on, Major

Adair ordered that his company had to hold until 2200 hours that night. Then, if they were still there, they could withdraw.

Lieutenant Ford slumped in his hole wearily and laid out what he had left to fight with – a few grenades, a clip of ammunition, his bayonet. He thought: 'If it's got to come, then let it ... but by God I'll show them!' Not far away Captain Starkey's thoughts were more ethereal. 'Now the gap between life and death had narrowed,' he recalled afterwards. 'I felt I knew and understood all of them here so well ... the mind went back over strange things ... there was no need to put on the shell of formality ... one was never more sincere ...'[7]

Adair, Ford and Starkey survived, but many of the infantrymen, trying to hold back the enemy so desperately so that the bulk of the BEF could escape from Dunkirk, didn't. By the time they finally got away, General Irwin's 2nd Division was reduced from 13,000 strong to 2,500 men. Individual battalions, such as the 4th Royal Berkshires, which had gone to France with the 3rd Division 800 strong, came back with 47 – a 95 per cent casualty rate!

But even terrible losses of this kind could not break the spirit of the infantry. What was left of the 3rd Division's 2nd Grenadier Guards was moving into the Dunkirk perimeter after much hard fighting when a German motor-cycle patrol, dressed in civilian clothes, roared up and shot the commanding officer and two company commanders. A burst of automatic fire ripped the Germans from their motor-cycle combination and they hit the cobbles – dead.

The damage had been done, however. Within sight of the beaches, the Grenadiers had lost Colonel Jackie Lloyd, whom they all respected and admired. They moved on miserably, ready to join the queues for the boats. Suddenly one of their number, Major Faure Walker, recognized a dejected figure to his front. It was the divisional commander, Montgomery. He swung round on his men and snapped, 'March to attention ... bags of swank now ... put it on ... It's the divisional commander!'

The Grenadiers squared back their shoulders, rifles at the slope, chins up, and marched towards Montgomery, who was depressed because his driver had just been killed in action. '*Eyes left!*' the officers barked and as each section marched by the little man standing there, they gave him a terrific salute. In his turn 'Monty suddenly straightened up and gave us a great salute.'[8] It was the style – even in defeat – that was expected from the Brigade of Guards.

But that moment of euphoria passed, as it did for most of the infantry, when they first saw the beaches. Everywhere there were dead and dying among the faeces; for the sand was covered with the waste products of thousands of men who had passed that way, together with a litter of abandoned gas-masks. Against a backdrop of a burning Dunkirk, a lurid red and black, the newcomers entered the beaches and felt immediately surrounded by a tangibly evil, threatening atmosphere. As one survivor recalled: 'A horrible stench of blood and mutilated flesh pervaded the place. There was no escape from it. Not a breath of air was blowing to dissipate the appalling odour that arose from the dead bodies that had been lying on the sand, in some cases, for several days. We might have been walking through a slaughter house on a hot day. The darkness which hid some of the sights of horror from our eyes seemed to thicken this dreadful stench. It created the impression that death was hovering around, very near at hand. ...

'On either side, scattered over the sand in all sorts of positions, were the dark shapes of dead and dying men, sometimes alone, sometimes in twos and threes. Every now and then we had to pull ourselves up sharply in the darkness to avoid falling over a wooden cross erected by comrades on the spot where some soldier had been buried. No assistance that availed could be given to these dying men. The living themselves had nothing to offer them. They just pressed forward to the sea, hoping that the same fate would not be theirs. And still it remained a gamble all the time whether that sea, close though it was, would be reached in safety. Splinters from bursting shells were continually whizzing through the air and occasionally a man in one of the plodding groups would fall with a groan.'[9]

Now at last the rearguard, which had fought so bravely to save their comrades who had gone before, was passing to the boats, attacked almost constantly by the dive-bombers – The Loyal Regiment, which had held the old fortified town of Bergues for two days, with the Deputy Chaplain and his padres holding one gate. Twenty-six officers and 451 men out of the original 800, a loss of 50 per cent of the battalion's effectives. The Duke of Wellington's Regiment, which had been the first to open fire on the enemy in World War Two and one of the last to disengage, 50 per cent losses. The 1/7th Royal Warwickshire Regiment, 15 officers and 220 other ranks – 60 per cent casualties. Its sister battalion, the 8th Battalion, eight officers and 134 men left, nearly 80 per cent casualties. ...

Still some of them fought on, such as the 40-strong force of the 1st East Lancashire Regiment, left behind to cover the retreat of what was left of the battalion. This rearguard was commanded by Captain Ervine-Andrews, a heavy-set Irishman. Before the war in India and China he had been regarded as a 'hard man'. He would walk 50-odd miles for a five pound bet or after having shot a black buck in the jungle carry the heavy burden home through the steaming swamps on his big shoulders.

Now with the building they had been defending burning all around them, the Irish captain called above the snap-and-crackle of the small-arms battle, 'Look, there are 500 of them, maybe 36 of us – let them get a bit closer and then here goes!'

Shrilling on his whistle, he dashed forward to the massed Germans. His handful of East Lancs didn't hesitate. They streamed after him, shouting crazily. Taken completely by surprise, the Germans fell back. Hurriedly Ervine-Andrews clambered up on to the roof of a nearby barn and started taking potshots at the enemy. He picked off at least 17. Then he seized a bren-gun and, according to the official citation, 'accounted for many more'.

But now his ammunition was nearly finished. As one of his men, Private Taylor, recalled later, 'It was a right do – when the ammo ran low we kicked, choked, even *bit* them'.[10]

In the end, the Germans gave up. The handful of East Lancs, led by the wild Irishman, were just too much for them. They ceased attacking. Ervine Andrews now sent his wounded back in the last remaining bren-gun carrier, leaving with exactly eight men still on their feet. But he still wasn't going to give up. According to the official citation, 'He then collected the remaining eight men of his company from this forward position and when almost surrounded, led them back to the cover afforded by the company to the rear, swimming or wading up to the chin in water for over a mile.'[11]

For his part in this action, Captain Ervine-Andrews of the East Lancashire Regiment, one of the last of the infantry formations to leave the burning beaches of Dunkirk, was awarded the Victoria Cross: the first British soldier to win it in World War Two.*

As soon as it was dark on 2 June, 1940, the remnants of the BEF embarked on destroyers tied up at the mole at Dunkirk, which was guarded by men of the 5th Green Howards, bearing fixed bayonets. 'There was to be no embarkation by the French until the British were finished,' the War Diary of the 1st Infantry Division states unequivocally. By 11.30 that night this had been done and Captain Tennant, RN, told his signals officer, 'Make to Vice-Admiral Dover – BEF evacuated'.

Now General Alexander and half a dozen others got into a motor-boat, after ordering the single remaining destroyer to wait for them at the mole, and set out on the last mission. Zigzagging wildly to dodge the shells which were landing in the water all the time, the little craft moved along the beaches. Twice the motor-boat grounded on sand bars and those in the boat later remembered the corpses of many soldiers floating silently in the oil slick. But Alexander persisted. Time and time again, shouting through his megaphone above the thunder of the guns and the shrill whine of the shells, *'Is anyone there? … Is anyone there?'* He called both in English and French.'[12]

According to Alexander's biographer, Nigel Nicholson, 'there was no reply' and 'at about 2 a.m. on 3 June, they left the harbour for England'.[13]

---

* The second, also awarded for his part during the Dunkirk evacuation, was given Lance-Corporal Harry Nicholls of the Grenadier Guards. His, like so many of them was awarded *posthumously*.

Of course there were. There were at least eighty thousand French soldiers in the area, some 50,000 of them holding the line to cover the British retreat and withdrawal. On board one of the last ships to go, author David Divine saw the silhouettes of at least a thousand Frenchmen outlined against the startling violet flashes of the shells exploding on Dunkirk. Still under fire and without any hope now, they withdrew to the shattered port – 'quite the most tragic thing I have ever seen in my life'.[14]

But Britain's alliance with France had about broken down. Within a month the Royal Navy would sink much of France's fleet, killing over a thousand French sailors, and France would consider bombing Gibraltar in retaliation. Now for Britain it was *sauve qui peut*, and at Dunkirk the country had succeeded in saving 338,226 men. Behind they had left 2,472 guns and 63,879 vehicles, plus 76,097 tons of ammunition and 416,940 tons of general stores.

So they went home to a heroes' welcome. Huge crowds lined the embankments and railway lines on the 40-mile stretch from Dover to London to see them pass. Bunting was strung between houses near the rails. Flags were waved. Children cheered. '*Well Done BEF!*' was scrawled on garden fences. Using a swear word for the first time in the British Press, the tabloid Daily Mirror's jubilant headline read: 'BLOODY MARVELLOUS!'

But it wasn't 'bloody marvellous'. It was a tremendous defeat. In Berlin Hitler told one of his generals confidently, 'We will not hear much more of the British in this war. ...'

VII

'Is there anyone there?'

While Britain deluded itself with this strange euphoria for the Defeat at
Dunkirk – 'if this is how the British celebrate a defeat, *how do they celebrate
a victory?'*, one puzzled French officer was heard to ask – there were still
thousands of British infantrymen in France. Indeed a week *after* Dunkirk
new units were being sent to that country, including a whole fresh infantry division, the 52nd Lowland Division, plus part of the 1st Canadian
Infantry Division.

But most of the new arrivals barely got further than their ports of disem-
barkation, Dieppe, Brest and Cherbourg, and were later withdrawn with
hardly a fight. It was different with that territorial division, which was
Scotland's pride, the 51st Highland Division. The 'braw laddies', whose
major concern back in January had been whether or not they should go
to war wearing the kilt, had been hurriedly withdrawn from the Saar as
soon as the BEF's front in Belgium had begun to crumble. By train and by
road they had been taken to the rear, where they had taken part in the only
successful counter-attack of the campaign in France, together with the
British 1st Armoured Division and the one commanded by an unknown
General de Gaulle.

Thereafter, however, the 51st had been unable to hold the tremendously
long, 20-mile stretch of the Somme front which had been allotted to them
by the French. One day after Dunkirk had been evacuated, June 4th,
two battalions of the Division – the 4th Seaforths and 4th Camerons, lost
between them 20 officers and 543 men. The long retreat to the coast had
commenced.

Now the Highlanders marched and fought 10 to 12 miles a day,
attacked all the time by Stuka dive-bombers, harassed by snipers and Fifth
Columnists, rarely out of range of the German machine-gunners, fighting
off German assaults, which often came in behind the cover of crowds of
refugees. The men were sleeping on their feet, completely worn out. Many
of them had not taken their boots off for six long weeks. And casualties
were mounting all the time.

On 5 June, the Division's 154th Brigade was struck by elements of *four* German infantry divisions. The pressure was tremendous. By the evening the 7th Battalion the Argyll and Sutherland Highlanders had lost 500 men, including 23 officers; while one company of their sister battalion, the 8th, was cut off in a village for 48 hours. Here 170 of them slogged it out with the enemy until finally they surrendered, having suffered a staggering 130 casualties!

On the night of 8/9 June, the Division retreated again, getting ever closer to the Channel. Now General Fortune, whose proverbial luck was rapidly running out, began to hope that the Royal Navy might evacuate what was left of his battered division. But that wasn't to be. Already the Germans had seized the cliffs to the west of their positions and had severely damaged the destroyers *Ambuscade* and *Boadicea*, which had been supporting the Highlanders, with their artillery.

Hurriedly General Fortune formed a perimeter around the little port of St Valery, a name which will be long remembered with bitterness in some parts of Scotland. He signalled the War Office that time was running out. He had rations left for exactly 48 hours. But he still hoped that the fleet of 70 merchant ships which was being assembled at Portsmouth would be able to take off the 51st.

He hadn't reckoned with a brisk, square-faced Swabian general, with the pugnacious, dimpled chin of a fighter. The commander of the German 7th Panzer Division had missed out in the campaign in Poland; he had been forced to take over the staff job of looking after the Führer's safety during his travels in that unfortunate country. It had been a job he hated, for he loved front-line service. Now with an active command at last, he was a general in a hurry, out to prove himself before he ran out of wars. His name was Erwin Rommel.

Now he thrust home his armoured drive to the coast, writing to his wife back in Stuttgart, 'The sight of the sea with the cliffs on either side thrilled and stirred every man of us; also the thought that we had reached the coast of France. We climbed out of our vehicles and walked down the shingle beach to the water's edge until the water lapped over our boots. Several dispatch riders in long waterproof coats walked straight out until the water was over their knees and I had to call them back. Our task was over and the enemy's road to Le Havre and Fécamp was closed.'[1]

It was, and with it the best port for the evacuation of a force as large as what was left of the 51st Highland Division had fallen into enemy hands. All that was left was the small port of St Valery itself, which as we have seen was under direct German fire. Of course, the Navy wouldn't let the 'brown jobs' down. They *did* try. The tug *Fair Play* brought in four craft to evacuate the waiting Highlanders. But there was no fair play in total war. Heavy fire was brought to bear on the small craft and they were hit and sunk almost immediately. The sloop managed to sail in under fire, take off

80 soldiers, and reach the exit to the harbour before she, too, was hit and sunk, taking with her her commanding officer. In the end the Navy gave up. As a soft, cold rain began to fall, it was announced that no more boats would be coming.

Rommel did not want to suffer any more casualties, so he tried trickery. He sent an emissary bearing a white flag to a battalion of the Seaforths, holding the woods near Le Tor. The emissary said blandly, the 51st had surrendered; why continue fighting? The officers of the Seaforths didn't know what to believe – communications were so poor. So they sent out their wounded and those who had volunteered to stay with them. Then the rest broke up and tried to slip through the German lines in small parties. Few succeeded. The 51st was beginning to crumble.

At 2 a.m. one of the many Jocks trapped, Private McCready, was told by his platoon commander, who distributed the last of his cigarettes among the men, 'it was a case of every man for himself. So we all bundled into the remaining five trucks, and I must say that I was completely unaware of what direction the coast lay or what was to be done, in fact, I was beyond caring about anything.'[2] But this escape party, like most of those which tried to get away, was unsuccessful. 'We had only gone half a mile when we were ambushed by a machine gun. I scrambled out somehow and dived into the ditch; then the enemy started using Very lights and picked the men off with Tommy guns as they jumped off the truck … I almost got a burst into my back.' The cocky little Jock managed to escape. But most of his party didn't. They either died or went 'into the bag'.[3]

At dawn on 12 June, Fortune received a message from his French Corps Commander, General Ihler, that he intended to surrender. Outside his own HQ there were French soldiers everywhere, waving white flags. Hastily Fortune sent a staff officer to the weary French general to inform him that the Highland Division intended to fight on. The staff officer returned with a message: '14 Juin 40. Le feu cessera à huit heures, Ihler.'

Fortune, who now felt he need no longer obey the French Corps Commander, considered what he could do next. The Navy couldn't take his Division off and he was surrounded on all sides, pinned down on the coast. Should he order a breakout in small groups or should it be a mass attempt? But before he could come to any firm decision, an evil-looking German tank rumbled up outside his headquarters. Its gun swung round and pointed directly at the door. Up in the turret an officer, clad in black, called in English, 'Where is General Fortune?' The big bluff officer, with his trim moustache, let his shoulders sag momentarily in defeat. He had been captured!

Now, after he had been taken to Rommel to be photographed with the future 'Desert Fox' (Rommel dearly loved to photograph battlefields, especially if there were a few dead bodies draped dramatically in the background), Fortune gave the order that those parts of the division which were still fighting should cease. The 'pride of Scotland', the 51st Highland Division, had surrendered.

Major Rennie of the Black Watch, one of his staff officers, was told to convey the order to Fortune's old regiment. They were to cease fire and surrender.

At first the weary soldiers were stunned. For a while most of them refused to believe Major Rennie. But then, as Rennie was well known and trusted in the First Battalion, they knew his word could no longer be doubted. With understanding came dismay. Tough infantrymen, old sweats with years of service behind them all over the Empire, broke down and wept openly. Some survivors refused to surrender and continued to fight for a while. Three hours after the official surrender, there were still men of the Black Watch fighting off Rommel's tanks, hopelessly outnumbered as they were. But in the end they too surrendered, followed a little while later by the last fragment of the Gordon Highlanders. They were disarmed and were allowed by Rommel, in a moment of generosity, to march past a gloomy Fortune, whose career was now ruined. Marching in a cold drizzle, they swung by their former divisional commander and gave him a smart *'eyes right'*, while the German cameras clicked and clicked. ...

While the Germans decided what to do with the 8,000-odd prisoners, plus the 40,000 others they had taken in the retreat to Dunkirk, some of the Highlanders escaped. Major Rennie was one. After an adventurous flight he managed to get back to England. One day he would command a re-formed Highland Division – and die in battle with them on the Rhine in March 1945. Instead of taking the long route he went through southern France and Spain; others got away directly across the Channel. One battalion adjutant, after first burying the unit funds, rowed single-handed to England. Others broke through the German cordon, such as Private McCready, who spotted a British ship off-shore ready to take him and his comrades off. But there was a problem.

'There was no way down the cliffs, which were 300 feet high and a sheer drop. Someone started making a rope of rifle-slings, and I joined in, but by the time we had it made it was daylight and the enemy was shelling from both sides. I was fourth man on the rope and it was two and a half hours before I got down. The first man to go met his death as the slings snapped, but it was either chance it or get caught, so over I went. What a drop; and the bullets spattering all over. We were being machine-gunned and sniped all the time. However, I got down without mishap and struggled along two miles of beach to the boats.

'What a lot of dead men on that beach – it was littered with them. I had just got into the small boat when the bombers came; one boat was sunk with about 30 men in it, only one man being saved. How I got on the ship is a bit of a dream to me, but get on I did, and soaked to the skin and simply covered with mud. I just sprawled to the deck, out for the count. I soon got a rude awakening as the enemy started shelling from the cliff-tops, but the destroyers put paid to their career. All those who had rifles had to get up on the top deck and fire at the planes. So I fired my remaining bandolier. ...'[4]

But the Rennies and the McCreadys were few and far between. Old sweat Percy Castle, who had been so contemptuous of the territorials' discipline back in '39 and who now woke up from an exhausted sleep to find himself a prisoner-of-war, thought angrily that '90 per cent' of his comrades, 'were completely apathetic'.[5] Tamely enough they filed by the grinning Germans to throw down their rifles on the ever-growing pile in the centre of a wet field. Private Castle did so with the rest, but the little man burned with rage. He had been caught on the hop and he didn't like it one bit. But for the time being he allowed himself to be herded along by the second-line German troops, who had now taken over, with the rest of the dispirited mob.

Separated from their officers, who had been sent to the prison camps in the Reich by train, the long columns of infantrymen started to slog north. In some places such as St Pol, the civilians took pity on them and threw them scraps of food. In northern Belgium it was different. Here the 'civvies' shook their fists at the dejected, beaten prisoners and sometimes spat upon them. Twenty-five miles a day they marched, often soaked by the rain, living off a cup of black coffee and a piece of bread. 'On many days' as Private Douglas Thow recalled long afterwards, 'there was no food at all and we were forced to forage in fields where there were potatoes, sugar beet, dandelions and nettles. Many of us had nettle soup, but often the beet and potatoes were eaten raw ... We had to wash the best we could – in the puddles usually.'[6]

By the time his particular column had reached the Belgian border Percy Castle had had enough. For a while, as he put it, he had 'come the old soldier', falling out of the column, looking wan and miserable, and taking off his battered boots to massage his feet. This had often aroused the sympathy of the civilians, watching the column shuffle by, and he had been given food and water. But he had fallen foul of a particular nasty German guard, who had snatched away his only blanket, knocked him down with the butt of his rifle and then had smashed his boot into the prostrate man's ribs.

Percy decided to 'hoof it'. The long column, one of scores now wending its way to the Reich, was guarded front and back by a solitary truck, with a machine-gunner posted on the roof. So Percy waited until the column trudged round a bend, when he couldn't be seen by the truck's gunner and swiftly sprang into a cornfield and hid in the standing corn till dusk when he was sure that there were no more guards bringing up the tail of the disappearing column. He then made his way to a wrecked railway station, where he started to bury his way into the rubble. He pushed a board aside and gasped with horror as his hand touched something soft, warm and living'. 'Christ Almighty, I nearly snuffed it there and then with a heart attack!' he recalled almost 50 years later as a very old but forceful man.[7]

But what he had touched was the bald head of a Frenchman hiding there. His adventures had begun. For two years he would be on the run in Nazi-occupied Europe. He would be captured yet again by the Germans, interned by the French and imprisoned by the Spaniards, finally to reach the safety of the British Embassy in Madrid, where he would be baked in wax all over to remove the many ticks in his emaciated body, only to find on his return to the UK in 1942 that he was to be arrested yet again – *by British Field Security*!

That was the last straw. Percy swore to his new CO 'I'll soldier no more' … 'Do what you like, sir, but I won't soldier no more!'[8] Three months later Percy Castle found himself back with the re-formed 51st Highland Division in North Africa, waiting for the invasion of Sicily. Percy would 'soldier on', whether he liked it or not, till May 1945. …

But because of his boldness, Percy Castle would be spared the horrors of becoming a 'kriegie'* for the next five years. He would not be cut off from the outside world, without women, existing on a minimum of poor food, at the mercy of his guards' whims. As one officer of the Highland Division recalled many years later: 'I can remember that in about November 1940 I had a bottom bunk. I had one blanket and I remember there was snow on the ground, and when the snow was carried in on the boots into the barrack room, the whole floor was covered with water. And I lay on this bottom bunk so cold and so hungry that I prayed that when I went to sleep that night I shouldn't wake up. That's how despondent I was.'[9]

Those thousands and thousands of 'kriegies' now in German hands had been condemned to waste some of the best years of their young lives behind barbed wire because their country had sent them to France ill-prepared, ill-trained and ill-led. They had no effective anti-tank weapons to stop the German panzer divisions (and would continue to be without suitable anti-tank guns right throughout the war). Even when they had the guns, they were not supplied with enough ammunition. Thirteen days after the start of the German offensive, the BEF was placed on half rations and Gort was forced to cable London that 'we have not, repeat not, ammunition for a serious attack'.[10] Twenty years of apathy, when the Army was starved of money, could not be rectified in a matter of months.

Back in England in 1939 Percy Castle, newly recalled to the colours, thought his territorial battalion 'more of a social club, where the Jocks

---

* POW slang taken from the German word *Kriegsgefangener*, i.e. prisoner-of-war.

called the Old Man (i.e. the colonel) by his first name, than a fighting regiment'.[12] In truth, for the average civilian the Army, regular or territorial, had been something of a joke up to 1939. As Mass Observation reported at the height of the 'phoney war', 'Before the war, even in the last weeks of August, the only response to shots of soldiers (in newsreels) was laughter. On not one occasion since the war has any soldier been laughed at.' But by then it was too late. Up to then the Regular Army had seemed to most civilians to be composed of work-shy dodgers, the unemployed or petty criminals – 'you will either join the Army or I'll sentence you to six months inside' – officered by upper-class 'chinless twits', who thought solely of horses and dogs and 'shooting things'.

In truth, there were plenty of officers who went to France in 1939 thinking it was going to be a great jaunt. Officers did take their horses and their dogs with them. Some took tennis racquets and golf clubs, too, as if they were off on a sports weekend in 'jolly old France'. One returned and wrote a book of his experiences, entitling it *'Grand Party'**. Officers of this kind fought bravely enough, it must be admitted, but they had not learned their trade. They were not fitted to lead men into battle against the Germans, who were highly professional and had been well and truly 'blooded' in the fighting in Poland the previous year.

High and low, they fell down on the job. Half-trained officers often leading virtually untrained men, however willing, were no match for the *Wehrmacht*, where officers had spent nearly two years in the ranks before being commissioned. The results were predictable. Because of a blunder by a senior officer, the 12th Infantry Division was destroyed in a single day on the Somme. The 51st Highland Division was forced into surrender because no one higher up the chain of command than General Fortune seemed capable of making a decision to save the Highlanders. Nicholson's Brigade was sacrificed at Calais for no real strategic or tactical purpose, in full view of the Kent coast, with the BEF only a mere 30 miles away! …

Back in England, however, they knew none of this. Montgomery, there too, was horrified when he saw 'British soldiers walking around London and elsewhere with a coloured embroidered flash on their sleeve with the title "Dunkirk"'. As he later recalled, 'they thought they were heroes and the civilian public thought so too. It was not understood that the British Army had suffered a crushing defeat at Dunkirk and that our island home was now in grave danger!'[13]

Montgomery's superior, General Auchinleck, who while in command in Norway during that equally ill-fated campaign had thought that 'Our men for the most part seemed distressingly young, not so much in years as in self-reliance and manliness generally; they give an impression of being

---

* Lieut-Colonel G. Brooks: *Grand Party*. Hutchinson, 1942

June 1940

callow and undeveloped, which is not reassuring for the future', [14] was also alarmed by the 'Dunkirk spirit'. 'By the way,' he wrote that summer, 'there is some bizarre "gupp" about a "Dunkirk Medal"... I hope it isn't true and I can't believe it. We do not want to perpetuate the memory of that episode, surely?'[15]

But the nation which had already sacrificed 60,000 young men in France did. They wanted to believe in the 'Deliverance of Dunkirk' and the 'Gallant Stand at Calais' (the loss of the 51st Highland Division at St Valery was quietly forgotten). 'To create heroic legends,' wrote the author of the history of that corps which lost so many men at Calais, 'successful and heroic objectives are necessary, and what better ones can there be than to sacrifice oneself so that others may escape?'[16]

For a good while yet they would continue to send their young men, still poorly armed, trained and led, on campaigns over half the world. An unthinking, perhaps even unfeeling, nation would commit them to battles that they hadn't a chance in hell of winning. And who, invariably, pays the butcher's bill? Why, of course – THE POOR BLOODY INFANTRY … !

BOOK TWO
1941–1942

Let the boy try along this bayonet-blade
How cold steel is, and keen with hunger of blood.

'Arms and the Boy', Wilfred Owen

I

'Will they never fight?'

'It is the will of the democratic war inciters and their Jewish-capitalistic wire-pullers,' Hitler thundered in his New Year's Eve radio message to his victorious soldiers, 'that the war must be continued. ... We are ready! ... The year 1941 will bring completion of the greatest victory in our history.'[1]

As the strains of that hoarse, hysterical Upper Austrian voice died away, the brass band broke into the bombastic blare of *Deutschland Uber Alles*. Grouped round their pear-shaped 'people's receivers', his happy, drink-flushed listeners in garrisons ranging from the Arctic Circle to the Mediterranean, and from the Channel coast to the Vistula in Poland, sprang to their feet and flung out their right arms in the 'German greeting'.

'*Sieg Heil!*' they bellowed confidently till the walls of their billets shook. Well they might. For this icy Tuesday, the last day of 1940, the Third Reich was the master of Europe. Germany had won all its battles; the Reich was virtually at peace. The Führer, in his infinite wisdom, had even demobilized half a dozen divisions after he had signed the peace with France.

Admittedly, while their newest ally Japan was beginning to carve up the Far East for itself, Italy, the other member of the 'Pact of Steel', was having some trouble in Africa. The Tommies were chasing them across the Western Desert this New Year's Eve. In Ethiopia – wherever that was, 'the spaghetti-eaters', as they called the Italians, were being beaten by a bunch of 'bush-niggers' and English, too.

But what did that matter? Who was concerned with what was happening to the 'macaronis' in Africa? The French had been knocked out of the war and the English run out of Europe for good. Let Fat Hermann's* flyboys bomb them into surrender. The *Luftwaffe* had been over London night after night for months now. Only two days before they had shattered Central London and killed over a thousand English civilians.

---

* The enormously fat head of the *Luftwaffe*, Herman Goering.

No, those happy drunken young men of that New Year's Eve so long ago must have told themselves confidently, this is peacetime with one slight difference. They were in uniform and could have the choice of women from a dozen different European countries. It was better than '*Mutti*' and her baggy flannel knickers any day. *Prost*!

On that same New Year's Eve and well into the morning of the first day of 1941, 'the democratic war inciters' in the shape of the 'New British Army', as it was being called, were slogging it out on training exercises. In the snows of Scotland, hogmanay ignored, the infantrymen of the 52nd Lowland Division, just like their comrades of the 3rd Infantry Division, down in the rain-sodden fields of the south, trained and trained as British soldiers had never trained before.

They ran five miles an hour, laden with 30 pounds of kit, steel helmet, and rifle. They slogged through the night, completing 20- and 30-mile route marches. They cross-countried in twos, with no money and no food, stealing to eat, with the police and the Home Guard on the lookout for them, trekking 50 miles without stopping. They practised bayonet-fighting in abattoirs, harassed by sadistic instructors, with warm animal blood thrown in their faces as they plunged home their bayonets. They fought vicious bouts of hand-to-hand combat with no holds barred. '*Go on, kick him in the fucking balls. ... Jab his bloody eye, out, willyer ...*' For while the German victors celebrated, a new spirit was beginning to animate the defeated British Army.

Back in the summer of 1940, a top secret conference, chaired by Eden, in the splendid pile of York's Station Hotel, had discussed the morale of the British Army. Eden had wanted to know if the troops would fight on in Canada if the Germans succeeded in conquering southern England. How loyal, in short, was the Army after the Dunkirk débâcle?

The results were very depressing. Commander after commander testified that, while the regulars would fight where they were told to fight, even in Canada, the wartime conscripts would fight on British soil – or not at all. In the last instance, they would simply desert to their families. At about the same time the Vice-Chief of the Imperial General Staff, Sir John Dill, told Chamberlain that the troops were 'demoralized ... and may not be steady when the time comes'.[2]

Returning from the Middle East, Captain Frost, who one day would command the 2nd Parachute Battalion in its epic stand on the bridge at Arnhem, noted to his dismay that 'all over England one saw dirty, untidy soldiers, slouching and slovenly. One heard stories of the wanton damage done to houses in which soldiers were billeted. In London it was the exception rather than the rule for an officer to be saluted by another rank.'[3] Frost, who would end the war wounded and in a German prison camp, thought 'To the uninformed it seemed as though there was something radically wrong with either the leaders and soldiers or the training and equipment of the army, and a whole host of self-styled military experts began to expound their views on the subject. One particular section of the press found opportunity to deride all forms of military discipline. According to them the custom of showing respect to and saluting officers was quite out of date in a democratic country. They saw no reason why half the regulations in the army should be enforced. In their opinion no soldier should ever clean or blanco his clothing or equipment and any form of drill was quite ridiculous. ... We were a democratic people fighting for freedom and must not tolerate any semblance of fascism in our army.'[4]

That had been in the summer. Now, however, new senior commanders like Montgomery, who had been personally booed by the Coldstream Guards on his return from France, were trying to put a fresh spirit into the Army. Montgomery tolerated no slackness from anyone, high or low. He fired generals as easily as he did second-lieutenants. He insisted that everyone, including staff officers in their fifties, should go on cross-country runs each week, to 'get rid of all the smoke and gin'.

Visiting one of the divisions of his new 5th Corps, General Martel's 50th Division, he could write of the unit which had seen much action in France: 'The standard of training in the Division is low. All energies have been directed to work on defence. The net result is that all the finer arts of how to compete with the Germans in battle have been put in the background. There are men who have never in their lives fired more than five rounds with the rifle; there are men who have never fired the bren gun; the use of carriers is not practised; the Headquarters of formations and units are untrained; the techniques of observation and sniping as learnt from the Germans are untouched; and so on. ...

'I met companies who had been in the same place for one month, doing nothing but dig and work on defences. The men had done no drill, no PT, no training. The men did not seem to be on their toes. I did not see the light of battle in their eyes.'[5]

After visiting the 4th Division, another formation which had been in France, Montgomery ordered the commander of the divisional artillery, the senior staff officer, the commander of the Service Corps and two regimental commanders sacked. He also discovered to his horror that the CO of the 8th Battalion, the Hampshire Regiment, was 63 years old and his second-in-command 59, and 'I interviewed several platoon commanders of 55'.[6] By the time Montgomery was finished, infantry battalions would go into action commanded by officers who were in their twenties.

The new generals like Montgomery insisted that training should not only be tough but realistic too. Exercises now were carried out with live ammunition. A bren gunner, firing live tracer, would be stationed at each end of a line of infantry. Once the order to advance was given, the gunners would fire a criss-cross of live rounds to the men's immediate front, while, from the rear, live mortar shells from the 3-inch mortars would be fired to give the trainees a taste of the real thing. Of course there were casualties, as the Canadian Farley Mowat, now training with the 'Hasty Pees' in England, found out.

'The *pièce de résistance* [of the training] was a half-mile obstacle course, mostly constructed of barbed wire that had to be surmounted or crawled under in four minutes flat. One day our personal demon of an instructor decided this was not enough and added a new wrinkle. As we staggered over the last barbed wire entanglement, he ordered us to double to the right, over a hill and swim a pond on the other side ... There was the pond – a huge open septic tank in which stagnated the sewage from most of the military camps in the Witley area!

'The leaders of our panting mob drew up in horror on the edge of this stinking pit, but the demon was right behind us, tossing percussion grenades under our tails, so in we plunged ...

'Before the first week was out, we had lost eight or nine of our number, three of them wounded during live firing exercises ... and I awoke one morning to find myself with the symptoms of a dose of clap, a discovery that shocked, disgusted and frightened me.'[7]

Young Mowat, who had had his virginity snatched the previous week by a hefty Land Army girl wearing manure-stained jodhpurs, need not have worried. His 'complaint' had been caused by the dip in the sewage pond, the MO assured him.

Another young infantry officer, Norman Craig, also noted the new spirit in the Army, coming especially from those senior officers who had been shocked by the débâcle in France. Normally, when the young officers of his brigade were lectured on the mistakes they had made on the most recent training exercise they fell asleep; for they were tired all the time. Not, however, when Brigadier Templer, one day to be chief of the British Army, came to talk to them. His lecture was on the 'Junior Leader in Battle' and he started off by saying, 'There is an old tradition that there should be no shop talk in the mess. I never want to hear you talk anything but shop, at any time! We have all got so much to learn, gentlemen, and there is so little time.'

Brigadier Templer went on to describe the infantry subaltern's first experience of battle, 'You are advancing peacefully with your platoon along a quiet lane. Suddenly all hell is let loose. You look up and your platoon sergeant's guts are hanging on a tree beside you! The platoon is turning to run – it is then, gentlemen, that you must *grip* those men!' Templer paused in absolute silence, and holding out his arm, tightened his fist slowly in a graphic gesture. Craig thought 'It was superb theatre and we sat enthralled'.[8]

But in spite of the reformers in a hurry, there was still a great deal of dead wood which needed trimming. The Army was still full of 'Colonel

Blimps', martial and patriotic, but clinging tenaciously to the old ways and outmoded traditions. Author Thomas Firbank, now an officer with the Brigade of Guards, found the Coldstreams stuck rigidly to their old style, as if the British Army had not suffered a terrible defeat in France. His adjutant's main concern with the young officers was to see that their hair was cut regularly, to amplify the knowledge of regimental history taught at the Depot, and to teach them a short glossary of words, the use of which would help to set them apart from the rest of the Army. Only four of these words were very important. 'London' was 'London' and not 'Town'. A 'service dress' was not a 'tunic', since the tunics of the Brigade are scarlet. A 'servant' was a servant and not a 'batman', and why not? And finally the Brigade wore 'plain clothes' when out of uniform. As Badger (the adjutant) said: 'Those fellows who live among the Wogs may wear mufti, but the Brigade has never served east of Suez.'

The Brigade of Guards still carried out its traditional functions, such as guarding the royal family at Buckingham Palace – 'Buck House', as Firbank now learned to call it. There 'there was a fine old-world air of privilege about the Mess at St James's. The food was good and the stock of wine still catholic. We invited mixed guests to lunch and men guests to dinner and wound up the day at the cleared dining table, circulating port by candlelight. This, I thought, was soldiering indeed.'[9] Perhaps, but it certainly did not fit men for the horrific stress of total war. ...

There was still too much bull, too. In training units men were expected to polish the *soles* of their boots and burnish the studs till they shone. The backs of the army-issued brushes had to be scrubbed till they were a bright white. In some units they even painted the top layer of coal (with which they heated the huts) with whitewash; and it was rumoured that when the Princess Royal came to inspect a unit in Catterick on a snowy day, men were detailed, once the battalion had gone on the parade ground, to cover their boot marks with fresh snow. When the Princess arrived, she was to be greeted by an immaculate battalion standing rigidly to attention in an expanse of virgin snow. No wonder the soldiers quipped; 'If it moves, salute it. If it stands still, blanco it. If it's too heavy to lift, paint it.' As they said in weary resignation: '*Bullshit baffles brains*'.

There were, too, still far too many men who were trying to stick it out in the depots for the 'duration', by 'swinging the lead', or inflicting diseases or complaints upon themselves so that they would be downgraded to 'C-3', or even discharged. There were those who rubbed diesel oil into their chests secretly in 'the ablutions' in order to cause an incurable eczema. Some who went to crooked doctors, who – at a price – could give a reluctant soldier hernia and his discharge. Others who faked mysterious complaints or even mental illness. Some even attempted to paralyse limbs by sleeping, for instance, with a hard cricket ball under the armpit. In 1941, as it became clear that there was still hard fighting ahead in the Desert and half a dozen other places in the Middle East, there were lead swingers and malingerers everywhere.

The Army reacted – predictably – by setting up a whole chain of new military prisons to punish those who would not serve in places such as Hull, Northallerton, Sowerby Bridge and Shepton Mallet (the latter was handed over to the Americans for the same use afterwards and became notorious for its sadistic commandant). These 'glasshouses' (named after the first military prison at Aldershot, which had a glass roof) were feared throughout the Army, even by hardened military criminals.

The days were long, starting at six with reveille and ending at nine with lights out, filled with hard physical activity, punctuated with short breaks for meals. Smoking was mostly forbidden. For most of the day talking between the prisoners – or 'men under sentence', as the Army liked to call them – was also prohibited until eight o'clock at night. Everything was done at the double. 'In the glasshouse we even go and shit at the double', was a common complaint. The slightest infringement of the rules could be punished with bread and water for three days or withdrawal of 'biscuits' and bedding so that the 'man under sentence' would be forced to sleep uncovered on the bare springs of his bed.

In spite of the fact that the Army insisted that as many as 20 per cent of the inmates were illiterate, verminous, and suffering from dirt diseases, and were men who already had a criminal record before they were called up, ordinary, intelligent young soldiers *did* find themselves in the glass-house. Mostly it was for 28 days for having overstayed their leave. And it was a shattering experience for most of them. One prisoner was quoted as telling the glasshouse authorities, 'Once you have been in detention, you know what it's like. When you haven't, detention frightens you more than you think.'[10] Another said, 'My spirit was completely broken and I never thought I could be made such an abject craven human being or that at my age I should ever shed tears. But so it was. The horrors endured in those detention barracks are so painful to me that I cannot bring myself to relate them.'[11]

One ex-officer, who was unfortunate enough to land in detention barracks in the Middle East (by the end of the war there would be British Army detention barracks in every theatre of the great conflict), wrote bitterly of his experiences there afterwards: 'Here when a prisoner passes the iron gate he is treated with total contempt for his identity as a man. He is made to strip naked and double mark time with knees up, arms held above his head while the sergeants watch, smoking cigarettes and yelling orders or abuse. Had not the material of these men been stronger than their tormentors they might have succeeded in bestializing them. They were mainly average disciplined young civilian soldiers who had not committed a crime, their chief fault overstaying their leave. Whistles got us up in the morning an hour before dawn and we doubled to the gatehouse to get razors. No knives, no mirrors were allowed and so we ate with a spoon and a piece of tin.'[12]

It was widely thought in the Army that the 'staffs' (whatever their rank, the guards were always assumed to be staff-sergeants) of the Military Prison Staff Corps routinely beat up their charges, especially if they were 'hard cases' who wouldn't soldier. The Army denied this or that any kind of physical punishment was meted out to the men under sentence, though they couldn't deny the men were locked up for a solid 42 hours at a week-end and that such establishments as the Aldershot glasshouse still carried on their inventories 'straitjackets', 'ankle cuffs' and 'chains'.

Under pressure they opened up the glasshouses for inspection by visiting journalists. The ex-war correspondent James Hodson visited one and reported: 'I visited one of their barrack rooms and have never seen such polished metal ... No smoking is allowed and no beer. They may write one letter a week, but can receive as many as they like ... They get no newspapers, but the headline news is read to them.'[13]

Journalist MacDonald Hastings visited Aldershot Detention Barracks for the *Picture Post*, which felt it was a crusading magazine on the side of the common man. His subsequent article, entitled 'Inside the Glasshouse: First Pictures ever taken', concluded: 'Reports that prisoners are physically knocked about by members of the prison staff – however justified such a measure might seem – are nonsense.'[14]

Yet in the same year that Hodson and Hastings visited the glasshouses and gave them a clean bill of health, a 40-year-old soldier under sentence was brutally attacked and killed by two 'staffs' of the Fort Darland glasshouse at Chatham.

Clarence Clayton was doubling up and down the square with his squad when he fell out in view of Regimental Sergeant Major Michael Culliney. The latter took the private to the huts on the side of the square and asked him again why he had fallen out. The soldier, red-faced and sweating, said he felt sick. Culliney lost his temper with the prisoner, for Clayton was a 'persistent malingerer'. He punched him and knocked him down so that he struck and cut the back of his head. Thereupon Culliney ordered the private to be conveyed to the sick quarters on a hand-cart.

On the way there the cart was stopped by CSM Leslie Salter. He was not going to allow Clayton to be 'driven' to the sick bay. He tipped over the cart and the private fell to the hard concrete, cracking the back of his head once again.

Now the CSM got worried. Clayton had gone strangely limp. He ordered a bucket of water brought up and thrown at the prostrate soldier. Nothing happened, save that this head fell to one side. Private Clarence Clayton was dead!

At the subsequent post-mortem it was discovered that Clayton should never have been in the Army in the first place. He had been a very sick man. The verdict of the medical examiner read: 'Death by tuberculosis, accelerated by violence.'[15]

In the end the Army was forced to institute an enquiry. Both the NCOs were court-martialled and stripped of their rank. Culliney got 18 months and Salter 12. One wonders if they spent them in one of their own glass-houses.

But before that took place, the Army wired the dead soldier's mother that he was dead and in that typical unfeeling manner of Army bureaucracy queried: 'Notify me as to your wishes, re burial … *Govt allow £7 10s Less cost of coffin* …'[16]

'*Less cost of coffin*'! How heartless …

But in spite of the new spirit abroad in the post-Dunkirk British Army and the draconian punishments applied for even the most minor infringements of the King's Regulations (*fourteen* days confined to camp for having bootlaces the wrong way round, for instance), the Forces were still not ready to fight.

General Alan Brooke, the new Commander-in-Chief of the British Army, told the tutors of the Staff College, Camberley, that their job was 'instilling a more offensive spirit into the army'. He felt that there was still a 'stagnation of higher training'.[17] Writing that February, Montgomery stated: 'We have today, divisional commanders and divisional staffs who have never handled a division under "full sail" at any time, not even in training'.[18]

Lower down, the situation was little better. A harassed Captain Frost, trying to set up the 2nd Battalion of the new Parachute Regiment, thought that 'our greatest problem in those early days was the lack of good reliable NCOs. With few exceptions, the other ranks were equally inexperienced and it was more by accident than design that some of them wore sergeant's stripes. Very few were able to enforce their authority unless an officer was actually present and a large number of them suffered under the misapprehension that military discipline was out of date.'[19]

The rank and file, some people thought, had turned 'bolshy'. Bolshy or not, it was with these men that the poorly trained commanders were going to have to fight the battles of 1941 and 1942. The disasters which would befall British arms in the next terrible 18 months would bear out the folly of her strategy, the failure of her higher commanders and the lack of training and spirit of her troops. Soon Churchill's demand that his infantrymen must be 'at least wounded before they surrender'. Would change to a helpless cry of frustration and despair – '*Will they ever fight?*' …

II

'We've taken a hell of a licking'

In Crete, Tuesday, 20 May 1941, dawned calm and cloudless. Over the stark-black jagged peaks of the mountains in the interior, the sun was rising a dramatic blood-red. Three weeks before, the mixed force of New Zealanders, British, and Australians had been hurriedly evacuated from Greece in another Dunkirk, after the Germans had chased them from that unhappy country. Now those in the know realized that it would not be long before the enemy attempted to do the same here in Crete, just off the Greek coast. Thanks to the top secret intercepts provided by Ultra back in Britain, General Freyberg, in command on the island, and his senior officers knew that they could expect trouble any day now. But how exactly they would invade still remained something of a mystery to them.

Brigadier Kippenberger of the 2nd New Zealand Infantry Division, one of those who knew what was coming, was shaving in his headquarters at the dusty little town of Galatos when it all began. Suddenly a German fighter came belting down the main street of the place, angry little flames crackling the length of its wings as the pilot fired quick bursts at anything that moved.

Kippenberger cursed and hurriedly mopped his face with his towel. He dashed to the open window. Further down the road which led to Canea, he could see other German fighters swooping down, with engines snarling and whining, ripping up the surface with vicious bursts of tracer. Kippenberger accepted the attack philosophically. He had been under fire often enough before. So he dressed and went down to breakfast, which consisted this morning of a cup of tea and a thin gruel of oatmeal and water. Even the 'hash-slingers' – the cooks, a long-suffering breed, used to the officers' complaints – grumbled about it.

But food was food for the old soldier Kippenberger and he set about tackling it eagerly. But not for long. Suddenly an officer near him cursed. Kippenberger paused somewhat stupidly with his spoon held to his open mouth. 'Almost above our heads were four gliders, the first we had ever seen, in their silence inexpressibly menacing and frightening.'[1]

71

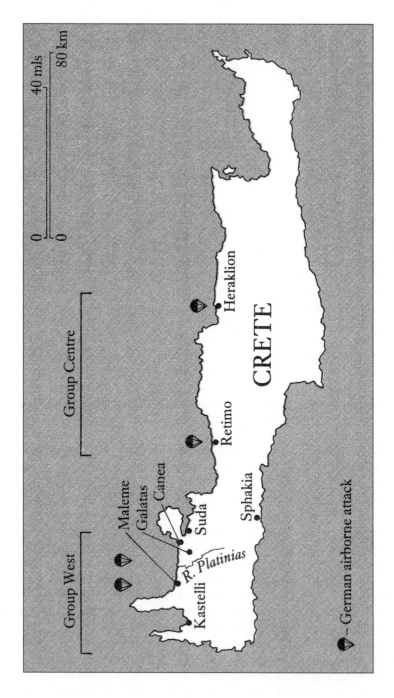

Crete, 20 May 1941

Abruptly, Kippenberger broke the sudden hush which had fallen over the little mess, as the thunder of many engines grew ever louder and he realized how the Germans were going to attack by parachute from the sky! He sprang to his feet and yelled, '*Stand to your arms!*' and then rushed upstairs for his binoculars and an old infantryman's favourite weapon, his rifle.

The German plan was typically bold. Fifteen thousand paras, the élite of the German Army, would be flown into the assault in two waves. 'Group West' would come in at dawn to attack the island's chief airfield at Maleme. It was vital for the success of the operation that this field be captured before the second wave came in. 'Group Centre' would also come in two waves to assault and capture Canea, Suda Bay and Retimo Airfield. Thereafter the men of the 5th German Mountain Division would be sent in by sea and by air. The whole plan was very risky, but German Intelligence had assured the planners in Athens that they could expect very little resistance. Crete was defended by a demoralized Greek regiment, some war-weary New Zealanders and Australians, and a couple of battered British infantry battalions newly brought over from the Western Desert, where they had already suffered heavy losses.

Now everywhere the *Fallschirmjäger* (including Corporal Max Schmeling, the former world heavyweight champion, whose part in the battle ended ingloriously right at the beginning when he twisted his ankle) came floating down to the stony, baked earth in their hundreds; while the gliders came swooping in at a hundred miles an hour, air brakes shrieking, the barbed wire wrapped around their skids snapping like string as they hit the ground.

After what they had suffered in the retreat through Greece, the New Zealanders were itching to get their revenge. Now the 'Jerries' were being presented to them on a silver platter. The sky was full of them and their transports. 'Like the sound of a swarm of enormous hornets rising to a crescendo of drumming, throbbing sound,' one of them remembered long afterwards, 'the sky was so full of enormous planes that it seemed they would crash into one another. Below them the air was full of parachutes dropping from the planes and flowering like bubbles from a child's pipe, but infinitely more sinister.'[2]

Immediately the ex-hill sheep farmers and country boys of the 22nd and 23rd Infantry Battalions took them under fire as they came floating down, a helpless, easy target. Colonel Leckie's 23rd Battalion found the III German Parachute Battalion landing right in its lap. In the first frantic, chaotic five minutes the Colonel shot five German paras himself without moving from his headquarters. His South Islanders, who were mostly old hands with a hunting rifle, did just as well. Later one of them thought it was 'just like duck shooting'. One after another they were slaughtered – there is no other word for it – as they lay sprawled on the ground or hanging from the olive trees, trapped and helpless, by their shroud lines. The III Parachute Battalion was virtually wiped out by midday.

'The sloping fields of the vineyards where the paratroopers had come down in the open,' one eye witness recalled afterwards, 'were littered with bodies, many of them still in their harnesses with the parachutes tugging gently at them in every mild puff of breeze and getting no response. Among the olives, corpses hung from branches or lay at the foot of the guarded trees, motionless on the trampled young barley. Only here and there a discarded overall, like the discarded shell of some strange insect, showed that its owner had got away and might be lurking in ambush in some gully or by a stone wall ready to sell his life dearly if discovered and, if not, to seek out his comrades when darkness came.'[3]

Everywhere that first day the German paras ran into serious trouble and suffered severe losses. As Major Nicholls of the Royal Leicestershire Regiment recorded, it was 'a fillip to morale'. The Regiment, which had just been sent from Africa together with the 3rd Hussars to bolster up the garrison of Australians and New Zealanders, now watched as 'One of the Junkers was hit just as it was about to disgorge its load. It crashed. Perhaps the death of those parachutists was preferable to the death suffered by those who came down with their parachutes on fire, going faster and faster as they neared the earth, only to be followed up by our platoons as they landed. One had the misfortune to land on top of company headquarters in some standing corn. He drifted to earth as I watched. When he was about 10 feet from the ground seven or eight Tigers, each with bayonet fixed, rose and approached him. That was the first time that I heard a man scream with fear ...'[4]

That Tuesday even Brigadiers went out to do battle against the Germans falling out of the blue sky on all sides. As paras started to fall on his HQ Brigadier Kippenberger started to sprint down the road to where they were landing. He burst through a gap in a hedge of cactus when there was 'a startling burst of fire fairly in my face, cutting the cactus on either side of me. I jumped sideways, twisting my ankle and rolled down the bank. After whimpering a little, I crawled up the track and into the house and saw my man through the window. Then I hopped out again, hopped around the back, and in what seemed a nice bit of minor tactics, stalked him round the side of the house and shot him cleanly through the head at 10 yards.'[5] On that first day even the dubious characters of the Field Punishment Centre proved themselves good soldiers, sallying out to kill paras after being hastily armed by the hardfaced 'staffs'.

That night General Freyberg, VC, the New Zealander commanding the Allied force, reported to his superior, the one-eyed General Wavell, in Cairo: 'Today has been a hard one. We have been hard-pressed ... Margin by which we hold them is a bare one and it would be wrong of me to paint an optimistic picture. Fighting has been heavy and we have killed large numbers of Germans. Communications are difficult. Scale of air attacks upon Canea has been severe. Everyone realizes vital issue and we will fight it out.'[6]

There was one fly in the ointment, something as yet unknown to the burly infantry general, who had been wounded three times in World War One. Colonel Andrews, VC, commanding the 22nd New Zealand Infantry, had withdrawn his battalion from the vital Height 107, which covered the airfield the paras needed so desperately at Maleme. In the chaos and confusion of that first attack, Colonel Andrews had withdrawn his A and B Companies because he thought HQ, C and D Companies had been wiped out. When the latter, who hadn't been wiped out at all, fought their way to these abandoned positions, they were bewildered. What were they to do?

As we shall see, the New Zealand infantrymen were highly rated by the Germans as first-class, aggressive soldiers, but again the lack of training in their leaders led to disaster. Bewildered and confused, the officers commanding the companies decided to withdraw instead of holding the vital feature. The Germans didn't hesitate. Even as Freyberg's message was on its way to Wavell, the paras rushed the vital height. The way was now open to bring Maleme Field under German control. The battle was beginning to sway in the enemy's favour.

But as yet the Germans were still mainly on the defensive, trying to consolidate their gains, while the Allied infantry counter-attacked. Under the command of New Zealand Brigadier Hargest, Maoris and white New Zealanders launched an attack on the German positions at Maleme at 3.30 on the morning of 22 May. Almost at once the infantry ran into trouble. From behind the cactus hedges and little white-painted Cretan houses, they were met by a hail of fire. As Captain Upham of the 20th Battalion recalled: 'We went on meeting resistance in depth – in ditches, behind hedges, in the top and bottom storeys of village buildings, in fields and gardens beside the aerodrome.

'There was TG (Tommy gun) and pistol fire and plenty of grenades. We had a lot of bayonet work, which you don't often get in war. The amount of MG was never equalled. Fortunately a lot of it was high and the tracer bullets enabled us to pick our way up and throw in grenades. We had heavy casualties, but the Germans had heavier. They were unprepared. Some were without trousers, some had no boots on. The Germans were helpless in the dark. With another hour we could have reached the far side of the drome. We captured as it was a lot of MGs, two Bofors pits were overrun and the guns destroyed.'[7]

But in spite of the boldness and daring of his infantry, Brigadier Hargest's plan was riddled with weakness, as were most British plans at that time. He had calculated, for example, that he could attack and capture the airfield during the hours of darkness. As it was, when the dawn came with that spectacular suddenness typical of the Mediterranean, he found his attack had bogged down in the open, exposed to any attack the *Luftwaffe*, which dominated air space over Crete, cared to launch.

Still he persisted. But the New Zealanders' élan was vanishing visibly, as if someone had opened a tap, and their spirit had begun to drain out at ever-increasing speed. The attack developed into a bloody slogging match – a corporal's war of sections fighting each other – and by early afternoon Hargest knew he had failed. There was nothing for it but break it off and try to hold what they had gained at such high cost.

Kippenberger's attack with his 10th Brigade was more successful. The Greeks in front of him had broken, but a Captain Forrester of the Queen's Regiment had 'begun tooting a tin whistle like the Pied Piper and the whole motley crowd of them,' as one eye witness recalled, 'surged down against the Huns yelling and shouting in a mad bayonet charge which made the Jerries break and run'.[8]

Now he set about recapturing the township of Galatos. To aid him, he had two old tanks from the 3rd Hussars, one of which had both its driver and gunner wounded. Kippenberger told Captain Farran of the 3rd Hussars he would provide two infantrymen to take their places. They should be able to learn to drive a tank and fire its gun in ten minutes. Then they would attack.

'We waited another ten minutes, the air filled with noise and tracer crackling overhead – and then Farran came rattling back. He stopped and we spoke for a moment. I said the infantry would follow him and he was not to go further than the village square. Now get going!

'He yelled at the second tank to follow him, pulled the turret lid down and set off. The infantry followed at a walk, then broke into a run and started shouting – and running and shouting they disappeared into the village. Instantly there was the most startling clamour, audible all over the field. Scores of automatics and rifles being fired at once, the crunch of grenades, screams and yells – the uproar swelled and sank, swelled again to a terrifying crescendo. Some women and children came scurrying down the road; one old woman, frantic with fear, clung desperately to me. The firing slackened, became a brisk clatter, steadily became more distant and stopped. The counter-attack had succeeded, it was nearly dark and the battlefield became suddenly silent.'[9]

But again Kippenberger could do little but consolidate his gains. The front settled down to a kind of armed, unsettled truce. Neither side was able to reinforce its men, the Germans because the Royal Navy sank their transports and the British because the *Luftwaffe* did the same with their ships. So they settled down for almost 24 hours of inactivity. One British officer recalled: 'After breakfast there was nothing to do except to go to sleep or try to, all except one who acted as sentry. I visited the posts and talked with the soldiers. It was always the same question they asked me:

"How was the battle going and what was the news?" Their high spirits had been replaced by a grim determination. For they were now playing the hardest of games – namely, sitting tight, under orders to defend their positions to the last man and with the prospect of no relief.'[10]

Freyberg, who three weeks before had remarked, when he knew from Ultra that the Germans were coming, 'Cannot understand nervousness; am not in the least anxious about airborne attack', now started to doubt. Hargest's counter-attack had failed and Kippenberger could do little but hold his positions. Moreover his forces were scattered over the island in penny packets, while the Germans were trying all the time to bring in more troops. He began to come to the conclusion that he had to 'concentrate'. But he knew what the connotation of that word was for his hard-pressed infantrymen. They had 'concentrated' before in Greece and North Africa and that had ended in withdrawal and then retreat. How would they take the order this time? Would it kill what was left of their determination and spirit? *The big retreat was about to begin*! ...

Captain Dawson of Brigadier Hargest's HQ brought the news to the 23rd New Zealand Infantry. Dawson was exhausted, but he tried to assume that stiff-upper-lip flippancy which the British like to assume in moments of great emotion or danger. 'I've got some very surprising news for you, sir,' he told the battalion commander Colonel Leckie.

Leckie kept the game going, 'What! Have they tossed it in?' he asked.

'Now we are to retire to the Platanias River line,' Dawson answered, explaining that the withdrawal had to start within thirty minutes.'[11]

Now the stiff-upper-lip flippancy was tossed to one side hurriedly. Now all was controlled chaos as the infantry spiked the guns they were being forced to leave behind them and set out, carrying their wounded with them, their rear covered by a small force of Maoris. But the paras had spotted the move. A battalion of fresh alpine troops was ordered to outflank the New Zealanders. This they did. The 23rd was ordered to withdraw once again. That night they did, 'carrying our wounded on improvised stretchers down the steep cliff face,' as one of them recalled, 'and then along a difficult clay creek bed to the road. Mile after mile we trudged. Everyone was tired. All were vaguely resentful, although none of us could have put a finger on the reason.'[12] Already the 'concentration' was developing into a retreat. ...

It was about this time that Private Williams of the Welch Regiment was captured, wounded, with a Corporal Jones and another man from the same battalion. Corporal Jones, a regular, ventured the opinion that their captors, 'could never beat our boys'.

'Against all evidence I felt he was right,' Williams wrote long afterwards. 'These were the crack troops of the German Airborne Division, the pride of their army and the envy of our own. Yet they did not impress me.' But when the three Welsh infantrymen were taken down to the cage, where there were other British prisoners, Williams found that 'a disconcerting feature was the number of men who, in spite of uniform, had lost all semblance of being soldiers. Some prisoners were in plimsolls, a couple were without boots or any kind of footwear, and one showed up vividly in kitchen whites. All looked wilted.'[13]

For now the Germans were attacking Brigadier Kippenberger's 10th Brigade, which was virtually shattered already, with six battalions supported by Stukas and an artillery regiment. He ordered Colonel Grey, commanding his 18th Battalion, which was down to 400 men still on their feet, to attack and try to hold the Germans. Colonel Grey, armed with rifle and bayonet, personally led the charge of his D Company. It failed disastrously. The company was overwhelmed.

'Suddenly,' Kippenberger, who was watching the attack, wrote later, 'the trickle of stragglers turned into a stream, many of them on the verge of panic. I walked in among them shouting, "Stand for New Zealand!" … and everything else I could think of.'[14] That stopped them for a while. But only for a while.

Just then the 18th's Regimental Sergeant-Major staggered up to the Brigadier. RSM Andrews said very quietly he could do no more. Kippenberger asked why. By way of an answer Andrews pulled up his sweat-stained shirt to reveal a neat bullet hole in the centre of his stomach. Kippenberger gave him a cigarette and told himself he would never see Andrews again.*

Andrews was followed a few minutes later by Colonel Grey, still holding his rifle, 'almost the last of his battalion and looking 20 years older than three hours before'…[15]

Slowly, inexorably, just like their forefathers before them at Gallipoli, the Anzacs and their British comrades were forced towards the beaches, fighting and retreating, fighting and retreating, their number growing fewer all the time, leaving behind them their dead and wounded to mark their passing.

Corporal Lewin of the Welch Regiment found himself left behind, nursing the bloody pulp of what was left of a foot severed by a mortar fragment. He was a regular soldier and did not moan his fate. He was alone, bleeding severely and trying to stop the bleeding by stuffing the gaping hole with bits of grass and dust. 'Not very hygienic, but better than bleeding to death, though I did expect to die. The Jerries weren't going to find me in time. Besides front-line infantry had no time for the wounded, especially if they were from the other side.' But they did. Three years later as a 'kriegie' on an outside working party near Munich, Corporal Lewin found himself liv-

---

* He would, three years later in Italy. Andrew's life had been saved because his stomach had been completely empty.

ing for weeks in tolerable comfort with obliging Bavarian ladies. 'Christ, if Patton hadn't come and liberated us,' he recalled many years later with a knowing smirk, '*I'd have probably shagged myself to death*'. ....[16]

Thus it came to the sad and inevitable end. While a cordon of heavily armed infantry was thrown around the beaches, Freyberg pleaded with Wavell and then directly with Mr Fraser, the New Zealand prime minister, for more ships to take off the troops. But the Royal Navy, which would lose 2,000 men, including Mountbatten's destroyer HMS *Kelly*, plus a lot of her crew, in the evacuation, would not make any more craft available.

Furtively those who were going to be taken off still made their way to the beaches. A Greek officer, Captain Stephanides, recalled slipping through Sphakia on his way to Suda Bay. 'It was an eerie experience as we groped our way through the streets of that murdered and deserted village, skirting huge bomb craters or clambering over masses of rubble and smashed brickwork. Every now and then the men in front would come to a sudden halt and then the whole column would stand stock-still for several long minutes before moving on again. Now that deliverance seemed so near everybody's nerves were on edge; people were cursing and swearing at each other at the slightest provocation in venomous whispers ... Each time the column stopped, I wondered if some hitch had occurred and if we were going to be told that the ships would not come for us after all. Yet in a way I did not feel things anywhere near as keenly as I would have done normally. I was so exhausted that I lived in a kind of daze, rather as if I were following the doings of someone else in a cinema film. As a matter of fact, to me the one concrete and all-pervading reality was the pain in my feet. ...[17]

On the beach itself lots were drawn to decide who should go. In the end Freyberg himself had to detail the senior officers who would be evacuated and those who would stay behind (17,000 would be evacuated and 15,000 would stay behind dead, wounded or captured*). Hargest was told he had to stay behind with those hundreds of New Zealanders who couldn't be taken across and he 'obeyed with a light heart'. Kippenberger's attempts to do the same were 'sharply overruled'.[18]

Sadly Kippenberger set about organizing what was left of his 10th Brigade for the evacuation. Many of his NCOs proudly volunteered to stay behind with the rank and file, who would soon be heading for the German cages. Then came the worse part, the march to the beach, which was some miles away. 'The last part [of the march] was lined with men who had lost their units and were hoping for a place with us. Some

---

* The German losses were estimated at 17,000. The paratroopers' losses were so high that the Germany Army never again employed mass formation of paras. Crete was Germany's Arnhem, with one difference – the Germans won!

begged and implored, most simply watched stonily, so that we felt bitterly ashamed.'[19] Thus the last of Kippenberger's men passed through the cordon of heavily armed men, who had orders to shoot any man who attempted to break through to the boats.

It was Dunkirk all over again, and although the New Zealanders lost a mere fraction of the Britishers who had been lost there – 6,000 men in all – New Zealand was a small country; and the loss was felt greatly. Indeed Mr Peter Fraser, their Prime Minister, was there to see them arrive in Africa.

Watching the scene, New Zealand Brigadier George Clifton, who had only escaped from the Greek débâcle himself the month before and who would end the war himself a 'kriegie', felt for the Prime Minister. 'Imagine his emotions,' he wrote afterwards, 'standing there waiting to greet these haggard, unshaven battle-stained fellow countrymen, many of them wounded; all badly worn physically and mentally; all worried by the loss of so many good "cobbers". Mr Fraser was responsible in part for all of this. Imagine the deep feeling stirred in that warm heart – because before all else he loved his fellow men. Yet walking among and talking to the survivors, he sensed their real reaction. "Bloody hard scrumming against a heavier pack, who had good backs behind 'em … We've taken a hell of a licking this game … Let's build the team up again, get down to hard training and bash them next time"'.[20]

Bold, encouraging words. But it was still the traditional language of the British infantry officer, who thought of war as some sort of game with lethal outcome. 'Hard scrumming … hell of a licking … build the team up … hard training and bash them next time'. It was as if they and the enemy were playing in the same league, following a list of fixtures. But the men who were to lead the Imperial infantry to final victory over the Germans and later the Japanese would have to learn before they beat them that this was not a game of sport.

Thousands of British infantrymen who had been evacuated at that first Dunkirk in 1940 never fired a shot in anger until they reversed the process in Normandy four weary years later. Now those who had managed to come back from the Empire's third 'Dunkirk' of Crete had indeed fired at the enemy and killed him sometimes. But they and their leaders had not yet steeled their hearts, become as ruthless and determined as the enemy. They still had not learnt that cardinal lesson of the fighting infantryman – *'Kill or be killed …'*

III

Up the blue

Back in 1939, the British minister in Cairo had told the Egyptian King that because of the new war the British would have to stay in control of the country until it was over. King Farouk, pudgy and decadent and at the age of 18 already an avid collector of pornography and a confirmed lecher, sneered in response. 'Oh all right. But when it's all over, for God's sake lay down the white man's burden – *and go!*'[1]

That had been two years before. But the war in the desert was still raging and the British had still not laid down the 'white man's burden'. Indeed for most of the war, from 1940 to 1943, North Africa, including Farouk's Egypt, would be the principal theatre of battle for the Empire's infantry.

For most of that time the battle for the desert – 'up the blue', the infantry called it – would consist of confident, bold advances over hundreds of miles, followed by headlong flights back the same way, month in, month out, year in, year out, carried out against a background of a featureless, arid desert, thousands of miles from the home countries of most of those involved – Germans, Italians, Greeks, French, Britons, South Africans, Australians and New Zealanders.

The Western Desert, to give it its official name, was nothing like those picturesque rolling sand dunes with which the average Briton was familiar from movies such as *Beau Geste*. Instead it was flat with yellow rocks, saltbush, grey earth and perfect beaches down on the coast. Here one perfect cloudless day followed another, with a slight breeze in the morning and another in the evening. In between the day was burningly hot and thick with flies. There was no mystery about the place and none of that subtle fascination which pre-war romantic novelists had imagined there. But when the fighting was over and the guns had stopped booming for the day, there was a sense of relaxation in the tremendous silence which followed at night. For the Great British Public it was a perfect place for the Army to wage war. It was a long way away, didn't involve them as a conflict in Europe would have, and allowed them to get on with their day-to-day life without bother.

The infantry looked far different from the hefty, pink-cheeked young men they had been when they had arrived 'up the blue'. Since then they had got their 'knees brown'. Their shorts were bleached to a dirty yellow and their boots had been worn a pure white by the gritty sand. Gone was the slouch hat or topee with which they had been issued right at the start. In its place there was a 'tin hat', painted yellow. When they took off their shirts they revealed skinny, toned-down bodies as brown as nutmeg. Their eyes were keener, their faces leaner than they once had been back in 'the UK', as they called that remote country that some of them wouldn't see for three or four years – or perhaps never again.

The desert had transformed them. In addition to the old soldiers' terms – 'bints', 'bondhooks' and 'gildys' and all the rest of that Anglo-Indian slang picked up in two centuries of soldiering in the subcontinent – they made frequent reference to 'sprogging up' and having a 'shufti'. Invariably they greeted each other with the Arabic phrase, '*Sayida*' and asked eternally, 'what's the griff?'.

The lived on corned beef, tinned sardines, tinned sausages, biscuits and two quarts of water per day for all purposes, drinking, washing (themselves and their clothes), and naturally 'brewing up'. Brewing up, or making tea, was the great blessing of life 'up the blue'. It had become something of a ritual, especially the early morning tea, which was the most impressive 'brew' of the day. The rule was that no fires could be lit before sunrise. But at 'first light,' as they called it, most of the infantry were up and stirring about their slit trenches or vehicles, waiting to brew up. Tins filled with sand were already soaked in petrol so that a porridge-like mix was ready to be ignited, with the brew cans in place on top. Here and there, impatient infantrymen waited with matches in hand. More often than not, before the platoon officer gave the signal to go ahead, someone would succumb to temptation and the match would be tossed into the sand and petrol mix. There'd be a whoosh, a burst of blue flame, and the brew-up would commence; while angry senior officers tore round in the morning haze trying to stop others following suit.

If they were lucky, there'd be real 'sergeant-major tea', a dark-brown rich brew, with plenty of condensed milk added, in which they boasted, 'yer can stand yer spoon'. This would wash down slabs of fried corned-beef or tins of 'M and V'* stew enriched with crumbled 'dog biscuits', as they called the issue biscuits, which replaced bread. Thereafter there would be a cat's lick with a mug of water, underneath the armpits, the genitals and the anal crack – and the face. When there was little water this would be carried out with sand. As a result most of them suffered from desert sores – scratches which readily festered and never really healed, reinfected all

---

* Meat and vegetable.

the time by the swarms of merciless flies which angered and irritated them all day long. Naturally, this being the British Army, they always shaved, however short the water supply. …

Eric Lambert, an infantry officer, pictured them vividly in 1941, as a platoon came limping wearily in from yet another skirmish in the desert: 'Down the wadi comes a file of men. They march slowly, out of step, and mostly in silence. The dull clink of their weapons is clear in the evening air. At first their faces look all the same, burnt deep, their eyes red-rimmed with the whites gleaming, cheeks hollowed, lips straight and grave. Their shirts and shorts are stiff like canvas with mingled dust and sweat, and streaked again with the sweat of that day. Their legs are bare and burnt almost black; their boots are worn pure white. Some who still have them wear their tunic, for the air will soon be deathly cold, and their headgear is, as before, motley: a steel helmet, a crumpled slouched hat and an Italian pith helmet. Their packs, haversacks and ammunition pouches have become as white as their boots and their weapons gleam dully in the spots where they have become worn, for they have had five months of use.

'They are a strange spectacle. They were once ordinary men, but now they do not belong among ordinary men; in the city they would seem like a vision. Their sameness is not only that of their dark-brown faces, their silence, their fatigue, for they have shared together, for many months, the most abysmal, the most terrible of human emotions; each has, in turn, and in his own way, been a hero, a panting coward, an entity with a mind crying its anguish at death. And while each has shown to his fellows most of his deeper self, each hugs to himself, grimly and pitiably, what is left. No one of them will ever be quite the same again.'[2]

'These no longer "ordinary men" would be cut off for months, even years from the customary amenities of their life hitherto, even when the desert war was not raging. There were no cinemas, no real NAAFIs, no "fags" save for the hated Indian "Victory" cigarettes, rarely beer – and *no women*! Their first enemies, the Italians, being more realistic in matters of sex, had brought up mobile whorehouses for their fighting men. After Tobruk surrendered to the British in 1941, one British commander was faced with a difficult problem when the madame of one such place offered to put her girls "at the disposal of the British Army".

'Thousands of prisoners had been rounded up. Now ten more were taken – the ten tarts of Tobruk. They stood in line in front of the white-washed, two-storied building which was both their home and red-light house. A woman of 50, grey-haired, hard-faced, tawdry in attire, played the role of a very nervous CO to the girls. A motley assortment, none of them was physically attractive. Their faces were hastily daubed with paint and powder, and the best one could say of them was that they looked the part – blowsy all of them. One, an ersatz blonde, might have been in her early twenties; a couple of others, brunettes, would have been passable had they been properly turned out. As for the others: they were human nonentities – and very frightened.

'The journalist who reported the piece translated for the British officer, who frisked his moustache angrily and said, "Tell them … tell them to take ten paces to the rear – immediately. … And tell them," the Colonel added, "they stink!"

'This I managed to break down, in translation, to a milder term which conveyed to the undermistress and the girls that their offer had been rejected. Before I left we found their books, or score sheets. They had all been very industrious. One girl named Antoinette had a pretty regular batting average of 50 *per diem*, which had been topped by only a few of the others on very rare occasions.'[3]

For the British and Empire infantry there was no such outlet for whatever sexual drive remained while they were still in the desert. There was masturbation, carried out furtively beneath their single blanket at night – a 'crafty wank' they called it; or done when they were alone, the only time they were thus, having taken 'a shovel for a walk' in the sands.* And there was homosexuality, of course. Not much because of the lack of privacy. But one homosexual major in an infantry regiment recalled just before the start of the Battle of Alamein that the thunder of the tremendous artillery barrage which preceded the battle seemed to have an aphrodisiac effect on the troops, so much so that a young married lieutenant crawled over: 'In a few minutes this boy was groping me and we were kissing passionately. It was a powerful emotional climax for both of us, although I knew he was married and not a homosexual at all.'[4]

But for most of the infantrymen the only sexual relief they received – often in months, perhaps even in years – was when they went on leave to Cairo or Alexandria. There 'back from the blue' after another session of the 'Benghazi Handicap', as they called the annual advance to and retreat from that town, they would indulge themselves, using up months of pay to do so.

They downed gallons of ice-cold beer on shaded café verandahs, served to them by obsequious 'wogs' in flowing white gowns and red tarboosh hats. They ogled the passing girls and cheerfully jeered the staff wallahs or 'gaberdine swine'.** Then, 'sand happy' as they were and now drunk, they would sally forth to find 'a bint'. For most of their progress through the swarming crowds they would be pestered by beggars and street

---

* This was when they defecated. If there was no 'thunderbox' they had to take a shovel to bury their waste products and help to keep the flies down.

** Staff officers in Cairo called thus from the material of their uniforms, with a pun on Gadarene.

salesmen, who pushed things in their faces with cries of 'Ili George ... Look 'are, George', while they sang drunkenly, *'when this fucking war is over. Oh, how happy I will be ... No more asking for a favour, no more pleading for a pass ... You can tell the sarn't major, to stick his passes up his arse ...'*

Sooner or later a tout, usually a small Egyptian boy, would latch on to them with a cry of 'Hi, George, you wan' a bint? My sister very nice, very clean. All pink inside like a white lady' and they would be led off willingly enough to the red-light district, the Burka, which the 'Aussies' had burnt down in the first war. Second war 'Aussies' from 'up the blue' were always boasting that 'Me old dad burnt down the Burka and Oi'm gonna burn it down agen!'

A few preferred the boy himself to the danger of catching the 'pox' from his sister 'all pink inside like a white lady'. But most didn't. They took their chances and enjoyed a brief, brutal commercial respite from the kind of all-male life they lived 'up the blue'.

Sergeant Coupe, who three years before had charged the sheep with his pike on the Lincolnshire coast, remembers with glee, even today, one of those 'all nighters', when 'in between sessions there was a little darkie boy who came in and brought us tiny cups of tea. I don't know whether it was the char or me, but by crikey, didn't I go at it after three months in the desert – *like a bleeding fiddler's elbow!'*[5]

But when their seven days were over, it was back to the 'blue' and the tough, rough all-male society which made up most of their lives, and where, especially if they were infantry, they would mostly die. Some of them simply 'dropped out', as the parlance of our own time would phrase it. They went 'on the trot' – deserted – and became 'the lost men', living off their wits and what they could pilfer. The CO of the 1st Battalion of the Black Watch, now re-formed after the St Valery disaster, felt the 'lost men' were 'immense fun'. 'Wherever you go in the desert,' he recalled long afterwards, 'you come across little pockets of men, camped by their vehicles; they are invariably unshaven, cheerful and brewing up tea in a petrol tin. Similarly they can *always* tell you which way to go. "Y Track, sir? Straight on till you get to the Rifleman's Grave. Can't miss it, sir." Or "Barrel Track, mate? H'y you just come from it." Nine times out of ten they give you the directions wrong. They appear to belong to nowhere and nobody and seem perfectly contented to camp out in the blue. Arthur (one of his officers) has now decided that they all are deserters from Wavell's first campaign.* He is planning for both of us to go "missing" one day. Then we'll ensconce ourselves in a jolly little camp and spend our days waving people in the direction of the Diamond Track or the Gebel Something-or-other'.[6]

---

* Back in 1939.

It would be a feature of most of the campaigns to come in Italy and north-western Europe that there would be a sizeable number of deserters behind the line (in 1944 there would be an estimated 20,000 alone living off their wits in Paris, for example; while in Naples at the same time American deserters had organized black-market gangs in company strength). But most of the young men who had enjoyed the fleshpots would not desert. Dutifully enough, like animals being led to the slaughter, they would take the 'Blue Train' from 'Alex', suffering from 'gippo tummy' and a tremendous hangover, to meet the enemy, the 'Teds' as they called the Germans,* once more. …

For most of 1941 after the defeats in Greece and Crete, the Imperial infantry fought the 'Teds' in the advanced supply base of Tobruk. Indeed, while the German and British armour 'swanned about' back and forth up the coastal road that eventually led from Tobruk to Alexandria, the only real fighting was taking place at the besieged port. Here the 'Rats of Tobruk', as they called themselves, 25,000 men in all, held out against Rommel, supplied solely by destroyers crammed with men and supplies. At night they would steam out of Alexandria or Matruh and risk the narrow channel, the only one, through the sunken ships and minefields, which led into the battered port.

By this time, after two years of desert fighting, Tobruk was a mess of broken, tottering buildings, though they still gleamed white and clear in the eternal sun. The place was being constantly shelled and was in full view of the enemy artillery observers, so that the reliefs at the front had to be carried out during the hours of darkness. Even the men's rations had to be cooked in the port and taken up at night. The men who had lain all day in their slit trenches and dugouts facing the enemy had to crawl down their trenches to the main dug-outs where brackish tea (water was rationed and in short supply) and bully beef stew were served. Here they could relax for a couple of hours and enjoy a smoke without fear of snipers, before crawling back to their positions – and the invariable German patrol activity and night attacks.

In charge of the besieged port for most of the time was General Morshead, who had formerly commanded the Australian 9th Infantry Division, which had taken an initial drubbing at the hands of the Desert Fox's *Afrikakorps*. (One of his battalions had lost its colonel and about a seventh of its strength because the former had insisted it stopped for breakfast. It became known as the 'Breakfast Battalion'. For the next four years the Aussies would partake of that meal in German prison camps – a long time to stop for breakfast.) But the tough Australian had soon learnt he was no longer fighting the 'Eyeties'. He had put iron into the

---

* From the Italian for German, i.e. *tedesco*.

Australians, Indians and 'Pommies' who now made up his garrison, nearly 40,000 of them. 'There'll be no Dunkirk here,' he had declared at the beginning of the month-long siege back in April 1941. 'If we should have to get out, we shall fight our way out. There is to be no surrender and no retreat.'[7]

And there wouldn't be – not *this* time, although Morshead found it very difficult, with the forces available to him (all supplied from the sea), to defend the 25 miles of perimeter. The defence lines were in the form of a semicircle, whose radius was about 10 miles, with Tobruk itself in the centre.

Morshead's Australians of the 9th Infantry Division hated the place. They sang:

This bloody town's a bloody cuss
No bloody trams, no bloody bus
And no one cares for bloody us,
Oh, bloody! Bloody! Bloody!
No bloody sports, no bloody games
This place gives me a bloody pain …

All raids all day and all bloody night
They give us a bloody fright.
Oh bloody! Bloody! Bloody!
Best bloody place is bloody bed,
With a blanket over bloody head.
And then they think you're bloody dead.
Oh bloody! Bloody! Bloody!

But in Tobruk they didn't stop in 'bloody bed with a blanket over bloody head', unless they were really dead. They fought and fought, while the Stukas hammered their positions day after day, falling from the hard blue sky like evil metal hawks of death. But in the end, after seven months of the siege, even the Australians had had enough. Secretly the 9th Division was moved out by night without a casualty by the Royal Navy, to be replaced by fresh British infantry – the HLI, the Bedfordshire Regiment, the Queen's … They quickly adapted to the life, but as one of them noted in his diary, 'Really this is a filthy place! It is quite impossible to keep clean and one's hair becomes a clogged mass of dirt. Washing one's head in sea water with soap is fatal, the whole thing congeals into a mass of semi-glue … How the Australians lived here for seven months under these conditions I cannot imagine.'[8]

But finally plans had now been made to break out of Tobruk, to link up with the relieving 8th Army coming from Egypt. On 20 November, 1941, the 2nd Battalion of the Black Watch started the attack into no-man's land.

For several hundred yards nothing happened as the Jocks, with bayonets fixed, marched across that flat, naked plain. Then all hell was let loose as the Germans spotted them in the darkness and brought a tremendous barrage down. 'With a series of rushes "B" Company went in – there was nothing for it but to go in with the bayonet. It felt like pressing against a solid wall of lead and it seemed fantastic that anybody should survive,' one survivor remembered many years afterwards. But survive some of them did, though every one of the Company's officers was killed or severely wounded and half the NCOs suffered the same fate. In the end the Company, which had started out well over 100 men strong, was down to 10 lone soldiers, led by the sergeant-major, CSM McKinlay. Behind them they left a forest of upturned rifles, stuck in the sand to indicate where a Jock had fallen. ...

Ever since they had arrived in Tobruk the Black Watch had been forbidden to blow its pipes. Now there was no stopping the pipers. Pipe-Majors Roy and McNicol swung into the regimental march *Lawson's Men*, followed by other rousing marches. Lying wounded in arm and leg one officer heard the pipes, and as he wrote afterwards, 'the playing was instrumental in kindling the spirit with which the whole attack was carried out. I heard *Highland Laddie* as I lay in Jill and it was the tune that got me on my feet and advancing again.'[9]

But what was left of the Black Watch couldn't go on much longer. Pipe-Major Roy was hit and carried back to the dressing station. In spite of the fact he had been wounded three times he still continued to play for the scores of wounded there. The adjutant staggered back. He had been shot in the leg. His wound was dressed and he went up front again – to be shot in the stomach. This time he didn't return. The slaughter continued, but in the end even the Black Watch could go no further. Out of the 32 officers and 600 men who had started out only hours before, there were now only eight officers and 160 men still left standing. Their casualties had been over 60 per cent!

But the infantrymen inside Tobruk, trying to break out, were not the only ones to foot that terrible butcher's bill. To the east, attempting to break in, the New Zealand infantry were suffering similar casualties. Brigadier Clifton, working his way forward through 'burnt trucks, tanks smashed open by solid shot, broken guns, dead bodies' to see how the New Zealand attack was going came 'across two very worn New Zealand officers'.

'Hallo, what's wrong?' he asked.

'Everything, sir,' answered the taller one. 'Our battalion has been overrun by tanks and shot to pieces. We're the only officers left.'

Clifton didn't believe them. He thought it was the 'only' survivors' usual hard luck story. 'No it can't be as bad as that,' he said cheerfully. 'I'll bet there'll be a dozen more, all *sole* survivors.'[10]

But the Brigadier was wrong. They *were* the only two survivors of the 24th Infantry Battalion from Auckland. It had been wiped out. 'No flowers by request,' the New Zealand infantry had joked grimly as they had gone into the battle. Now there was no one left even to send flowers. ...

On 27 November, 1941, the 19th New Zealand Infantry Battalion and a squadron of tanks from the Royal Tank Regiment made the final attempt to link up with the battered 'Rats of Tobruk'. All that night, the tanks attacked and attacked and the infantry charged with fixed bayonets until at one o'clock, they made the link-up with the men of the British Essex Regiment. Back at HQ the corps commander responsible for the thrust signalled, 'Tobruk and I both relieved.'[11]

Since the end of April the garrison had held out against everything the Desert Fox could fling at it. Now he was on the run for a change, retreating back into his original starting positions. In that long black year of defeat after defeat it was the only victory, if it really could be called such. As Alan Moorehead, the Australian war correspondent, wrote that year, 'The first stage of the battle was over. No one could say clearly who had won. British, Germans and Italians lay around Tobruk too exhausted to go on, almost too tired to pick up the spoils of war. As December came in the coldest month of the year, the semi-quiet of utter weariness had settled over the front.'[12]

But as the African front settled down into a weary, exhausted truce, on the other side of the world another great conflict had broken out which would shake the British Empire to its very foundations. In the end, in spite of the bravery of its fighting men, these new and terrible defeats in the Far East would signal the downfall of that Empire – 'all that red on the map' – on which, as generations of patriotic little British schoolboys had learned, 'the sun never sets'. Now the sun was beginning to set. ...

IV

Black Christmas

Hong Kong, Christmas Day 1941.

It was now the third Christmas of the war and for nearly two thousand British infantrymen the last of their lives. With the temperature in the seventies, it could not be called a white Christmas. Indeed, afterwards most people would consider it the blackest Christmas in the whole 300-year-old history of the British Empire.

Seventeen days before Hong Kong had been almost a peacetime garrison for the men of the East Surreys, South Lancs and the Highland Light Infantry. Although most of them didn't earn more than 14 shillings a week, their pay went a very long way when beer was twopence a pint in the 'wet canteen' and every infantryman could afford a servant at 1s 3d., who did all the unpleasant chores of military life – blancoing, polishing, shining and the like. Ten shillings a month would provide a willing young Chinese woman – 'a down-homer' – who not only washed and cooked for the infantryman but also provided other 'comforts' in bed too. It had all been a nice comfy little existence, with the afternoons given over to sleep or sport and the evenings to drink and lechery. No one had really seriously considered that these men would actually one day have to go and fight.

In October 1941 this carefree doomed garrison had been joined by nearly two battalions of Canadian Infantry, the Royal Rifles of Canada and the Winnipeg Grenadiers, who were not the most able of combat soldiers. Before sailing, the sick – those with syphilis, hammer toes and duodenal ulcers – had been weeded out, while the rest of this untrained reluctant force had been kept from jumping ship at gun-point! Even then 50 Grenadiers and one Royal Rifleman managed to avoid the police and desert.

Now this mixed force of regulars, unwilling Canadian volunteers, plus the locals of the Hong Kong militia had waited on the morning of Monday, 8 December for the Japanese to attack from across the mainland. They came surprisingly enough in columns of route, without making the slightest attempt to take cover, as if they were on some sort of ceremonial parade.

Major George Gray of the 2/14th Punjabis had not dared to believe the evidence of his own eyes. Then he had waited until the Japanese were within 300 yards before bellowing at the top of his voice, '*FIRE!*'

His men needed no urging. They poured a devastating hail of fire into the enemy, and at that range they simply couldn't miss. As the infantry worked their bolts and pressed fresh clips into their rifles, the bren gunners hosed the Japanese. Their mules bolted. In an instant all was death and destruction. Hurriedly the surviving Japanese fled the field, leaving over 100 of their own dead behind them, littering the trail like sodden bundles of khaki rags.

It was the defenders' one and only victory. The next day disaster struck as the Army's oldest regiment, the Royal Scots – 'Pontius Pilate's Bodyguard' as their nickname had it – was attacked and caught completely by surprise. The official communiqué stated that the Royal Scots 'fell back in disorder and confusion'. In fact, some who were there thought that the First of Foot ran like hell and earned for themselves the derogatory nickname of 'The First to Foot it'.

But it didn't stop there. On the 11th, the Japanese launched a ferocious attack on the Regiment's B and C Companies, their officers swinging their swords and yelling '*banzai*', the rank and file shrilling on whistles and yelling obscenities. Both company commanders fell under the savage assault and a further 60 men were slaughtered in fierce hand-to-hand fighting. It was too much for the Royal Scots. The survivors fell back in ignoble confusion.

Now it was decided, after two days of defeat, to pull back from the outer defences to the main island. A mini-Dunkirk was organized and the Army pulled back, together with thousands of refugees clamouring fearfully that they had to escape, too, or be slaughtered by the sons of the Rising Sun. As for the latter, they thought resistance was about finished in Hong Kong. They sent a letter to the Governor, Sir Mark Young, and demanded the surrender of the port. If he didn't do so, they would launch an all-out aerial and artillery attack. Curtly Sir Mark refused.

General Sakai now prepared for the attack. He would use his crack 88th Infantry Division, which presently was enjoying itself raping the Chinese women in the outskirts and pillaging their villages. At the front in the meantime his propaganda companies bombarded the defenders with appeals to surrender and references to home at Christmas – 'The naked girls of the Windmill swaying backwards and forwards. ...'

'That's all he knows about it. They ain't allowed to move.'

'I saw one move once – *she got a wasp on her tit.* ...'

One day later the joking and jibing was over and the Japanese attacked in earnest, three whole regiments of them, all of them infantry veterans of the long, drawn-out campaign in China. Swiftly, ignoring their casualties, the Japanese swept over the first British positions, and on 18th December carried out their massacre: the first of many that would mark their progress throughout South-East Asia.

Twenty-five anti-aircraft gunners, who had surrendered, were ordered to come out of their position one at a time. As the first man came out, a Jap charged him with a bayonet. The gunner screamed as the long bayonet went straight into his guts, and he doubled up, trying to hold in his entrails. One by one the men were systematically slaughtered. Their blood up now, the Japanese infantry advanced on the nearby advanced dressing station, where they slaughtered the wounded and the staff, including the women nurses.

Those who could fought back to the bitter end. Brigadier Lawson, commanding the Canadians, was overrun at his headquarters, where even the bandmaster fought to the last. During the fight, Lawson managed to telephone the commanding general, who could hear the screams and shrieks of the massacre taking place there. Lawson gasped, 'They're all around us ... I'm going outside to shoot it out.' His voice General Maitby remembered afterwards was 'completely matter-of-fact and unemotional'.[1] Lawson then smashed the telephone switchboard and went outside into the confused throng, a revolver in each hand. His body was not found for six days. Both his revolvers were empty and eight very dead Japanese lay around him. ...

On that day another Canadian died gloriously. B Company of the reluctant, ill-trained Winnipeg Grenadiers had already taken a bad beating and had been reduced to a couple of score soldiers under the command of a bewildered 19-year-old second lieutenant. Now they were ordered to retake a hill held by the Japanese. They didn't get far. Their attack had hardly jumped off when the young company commander's body was ripped across by a cruel burst of machine gun fire. All around him the survivors started to go to ground.

Not CSM John Osborne. By the dint of much threatening, cursing and promising, the NCO kept the men moving. Half an hour later they had driven the Japs off the hill and a happy Osborne gasped. 'Now, you bastards, we're here and we're *staying* here! Any guy who thinks different, say no.'[2]

No one dare contradict the Sergeant-Major.

Soon afterwards the enemy counter-attacked. They forced their way back up the hill to within hand-grenade distance of the defenders. The grenades began to sail through the air like evil metal eggs. Time and time again Osborne, disregarding his own safety, snatched a grenade up at the very last moment and slung it back down the hill.

For eight and a half hours Osborne and his remaining 12 men, all that was left of a full company, held the hill as the Japs attacked and attacked until finally, when he was down to eight Grenadiers, a grenade fell where he couldn't sling it back. Osborne shouted a warning to his survivors to duck and then he flung himself on to it. The grenade exploded. Sergeant-Major Osborne's body was tossed into the air like a lifeless doll.

A little later the remaining five grenadiers surrendered. This time their lives were spared. They were not bayoneted to death like so many of the Hong Kong garrison were. Their captors admired courage, and in the manner of his death CSM Osborne had saved their lives. The British government admired it, too. Later John Osborne would win Canada's first VC of the war for the 'highest quality of heroism and self-sacrifice'.

But the rest of the Canadians were now about beaten. Virtually leaderless, demoralized and exhausted, they scattered all over the island, leaving the rest of the fighting to others, to find solace in sleep and looted drink. When the Japanese took them prisoner, they had no compunction about slaughtering them. One party was roped together and used for living bayonet practice by their sadistic captors; another was lined up on a cliff facing the sea. Then they were systematically shot in the back. Horror upon horror. ...

But as Christmas Day dawned, with people back in Canada and Britain thinking of preparing Christmas dinner with all the trimmings in spite of wartime, wondering if there would be enough to drink and sufficient cigarettes to go round and if the ham and mince pies would stretch for both tea and supper, the Japanese atrocities in Hong Kong mounted to a final cataclysmic crescendo.

That morning 200 drunken Jap infantrymen stormed into Hong Kong's St Stephen's College, which had been converted into a makeshift hospital, and which was full with 95 wounded British soldiers. Two doctors, Colonel Black and Captain Whitney, tried to bar their way. They were shot down mercilessly. Now as most of the terrified nurses watched in horror, the drunken Japs ripped the bandages off the men's wounds, revealing bloody gory stumps and great gaping holes. One nurse, less terrified than the rest, flung herself over one of the wounded trying to protect him. She was bayoneted where she sprawled, the blade passing through her breast into the body of the wounded soldier. In a space of 30 minutes, 56 wounded men were brutally butchered.

Then it was the turn of the nurses. They were locked in a room and systematically raped by the Japanese throughout that terrible Christmas Day right on through the night until the following Boxing Day.

By then most of Hong Kong had surrendered. But although the commanding general ordered the official surrender to take place at three that afternoon, while back in Britain people listened to their poor stuttering monarch giving his Christmas radio message to the Empire, their stomachs swollen with food, some did not obey. A platoon of the Middlesex Regiment fought to the last man. *They* lived up to the regimental nickname the 'Diehards'. A company of the Royal Scots, 11 men in all, commanded by a second-lieutenant, were last heard of still fighting two hours after the official surrender. Four Royal Marines barricaded themselves in the Garrison Sergeants' Mess, which was well supplied with booze. Here they held off all comers, drinking and fighting, drinking and fighting until a whole Japanese platoon, supported by a light tank, firing its cannon at point-blank range, put an end to their party. A lone officer, whose fiancée was one of the nurses slaughtered at St Stephen's College, armed himself with a Tommy gun and as many grenades as he could carry, and went out long after the surrender looking for Japs to kill. He was never seen again. Finally an exhausted silence fell over the newly captured colony, broken only by the scream of some helpless victim and the dry crack of a pistol as the Japanese administered the *coup de grâce* to some poor unknown.

One day later the victorious Japanese paraded their sorry captives in triumph through Hong Kong. Here and there an officer or NCO tried to keep up the spirit of the beaten soldiers. The old familiar cries rang out ... 'swing them arms' ... 'a bit o'swank, lads!' But it was no use. The day was too hot, their loads were too heavy and their humiliation too great. They struggled on, leaving behind a khaki-coloured trail of abandoned kit, prodded forward by the bayonets of the squat, grinning little yellow men.

Some of the crowds of Chinese who watched them stagger by averted their eyes rather than see white men humiliated like this. A few risked beatings by the Japs or the butt-end of a rifle for throwing packets of cigarettes to the captive soldiers. But many were glad to see them go, happy that the cocky British infantry had been humbled and crushed. They sneered at the captives in what English they knew. Some threw rotten eggs and stones.

But not only the Chinese. The many Indian shopkeepers who had lived off them and the white civilians for years now festooned their houses and shops with the Rising Sun of Japan – 'the poached egg', as the prisoners would soon begin to call it – in an attempt to curry favour with their new masters. Not only that, they exploded too into a rash of nationalism. Everywhere the red, white and green colours of the Indian independence movement started to appear. Soon they and the many thousands of Indian soldiers who would be captured in the Far East would be flocking to the flag of the Indian National Army. It would not be long before these turncoats would be fighting against the very men with whom they had once served. British rule in the Far East was beginning to break down. ...

Ironically enough it had been Indian troops of the 1st/14th Punjab Regiment who had fired the first shots against the advancing Japanese as they had crossed from Thailand into the Malay Peninsula in that same December. Now, as December gave way to January 1942, they and their erstwhile comrades of the British and Australian armies were retreating everywhere. For the Japanese infantry, pictured up to then as bespectacled and blind as a bat, had consistently outfought his Empire opponent.

Lightly armed, employing a great many bicycles, living off the land, they were much more mobile than the British infantryman. He went to war in this tropical area, borne down by his heavy boots, tin hat, gas-mask, heavy pack, rifle and bayonet. He had also been trained to be very dependent on his vehicular transport and this complicated things. So he dug in along the few roads heading south towards Singapore, ignoring the jungle to left and right, because everyone knew it was 'impassable'. But it wasn't, not for the Japanese at least. And suddenly the British troops would find their flank had been turned and the Japanese were behind them yet again.

Occasionally the British and the Australians were lucky. They surprised the Japanese. North of the village of Gemas, for example, General Bennett, commanding the Australian Infantry Division, set up an ambush along the road leading over the bridge there. At 4 o'clock on the afternoon of 15 January, 1942, as one eye-witness recorded: 'Several companies came over the bridge and walked down the road blissfully unaware that keen eyes were watching them from out of the jungle on each side. The officer in charge of blowing the bridge decided to let enough Japanese over. He waited until there were as many actually on the bridge as he thought there were likely to be at any one moment and then released the fuse. There was a tremendous explosion. The Japanese on the bridge were blown sky-high. Bridge, bodies and bicycles went soaring up. The explosion was the signal for the battalion to fall upon the Japanese, which they did with loud yells. Rifles barked, Tommy guns sputtered, many of the Australians dashed forward with their bayonets. Nearly all the Japanese who were on the other side of the bridge were killed. Later it was estimated that between 800 and 1,000 of the enemy were killed, while the Australians suffered less than 100 killed and wounded.'[3]

But a day later the 45th Indian Brigade, recently raised and raw, was struck by a devastating Japanese attack. It fell back in confusion, having lost most of its white officers, and was withdrawn to Singapore, where it played little further part in the battle. The Australians were forced to pull back again.

Now, however, with the Japanese seemingly successful everywhere, making a surprise appearance to the defenders' rear time and time again so that they were forced to pull back, the withdrawal was becoming closer to a retreat, even a rout; though here and there troops fought bravely to the last. A Colonel Dalley in charge of a section of the front found that one of his companies, a locally raised Chinese unit, had slogged it out with a whole Japanese battalion. 'It was a frightful sight,' he reported afterwards. 'They'd been blown to pieces. They'd used up all their ammunition. There were no wounded to bring back. They'd stood their ground. They'd had orders to stay and they stayed. And they all died.'[4]

Unlike the Australians of a machine gun battalion close by. Colonel Dalley remarked to their CO, Colonel Asherton, that 'I don't think your chaps are happy.' They weren't, but as the sound of firing came closer, the two colonels managed to hold the men. But as soon as the fighting commenced and Colonel Asherton was killed, there was no holding the Australians. Less than an hour later the Australians came down the road from the front line, 'It is the most vivid memory I have from the Singapore campaign ... They came moving at a half-trot, panic-stricken. I've never seen anything like it. It was pouring with rain and most of them were clad only in shorts. Few were wearing boots, and some of the men's feet were cut to ribbons – they'd come across rivers, through mangrove swamps, through the bush. They'd scrapped everything that could hold them back. They'd thrown aside their rifles and ammunition. ...

'Among them was one Aussie soldier fully equipped: rifle, ammunition, cape, shirt, shorts and boots. He came across the road to where three of us were standing, watching. "What's happened?" we asked him. He looked at his fellow Australians. "They're finished," he said. He was quite calm. He was a boy of about nineteen, a private. He seemed sorry for his mates. "Can I join up with you blokes?" he asked.'[5]

That nameless lone Australian infantryman was a real soldier. But behind him came a rabble of demoralized, panicked soldiers. 'Behind the Australians came the Indians. The Australians had come through their lines and the Indians had caught the panic. The Indians were mostly young boys and they were without officers. They didn't stop. They just went hurrying down the Jurong road, heading for Singapore.' Watching the terrible scene a civilian correspondent saw a bren-carrier of the Argylls come clattering up to check whether the Japanese were really on the fleeing men's heels. 'The Aussies saw it first, thought it was the Japs and just seemed to dive head first off the road. "Look out," they yelled, "It's the Japs!" They dived into the storm ditches, into the bush, anywhere out of sight. In seconds the road was clear as if the rabble had never been there ...'[6]

On 30 January fewer than 200 survivors of the Argyll and Sutherland Highlanders came down that road wearily. As they started to cross the Causeway on to Singapore Island, their pipers began to play. They were the last of the British Army to cross. Behind them the sappers blew the Causeway and cut Singapore off from the mainland.

One day later, the buck-toothed, weak-looking General Percival, an infantryman who now commanded the Singapore garrison, spoke over the radio to his troops. 'The battle of Malaya has come to an end,' he said in his weak voice, 'and the battle of Singapore is started ... Today we stand beleagured in our island fortress until help can come, as assuredly it will come. This we are determined to do. In carrying out this task, we want the active help of every man and woman in the fortress.'[7]

'It's a bit late in the day for Percival to call on "every man and woman" of the 700,000 natives,' one of his listeners commented realistically, 'Their will to fight is gone.'[8]

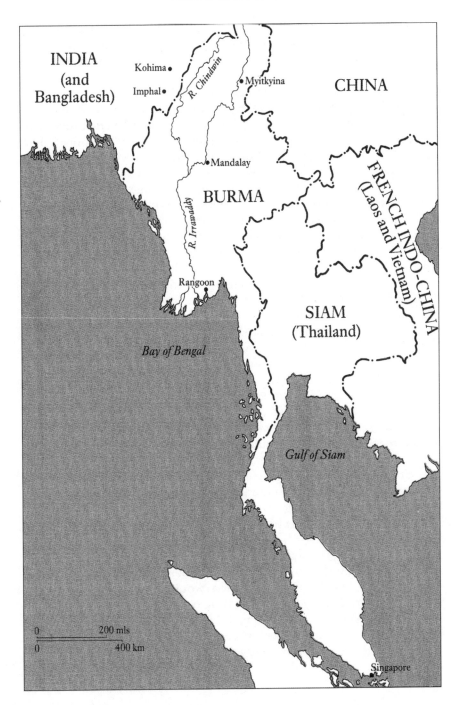

Burma, Singapore and surrounding countries.

Although on paper Percival had enough men to match the Japanese massing to attack him, it was on paper only. At least 15,000 of his 85,000 men were non-combatant, unarmed troops. His infantry battalions who were going to the fighting (thirteen British, six Australian, seventeen Indian and two Malay) were in a pitiful state. Six of the British battalions of the 18th Infantry Division, who had just arrived there, told to expect *'Chinks, stinks and drinks'*, were soft from weeks at sea; the other seven had suffered severe losses in the previous fighting. The plight of Australians was even worse. With the exception of one battalion they were all made up of raw recruits, some who had been in the Army only two weeks and had never fired a gun. And there was a desperate shortage of good officers.

The troops were resentful too of the people they had come to defend, the white administrators and planters whom they thought snooty and unrealistic. The Secretary of the golf club refused them permission to chop down some club trees to give them a better field of fire. Other ranks were barred from the clubs, where they still dined – with the Japs at the gate – in evening dress. Snooty English women refused to dance with the 'Colonials' – the Australians, etc. etc.

But more than anything they were nervous. By now the Japanese infantryman had a tremendously inflated reputation as a fighter. From being the 'little slant-eyed yeller bastard', he had become the superhuman fighter who never surrendered, when wounded killing himself rather than be taken prisoner. Always he was quicker off the mark than his opponent. Moreover he was vicious and cruel. If you fell into Jap hands, you could expect to be beaten up, tortured – or worse. Even the generals were nervous. Gordon Bennett, who commanded the Australians, already felt they had no chance. One day he would quietly slip away from Singapore with one of the last craft to leave, abandoning his leaderless unlucky infantry to their fates. 'I must at all costs return to Australia and tell our people the story of our conflict with the Japanese.' The escape would ruin him. But at least he was able to grow old and die in bed. Hundreds of the men he left behind would never see the end of the war massing on the other shore only a thousand yards away. Singapore island, he insisted, 'must be fought for until every single unit and every single strong point has been separately destroyed'.[9] He reckoned, as did the Imperial General Staff (at least officially), that the 'City of the Lion' would be able to hold out for at least six months. During that period he and the Americans would be in a position to relieve it. It was Sunday, 1 February, 1942. In two short weeks it would be all over, and a shocked Winston Churchill would never completely trust the British Army ever again. ...

V

'The honour of the British Empire and the British Army is at stake'

At first the Japanese concentrated on 'softening' the garrison up. There was Japanese long-range artillery sited so that it could cover the entire city and Singapore's four airfields. These guns now opened up, lobbing huge shells into the garrison, which, in spite of the 12-inch guns that the Navy had installed in Singapore back in the thirties, could not answer back. The naval guns were in fixed sites, *pointing out to sea*! The artillery bombardment was complemented by almost constant attack from the air. Not only did Japanese dive-bombers come hurtling down from the heavens to attack military targets, but Zero fighters came zooming in at tree-top height to machine-gun individual civilians cowering in the streets or to drop small anti-personnel bombs which burst in the air, scattering hundreds of tiny razor-sharp metal shards that scythed down everything before them. By the second day of the siege, it was estimated that roughly 200 people a day were being killed by the bombardment from the air and land.

Morale slumped, not only among the native population but also among the troops. Men began to desert their units. One observer noted bewildered knots of men wandering 'grimy, lost, leaderless and without orders'. Another found his bungalow invaded by a gang of 'convalescent soldiers' who 'all looked hale and hearty'.[1]

Many who had fought the length of the peninsula down to Singapore were desperate with fatigue. They just bedded down where they were, not making any attempt to find their units. Others went on a weekend-long binge, looting anything alcoholic, including *crème de menthe*. With every fresh raid and each new rumour, there seemed to be more and more unkempt, drunken soldiers on the streets, reeling along, waving their looted bottles.

Sometimes these drunks, who seemed to belong nowhere, became violent. An air-raid warden, who happened to be grey-bearded, was hurrying to yet another blaze started by the bombs, when a bunch of drunken soldiers, amused by his beard, jeered: 'Let it burn, dad! It's too late!' Then they started to pelt him with oblong 'missiles'. Two of them landed on the front seat of his car. Later he examined them and found them to be cartons of looted cigarettes.

But in spite of the shells, the bombs, the looters, the disgruntled troops wandering aimlessly through the streets, civilian life seemed to go on in Singapore, as if the war were a thousand miles away. Raffles was always full at night, so much so that you had to book a table in advance if you wanted to eat there. Drinkers swarmed into the Cricket Club at night and the 'World' was packed with men standing in line to dance with a 'taxi' girl for 7d.

And all the while General Percival just waited. In that period of days before the Japanese Commander of the assault force launched his three-division attack, no attempt was made to take any deterrent action. Percival just sat passively in his headquarters, letting events take their tragic cause.

At half-past ten on Sunday, 8 February, General Yamashita launched a wave of 4,000 men, all veterans of the fighting in China, across the water against the 22nd Australian Brigade holding the north-western area of the island. Almost immediately they were spotted. The Australian infantry opened up against their boats with all they'd got. Tracer zipped lethally across the black water. Machine guns chattered viciously. Boat after boat was sunk; Japanese, laden with their heavy equipment, went under, screaming for help that didn't come. Others, filled with dead and dying infantrymen, simply floated away. Within minutes the first wave had been virtually wiped out.

It was now that it had been planned to switch on scores of searchlights to turn night into day. At the same time the batteries of guns supporting the Australians were scheduled to open fire on the other shore. Neither happened. So the Australians fought on in the darkness as the second wave of invaders was wiped out, only to be succeeded by the third. Desperately infantry commanders along the Australian front sent red alarm flares sailing into the night, summoning help from the guns. Here and there a British 25-pounder spotted the frantic plea for assistance. Shells sailed over the heads of the sweating, anxious Australian infantry, throwing up huge spouts of wild water and flailing Japanese bodies.

But already it was too late. The Japs were already across! Now instead of attacking the Australian positions frontally, they did what they had done so effectively in the jungle. They slipped through the crumbling pockets of defenders, each small party led by an officer, carrying a sword, with a compass strapped to his wrist.

By 1 a.m. the Australians, confused and nervous, were beginning to withdraw from their positions, trying to find their way to the rear in the maze of the jungle. Many died in that flight, hacked to death in hand-to-hand combat with the Japanese as parties bumped into each other in the confused darkness. Others fled. By mid-morning it was clear to a dismayed Bennett that the 22nd Australian Infantry Brigade no longer existed as an effective fighting force and that the enemy had a firm footing on the island.

Now as a hastily organized defensive line further inland was set up the Japanese Imperial Guards landed in the north-east and rapidly broke the Australians' defence position there, only to be thrown back by Brigadier Maxwell's infantry. It was the only victory of the whole sorry battle for Singapore. So doggedly did the Australians fight against these crack Japanese troops that their commander asked for permission to give up his attempts to land troops there. But before that permission could be given, the Australians had disappeared, as if by magic.

How this happened is still unclear. Brigadier Maxwell later stated he had given the command to his brigade to withdraw, but he had approval to do so from his superior General Bennett. The latter denied he had given that permission. To the jubilant Japanese it didn't matter what had happened behind the scenes, they pressed on virtually unopposed.

Now the one-eyed Commander-in-Chief Wavell flew in from India. An unlucky general, who wrote poetry, he ordered an immediate counter-attack. Again he was unlucky. The counter-attack was a failure and added even more to the impending disaster.

Just before he had ordered the immediate counter-attack he had received a cable from Churchill, who was worried about the effect of the fall of Singapore on American public opinion. He cabled: 'There must be at this stage no thought of saving the troops or sparing the population. The battle must be fought to the bitter end at all costs. The 18th Division has a chance to make its name in history, commanders and senior officers should die with their troops. The honour of the British Empire and the British Army is at stake. I rely on you to show no mercy to weakness in any form ... The whole reputation of our country and our race is involved. It is expected that every unit will be brought into close contact with the enemy and fight it out.'[2]

Now Wavell put out an order of the day which used Churchill's arguments, even the same words, and which ended 'I look to you and your men to fight to the end to prove that the fighting spirit that won our Empire still exists to enable us to defend it'.[3]

But apparently the troops were no longer prepared to fight to prove that the spirit which had 'won the Empire' still existed. The 18th Infantry Division would never make its name in history, save to be recorded as a whole division which went virtually from the troopships into Japanese captivity. To the very end Percival and the civil government failed to call on the fighting spirit and patriotism of the British civilians and the Chinese whose compatriots had been locked in a bitter war with Japan for over half a decade.

On Friday the 13th, those who could began to leave the doomed city in earnest. In fact, as the Japanese began to bomb the docks, panic broke out among those who felt the ships might be sunk or leave without them. In the end the police had to fire over the heads of the frantic crowd. But not only civilians left. Senior officers of the Royal Navy, including an admiral, and the RAF did too. Things were falling apart.

But if some were panicking, part of the defending infantry was fighting back at last. The Malay Brigade, a regular, locally raised unit, officered by Britons who spoke the language, fought that day until it was 'almost obliterated'. Even Percival, not much given to praise, noted that the Brigade 'showed what *esprit de corps* and discipline can achieve. Garrisons of posts held their ground and many of them were wiped out almost to the man.'[4] But the Malays were in direct contact with the enemy. Many of the Australian and British infantry could not see their enemy. They simply sensed him somewhere in thick luxuriant jungle around their perimeters.

Some couldn't take the nerve-wracking tension of waiting for the next Japanese sniper to open up or the sudden chatter of a machine gun like an irate woodpecker, followed by taunting calls in broken English, '*You no fight, Johnny … Why you now no fight, Tommy bastard*?' And again there'd be the dry harsh crack of the sniper's rifle and some poor unfortunate would scream and die, clutching his holed forehead. They cracked and stole off back to the city. The number of desertions increased. Even a few officers left their units to their fates. And at the docks there were ugly scenes when armed deserters tried to drag screaming women off the escape launches.

But it wasn't only the ordinary 'other-ranker' who no longer wanted to fight and was prepared to go to desperate lengths to escape before the inevitable happened. After the first offer by the Japanese to surrender (at which he fought hard to convince Percival to do), General Gordon Bennett decided to go behind the Commanding General's back. Without consulting Percival he wired the Australian Prime Minister in Canberra that 'in the event of other formations falling back and allowing the enemy to enter the city behind us,' it was his 'intention to surrender to avoid further needless loss of life'. It was an unprecedented move, though in the past other dominion commanders had appealed directly to their own premiers. Now while he waited for an answer, Bennett asked the Sultan of Johore, with whom he got on very well, if he could provide a boat for him in case he wanted to make an individual escape. The rot was setting in right at the top!

While this was going on, the Japanese finally broke through what was left of the Malay Brigade and headed straight for the Alexandra hospital, which was crammed with wounded. The medics surrendered and the usual massacre of the wounded occurred. First they slaughtered the surgeons in the operating theatre and bayoneted to death a wounded soldier of the 2nd Loyals *on the operating table* itself! Then they started moving out the wounded, mercilessly bayoneting those who couldn't be shifted. Those who were left were crowded 60 to 70 in tiny rooms and left there without food or water or attention in the stifling heat in a kind of latter-day Black Hole of Calcutta. At times, when it took their captors' fancy, small groups of them were led out to be stabbed to death. A shell struck their prison some time during that terrible night and gave some of the fitter patients a chance to make a dash for it through a hole opened in the wall by the explosion. Eight tried and five were mown down. Those three were the only survivors who lived to tell the tale after the war. ...

On the weekend of 14/15 February the end was near. The streets of Singapore were filled with thousands of confused, dejected soldiers with nothing to do and nowhere to go. One stripped to the waist harangued the crowds, telling them: 'It's time to surrender – we're fighting for a way of life that's finished anyway.'[5] And he was right, too. Some washed and did their laundry at the sides of busy roads like a lot of khaki-clad coolies, though not many, for water was running out now. Percival was informed and made a kind of decision. 'While there's water', he announced to his chief engineer, 'we fight on.'[6]

Sunday came. Bennett remembered it as a 'hopeless dawn of despair'. Percival went to church in a freshly starched uniform, trying to the very end not to alarm the civilians and succeeding in concealing the real gravity of the situation from them to the very end. He knew now, however, he had been granted wider discretion. Earlier he had received a telegram from Wavell reading: 'So long as you are in a position to inflict losses and damage to enemy and your troops are physically capable of doing so, you must fight on ... When you are fully satisfied that this is no longer possible, I give you discretion to cease resistance. Inform me of intentions. Whatever happens, I thank you and all your troops for gallant efforts of the last few days.'[7] Now it was up to hum.

In the end – 'pale and with bloodshot eyes' – he personally made an approach to Yamashita, with his party carrying the Union flag – and a white one!

The Japanese newsreel camera man recorded that meeting for all time. Percival, skinny to an extreme, looking foolish in his long khaki, army-issue shorts facing a bull-like, determined General Yamashita, right fist clenched on the table in front of him, as if ready to pound it at any moment. It was a classic scene: the vanquished and the victor.

Both were infantryman with military service going back to World War One. But one came from a nation which had not been prepared to face up to the realities of mid-twentieth century warfare; a nation which had not been ready to defend with a rifle in hand that which it had once conquered by force. The other came from a completely different race, cruel, grasping, ready to die, willing to create a new empire. Here two totally different worlds faced each other and the new one had triumphed; and even after

103

defeat in the years to come would continue to triumph – economically this time – right up to our own time.

Yamashita barked in that harsh grunting manner of the Japanese military: 'The Japanese army will consider nothing but unconditional surrender at 3 p.m. Nippon time.'

'But I can't guarantee it.' Percival objected. 'We can't submit our final reply before midnight.'

The victor wasn't having it. He thumped the table with his fist. 'Are our terms acceptable or not? Things have to be done quickly. We are ready to resume firing.'

An aide pushed forward and demanded in English, 'Does the British Army surrender unconditionally?'

Desperately Percival cried, 'Please, wait until tomorrow morning for the final answer.'

But there was to be no more waiting. Threateningly Yamashita leaned forward. 'In that case,' he retorted, 'we will continue the attack until tomorrow morning. Is that all right, or do you consent immediately to unconditional surrender.'

Percival let his head drop in defeat. For years he had commanded the destinies of hundreds, then thousands of men. His every word had been obeyed instantly. He had had the power to make and break men at the snap of the fingers. Now he was a nothing. In a faint voice, he gave his consent to an immediate surrender.[8]

Later, before he, too, went into the prison camp, where he would spend the next four years, he drafted a final signal to Wavell in India. It read: 'Owing to losses from enemy action, water, petrol, food and ammunition practically finished. Unable therefore to continue the fight any longer. All ranks have done their best and grateful for your help.'[9]

But all ranks hadn't done their best. Many of the 85,000 soldiers who now entered the captivity of these most cruel captors had not fired one single shot in the battle for Singapore. Even those who had felt a sense of relief. There were only a few who were not prepared to surrender and wanted to fight on. As one Australian officer in an infantry battalion recorded, as the surrender came into effect: 'A strange quiet settled over the Battalion positions. The men could not but feel thankful for the relief from the bombs and shells and the continuous strain of the past five weeks, but to the many who had never entertained the idea of capitulation, it came as a staggering and sorrowful blow. It was difficult to realize that they were beaten and were prisoners of war. They were prepared to fight on the streets but they had no choice.'[10]

But why didn't they fight on the streets? Why had they obeyed the orders from the top to surrender so willingly, almost gratefully? In 100 days the British Army had lost the Far Eastern Empire and had, in Singapore, been beaten by a smaller army. What was wrong with the British fighting man?

Churchill knew why. Publicly he called the capitulation at Singapore 'the worst disaster and largest capitulation in British history'.[11] He even hinted to the editor of *The Times* that he might now lay down his office, 'I am an old man. No man has had to bear such disasters as I have.'[12] Privately the fall of Singapore, after the shameful defeats in France, Greece, Crete and North Africa, confirmed his fears about the spirit of the British fighting man. Something had gone drastically wrong with it. The British soldier simply would not fight.

The Top Brass knew it, too. In a letter at that time to Sir John Kennedy, chief of plans at the War Office, Wavell wrote: 'The real trouble is that for the time being we have lost a good deal of our hardness and fighting spirit. I am sure that you realize this and that in your training and teaching at home you are doing everything possible to restore it. Until we have again soldiers capable of marching 20 to 30 miles a day for a number of days running and missing their full rations every second or third day, and whose first idea is to push forward and get to grips with the enemy on any and every occasion and whatever the difficulties and odds, we shall not recover our morale or reputation.'[13]

Kennedy raised the point with the Chief of the Imperial General Staff Brooke. He agreed that 'we are undoubtedly softer as a nation than any of our enemies except the Italians. This may be accounted for by the fact that modern civilization on the democratic model does not produce a hardy race.'[14]

Later Brooke produced a paper on the subject, in which he stated, 'The morale and the discipline of the Army must be vastly improved ... There is much we can do ... to raise the morale and tighten discipline. It is, I fear, true to say that our troops have not always in this war fought as well as they could and should. The reason, in my opinion, has been directly due to a low standard of leadership and true fighting morale.'[15]

Of course it went deeper than that. Since 1918 and victory in World War One, the average working man had gone slightly 'bolshy' (as his superiors put it) and lost his old traditional sense of deference and service. 'Among servicemen,' as ex-Major Denis Healey reflected just after the war, 'there was a feeling that they were as good as anyone else.'[16] Dunkirk had confirmed for many 'other rankers' that officers could show the yellow streak and that rank and birth didn't automatically guarantee firm, reliable leadership. 'The chinless wonders' and 'upper-class twits', as they called some of their officers contemptuously, could make just as much a mess of things as any working-class man.

Too many of these 'other rankers' and their officers as well had wanted the easy life that democracy afforded without feeling any obligation or need to defend that way of life. Consistently they had wanted butter and not guns, unlike their enemies. They had not been prepared to re-arm. They had not been prepared to serve and in the end they had not been prepared to fight, either. In the end, all Englishmen of all classes, rich and poor, intellectual and worker, conservative and left-winger, they had all contributed to what had happened in Singapore.

That dreadful winter a book written by a young American, while still a student at Harvard, was still leading the best-seller lists in the United States. Entitled *Why England Slept*, it detailed with amazing clarity for one so young what the British had done wrong in the years leading to the outbreak of World War Two and her series of terrible defeats. The young author pointed out just how much the leadership was to blame for the mess Britain now was in. 'But the English people must bear the responsibility as well,' he maintained. 'They had been warned. Churchill and others had pointed out to them the dangers that had menaced their country ... The failure of their leaders to grasp the true situation is grave enough, but the English public cannot be exonerated of their share of the responsibility. They gave the stamp of approval to the policy which has brought them so near disaster.'[17]

Twenty years later that same young man who was now the 35th President of the United States would demand of his nation that which no one had been prepared to ask of the British, '*Don't ask what America can do for you, ask what you can do for America!*'

VI

'They might look like scarecrows but they look like soldiers, too'

On a secret radio some of them had listened to Churchill broadcast to the world what had happened. 'I speak to you all under the shadow of a far-reaching defeat,' he had intoned sombrely. 'It is a British and Imperial defeat. Singapore has fallen. All the Malay peninsula has been overrun.' Outside their jail some of them had heard their womenfolk being marched off into Japanese captivity bravely singing that cult song of those years: 'There'll always be an England ... and England will be free.' And it had seemed to them behind the barbed wire to be more than a tune, but a way of life which had been put to words and music.

But now that way of life was to vanish for three years – and for perhaps nearly a third of them for good. For now they were going to experience the full misery of captivity in the hands of such a sadistic and cruel people as their jailers. Later many of them may well have thought it would have been better to fight, perhaps even to die, than endure the horrors of what was to come – those who survived.

Some were savagely murdered straightaway. A group of infantrymen were flung into the back of a truck by the Japanese and had blankets piled on top of them. They could hear their captors laughing and whispering outside and unscrewing the British two-gallon tins of petrol. The driver was the first to be suspicious. But it was only when the Japanese started to soak the blankets with the petrol that he rumbled what was going to happen.

'The sudden knowledge,' as one of the eye witnesses was to write later, 'seemed to separate his mind from his body and he started jerking and heaving to escape from the stifling horror of the blankets, and the sounds that came from his throat and filtered through the gag infected the others and they, too, began to writhe in terror, strange sounds pouring from their blanket-stuffed mouths. There was a muffled explosion and they heaved their bodies this way and that; the flames reached down quickly but to them, the interval was timeless. The blankets blazed on their bodies and as the fire scorched them they made a last effort to burst loose and the driver stood upright in an oven of fire, blinded by the flames, his arms and body blazing like a torch. He managed to turn towards the open back and tried to step forward, he toppled across the burning cases and fell to the ground. His head lay in a puddle of fire ...'[1]

But for most of them death came slowly, as the Japanese, ignoring every article of the Geneva Convention and contemptuous of these soldiers who had surrendered to them with hardly a fight, starved and worked them till they were dropping like flies, succumbing to the tropical diseases which raged in the camps. Pellagra, the vitamin deficiency disease, was almost universal. Red, weeping sores appeared all over their emaciated, nearly naked frames. Ulcers formed on the tongue, the gums, the throat. In the medical profession the disease is sometimes refered to as the 3-Ds, for that was the form it took – dermatitis, diarrhoea and dementia. There was a fourth D too – *death*!

But there were other diseases, some of which the survivors would still be suffering from nearly 50 years afterwards: amoebic and bacillar dysentery, the attacks of which left them squatting exhausted, unable even to press back in their anal sphincter, which had been forced out by the frequency and the violence of their spasms. Beri-beri, malaria and diphtheria, which closed the throat so that the victim died either of starvation or the disease itself, drowning in his own fluids as the lungs gradually filled up with them.

Blindness became commonplace. It started with night blindness, the result of a deficiency of vitamin A. Thereafter followed the shooting pains at the back of the eyeballs and objects began to look as if they were floating in a thick grey mist. In the end, with no drugs to help the doctors, who tried to do their best for their helpless patients, total blindness followed.

Some fought back the best they could – the 'hard men'. 'The Bolshie bastards' or the 'naughty boys", as they were sometimes called by the others, were determined to survive, cost what it may. They stole and they bartered and tricked, not afraid even of pulling fast ones on their cruel Japanese and Korean jailers. They ate skinned cats and rats, snails and worms, as much grass and weeds as they could get down. Probably they would have eaten each other if it had been possible.

Terribly emaciated, half-naked and covered with suppurating ulcers, they stole banana skins from Jap refuse barrels and boiled them into a soup. When they were sent out on working parties, labouring from dawn to dusk like slaves, they stole anything and everything they could lay their hands on. And not only food. In one camp they pilfered enough bits and pieces to make a radio which they code-named 'The Old Lady'. The receiver was made from the stolen steering damper knob of a Norton motor-cycle; the ignition coils were 'whipped' from an old gun battery; the insulation was supplied by pieces of aeroplane glass similarly 'whipped' or 'flogged' on an airfield where they were forced to work, etc. etc.

With their bones showing through like skeletons, testicles gangrenous, their fingers and toes slowly dissolving away, the tips open and bloody, these 'hard men' fought back. In this terrible adversity they showed the true British fighting spirit which had been so lacking before.

An Australian infantryman, Harold Ramsey, remembered years later how he and his four mates, who had snatched out frogs from a dirty river to eat – 'the five biggest thieves in the camp' – stole a scrawny chicken one night. 'Our chap grabbed the chicken by the arse instead of the neck. It made a terrible noise. A Jap guard approached. We let the chicken go. Then I told the chaps to kneel down and fold their hands and close their eyes. When the guard reached us, I told him that every night at that time the five of us met at that spot to pray. So it was okay. He left us alone.'[2]

Some of the 'hard men' became so tough and unfeeling that their hardness verged on paranoia. Russell Braddon, the writer, recalled one later who was given the job of looking after the bodies – 'the stick-like bundles' – awaiting cremation in a camp in Thailand. This fellow Australian, being 'without brains or emotions or finer susceptibilities of any kind" was more than happy at his ghastly work.

'He stripped the dead of their gold teeth caps; he stole fearlessly from the guards, who dare not touch him lest he contaminate them; he cooked what he stole ... on the fire where he burnt the bodies. He was a complete moron.

'It was his practice before dealing with the fresh batch of bodies that arrived each morning to boil himself a "cuppa cha" and watch the working party fall in to be marched away to the cuttings. He liked watching the working parties fall in to march away because *he* stayed at home by his fire, where, even in the monsoonal rains, he could keep warm and do his cooking. Upon one particular occasion, he sipped his tea out of the jam tin that served as a mug and watched the parade. As he watched he rolled some tobacco in a strip of tissue that clings to the inside of a bamboo, then his fag completed his picked up a body and tossed it easily from yards off (for it was only light) on to the fire. He enjoyed the revulsion this caused. He did it every morning just before the workers marched out. Grinning at them as they glowered angrily, he then shambled to the fringe of the fire to light his cigarette.

'As he leant forward to pick up a faggot, the body he had just tossed into the flames, its sinews contracted, suddenly sat bolt upright and grunted, and in its hand thrust out a flaming brand on to the cigarette IN THE MORON'S MOUTH!

'With a scream of terror, the man who had burnt hundreds of bodies with callous indifference fell backwards, his hands over his eyes. When the workers reached him, he was jibbering and mad. ...'[3]

But even the hard men succumbed in the end. Of the 6,000 British prisoners of war building part of the 'Railway of Death' in Thailand, 2,742 died of malnutrition and disease, an appalling death rate of 45 per cent! Ironically enough most of them came from the 18th Infantry Division, which had barely fired a shot in the battle for Singapore.

In Borneo the death rate was even higher. Of the 2,000 British soldiers from Singapore who had been transported there to work as slave labourers, only 750 survived to the end of the war. Of these, 650 were ill. In 1945, after three and a half years of captivity, there were not 30 soldiers in the whole camp fit enough to be sent out on a working party! There, in one of the periodic marches to a new camp, 2,970 prisoners of war set out on the long journey. Day after day they staggered on under the burning heat, sick, hungry, and exhausted. When they fell out, their skulls were smashed with rifle butts or shovels and they were left to rot on the trail, unburied. In the end only *three* reached their destination. ...

Of course there were a few good camps and gentle guards. In Saigon, where 2,000 men captured in Singapore had been transported to work on the docks, the Britons were decently housed and fed by their guards. Here there were few beatings and no torture. Only one or two died – of natural causes. The prisoners had established secret contacts with the Free French outside and had been helped with food, medicines, tobacco, etc. Many of the POWs went 'under the wire' at night, dressed in civilian clothes given them by the French. Naturally they wanted women – and they found enough of them in the capital's many brothels. Unfortunately far too many of the local whores were diseased and VD became a problem in the Saigon camp. As a result the men were forced to slip back under the wire, not to visit the whores this time but to be treated by sympathetic French doctors!

There were men who grew fat in the camps, while their fellows wasted away, because they toadied to the Japanese and did their dirty work for them. In the Shamshuipo Camp, which housed the British and Canadian infantrymen captured at Hong Kong, there was one such 'king rat'. He was a major, the only officer left, who was weak, vacillating and subservient, willing to carry out any order the Japanese imposed, maintaining he owed no further allegiance to 'King and Country'. The men under his command called him 'Major Disaster' or 'Major Benjo' *benjo* being the Japanese for latrine. He waxed fat for four years. Then came the reckoning after liberation. He was denounced, court-martialled, and disgraced.

Around him though at the height of his power, he gathered a little coterie of like-minded toadies. They got the cushy jobs of clerks, runners and orderlies and reported to 'Major Disaster' 'treacherous' remarks against their masters the Japanese. These were 'the Benjo narks', as the other men nicknamed them bitterly: men who always seemed to eat and smoke more than the rest; men who were going to survive cost what it may. 'Arsehole crawlers', the infantrymen called them contemptuously.

Some neither fought back like the 'hard men' nor toadied like the 'Benjo narks'. They simply resigned themselves to their fate and allowed themselves to die; for they had lost the will to live. The infantrymen of the Winnipeg Grenadiers and the Royal Rifles of Canada, who were interned in that same camp run by 'Major Disaster', belonged to this group. They had suffered 800 casualties, many of them officers, in the brief battle for Hong Kong. They resigned themselves to the dirt and disease and made little attempt to better their conditions, as did the regulars of the British infantry. As one of the latter, RSM Challis, remarked: 'I thought our blokes looked rough until I saw those Canadians.'[4] Over the next three years 264 more Canadians would die there as POWs and a further 300 passed away after their return to Canada. It was a tragic, miserable record, with only a mere 500 men surviving out of those who had sailed to war from Canada originally.

But most of them managed to keep up their spirits right to the end, in spite of the terrible conditions. Alf Allbury, captured with the 18th Infantry Division, had slaved in various camps for two years when he was ordered to join a party of POWs being sent to work in Japan. This was considered a high honour – by the Japanese. They ordered the whole camp to parade to witness the send-off of the 'Japan Party'. The camp's six-man band was positioned just below the saluting base, where the Japanese officers, complete with sword, stood fiercely erect as the 'Japan Party' started to move off.

The prison band struck up the 'Colonel Bogey March'. Now, as the column approached the platform with the Japanese officers, the British officer in charge yelled 'eyes left!' Behind him the infantry clicked their heads woodenly in the direction of the Japs and spontaneously broke into the insulting obscene words of that march. *'Bollocks – and the same to you ... Where was the engine driver when the boiler bust? They found his bollocks and the same to you ... bollocks ...'*

That moment was impressed on Private Allbury's mind for ever. Many years later he recalled: 'There was a confused blur of pinks and yellows and greens, the bobbing of broad straw hats, the clatter and din of pots and pans tied to our packs, as triumphantly we passed through the gate still raucously paying tribute to our conquerors. It was for everyone, including those left behind us, one of the most uniquely moving moments of the war. Whatever tomorrow might bring, today had been ours ...'[5]

But whatever flashes of defiance and spirit the emaciated sorely tried prisoners of the 'Sons of the Rising Sun' showed in their prison camps all over the Far East, the comrades who were still free continued to be defeated everywhere. In Burma, fleeing towards India all that winter and spring of 1942, they ploughed their way up sheer slopes, down tracks, ankle deep in slippery mud, soaked to the skin, rotten with fever, their progress marked by the hundreds of corpses, both white and brown, their depleted formations left behind them.

Here again discipline broke down. Mandalay, abandoned and about to fall to the Japanese, was filled with looters from the Indian Army. In the villages around, deserters from that Army, mostly native soldiers, terrorized the villagers, often murdering them when they refused to hand over food, drink or gold. It was not surprising that the locals turned against the retreating troops, carrying out their own kind of scorched-earth policy in their path, betraying them to the Japanese when it suited them. Forty-odd years later a former officer of a British infantry regiment would confess he ordered his soldiers to massacre the inhabitants of a whole Burmese village because he was afraid they would betray his company to the Japanese.*

Watching them retreat through this impossible hostile terrain, American war correspondent Jack Belden thought: 'The physical condition, morale and spirit of the British Army was at a low ebb. Three months of bitter campaigning and worse hardship had enfeebled the whole Imperial Army and exacted a heavy toll in fighting fitness. Moreover the average soldier in the Imperial Army no longer wanted to fight in Burma. The Indians were anxious to get back to their native land and the British wanted to clear out of that forsaken country. This was obvious from their oft-repeated greetings of "See you in India", but it was more apparent from hundreds of bitter comments that increased in violence as the days wore on. Though the high British authorities had delayed the Chinese** from originally coming into Burma, a typical comment heard on the retreat past Mandalay was: "If the Chinese want the goddam country, give it to them!"'[6]

For 900 miles the infantry marched and fought, desperately trying to reach India before it was too late and they were trapped by the Japanese, who had defeated them time and time again and had now become supermen in most of their eyes. In the end they reached India at Imphal. But as they marched in through the pouring monsoon rain, they were told to make their way into the jungle and set up their bivouacs there.

It seemed that no preparation at all had been made for them in India. As one of their Corps Commanders, General Slim, an infantryman himself, remarked: 'They had arrived with nothing but the soaked, worn and filthy clothing they stood up in; they had no blankets, no waterproof sheets, no tentage. Nor did they find any awaiting them. On those dripping gloomy hillsides there was no shelter but the trees, little if any clothing or blankets. As Taffy Davies***, indefatigable in labouring to ease the suffering of our

---

* Upon his confession in 1985 there was no immediate decision as to what, if any, legal action should be taken against the ex-officer, by then in his seventies.

** The US General 'Vinegar Joe' Stilwell had led the Chinese Army, supplied by the US, into the battle of Burma.

*** Major-General Davies.

troops, wryly said: "The slogan in India seems to be, 'Isn't the Burma Army annihilated yet?"'[7]

But in spite of the fact that many of his men were bitter at this reception and that eight per cent of them would now fall sick, many of them dying in India, General Slim still felt proud of them as he stood on a bank by the road and watched the rearguard march into India. 'All of them, British, Indian and Gurkha, were gaunt and ragged as scarecrows. Yet, as they trudged behind their surviving officers in groups pitifully small, they still carried their arms and kept their ranks, they were still recognizable as fighting units. They might look like scarecrows, but they looked like soldiers, too.'[8]

But as 'Vinegar Joe' Stilwell, notorious for his sour disposition, who reached India with his corps at the same time as Slim, remarked realistically, for retreats, however heroic, don't win wars: 'I claim we got a hell of a beating. We got run out of Burma and it is humiliating as hell. I think we should find out what caused it and go back and retake it ...'[9] But there was to be no advancing for the Allied armies on *any* front yet. For they were still retreating everywhere.

VII

'The very earth was exhausted'

On this night of 4/5 June, 1942, the moon was late and the night was chill as the forces concentrated for the attack. A great quiet hung over the Western Desert, broken only here and there by the rattle of a tank or bren gun carrier taking station. The previous evening they had lightened their vehicles, throwing away unnecessary equipment, even precious personal possessions, to make room for the extra ammunition and two-gallon 'flimsies' they would need for the attack on Rommel's positions. Now the infantry, huddled in their greatcoats slumped in sleep – those who could sleep – or puffed moodily at their cigarettes, each man wrapped up in a cocoon of his own fears and apprehensions.

The moon finally appeared, full, spectral, casting an icy cold light on those waiting below. Everywhere the artillery officers, tensed near their 25-pounders, flashed glances at the green-glowing dials of their wrist-watches. It wouldn't be long now. In their tanks, other officers made a last check of the steel-cluttered interior – extra shells, Very light flares, first-aid kits, morphia. And in the trucks the infantry smoked and smoked. ...

At precisely ten minutes to three, exactly as General Ritchie, commanding the Eighth Army, had planned it, the night exploded with the shock of heavy guns. Suddenly the whole horizon seemed to blaze like the opening of so many enormous blast furnaces. The infantry started, threw away their cigarettes, gasped, as the shells shrieked their banshee-like howl, heading straight for Rommel's positions. Soon the signal to advance would come and two whole divisions of infantry, the British 50th Division, which General Montgomery had not thought so highly of two years before, and the rested, somewhat green 2nd South African Division, would commence their advance.

Dawn came early. Now the tanks rattled forward. To the rear, as they disappeared over the abruptly burning horizon, the infantry could hear the angry thump of enemy guns and that unmistakable ferocious sound that their 88-mms made – like a huge piece of canvas being ripped apart.

Then the hysterical high-pitched hiss of their Spandaus, followed by the first shower of red flares soaring into the dawn sky, as the 'Teds' signalled for help. The battle had been joined!

At midday some of the tanks returned, their metal sides scored deep with gleaming silver wounds where armour-piercing shells had bounced off them, to refuel. All of them bore with them heavy loads of badly wounded men, a grim and weary lot. They were the survivors of the 'Hell's Last Issue' – the Highland Light Infantry – which had been caught in the open between the opposing tank forces. The Germans had shot them to pieces. That afternoon their colonel, blood streaming down his wounded face, passed back and forth three times collecting what was left of his shattered battalion.

As darkness approached, Indian troops – Jats, Baluchis, Gurkhas – and men of the Northumberland Fusiliers moved forward to back up the tanks. Almost immediately the Indians were attacked by German tanks. The anti-tank guns of the Northumberland Hussars were rushed to meet the new challenge. To no avail! The German tanks overran a nearby infantry battalion and started shooting the Northumberlands up. In vain they tried to knock out the German Mark IIIs and Mark IVs, but their shells bounced off their thick steel hides like glowing ping-pong balls. A sergeant of the Recce Regiment, with what was left of his section, sprang on one lumbering monster and tried to ram grenades inside the turret. Behind them another tank spotted the attempt and scythed them from the deck like someone swatting flies.

The Indian Brigade was overrun. A young soldier with his arm blown off tried to man the one remaining anti-tank gun. He didn't make it. A ding-dong tank battle was now raging and the British were getting the worse of it. Instead of concentrating as Rommel did, Ritchie was dispersing his tanks into small groups to aid his hard-pressed infantry, crying out for help on all sides. Swiftly the senior officers were losing effective control of the battle. Now it was up to individual officers and units to slog it out.

Saturday 13 June – the ninth continuous day of battle – dawned warm and clear. Immediately at first light, the two armies engaged. At once the battlefield became a confused mess of flying sand, tanks scurrying back and forth, mushrooms of black smoke ascending to the hard blue sky. To the rear, the expectant, tense British commanders could hear the frantic calls for assistance from the tank commanders crackling over the ether. They had run straight into a line of concealed 88mm guns. They were picking off the British tanks like sitting ducks. Startlingly, frighteningly, a wedge of sand-coloured steel monsters started to lumber straight towards the HQ of the British armour. *Germans!* The headquarters fled in their vehicles. Communication broke down.

Desperately the British tanks tried to break through the German anti-tank screens to get at their tanks. Tank after tank shuddered to a stop.

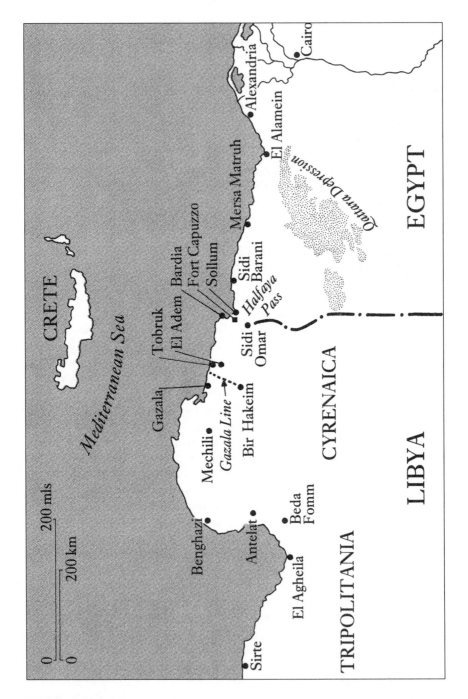

The Western Desert

Screaming burning men flung themselves out of the escape hatches to be mown down cruelly by the waiting German machine-gunners. Solid shot slammed into tank turrets like blows from a giant fist. Inside, the metal glowed a menacing red. Tensely the trapped crews waited for their fate to be decided. If the shell penetrated, it would break up into scores of burning steel shards. In that confined space they would be flayed to death. One day the recovery crews – British or German – would *hose* what was left of them in a bright red, ugly flurry.

Finally they were through. But their losses had been tremendous. They were easy meat for the massed German armour. Cohesion broke down yet again. No longer were they fighting in regiments or even squadrons. They were isolated in desperate little groups, their vision limited in the swirling sand, fighting not for victory now, but to save their lives. Everywhere the desert was littered with burning or disabled British tanks, their tracks sprawled behind them in the sand like broken metallic limbs. Over and over again there was that ominous hollow boom of steel striking steel and yet another of the lighter British tanks would shudder, rear up on its rear sprockets, a gleaming silver wound gouged and smoking in its metal hide, its gun suddenly drooping in defeat.

Now as little groups of broken, wounded tank corps men started to drift back to the rear, it was the turn of the German armour to surge forward, full of that brutal national socialist confidence. This time, Rommel had promised them they would break the Tommies for good; this time they were going to chase them right into the Suez Canal!

A desperate General Ritchie, realizing his plan had failed, signalled urgently to his armour. 'Abandon the Gazala Line! *Get out and get out before it is too late!*'[2] Here and there among the armoured and motorized formations a near panic broke out, while senior commanders racked their brains trying to work out how they were going to get their battered formations back to the Egyptian frontier. 'In the midst of the confusion, the sickening sense of defeat and doubt, the breaking of communications and the spectacle of the incoming wounded,' Alan Moorehead noted at the time, 'the British commanders got to work. It was the blackest night they had had in more than two years of fighting'.[3] There was worse – much worse – to come!

By Sunday the great flap was in full swing. It was the 'Benghazi Handicap' once more, but in much more terrible form. Everywhere stores and equipment intended for the great push were blown up hurriedly or simply abandoned, thousands, hundreds of thousands, millions of pounds worth of material. The sky was black with the smoke of burning fuel dumps. Men cursed as they were ordered to abandon their guns, because there was no transport for them, yanking out the firing pins and smashing them on the barrels and then joining the great flight eastwards to Egypt. Everywhere ambulances, armoured cars, tanks, mobile workshops, trucks and jeeps fought and jostled for position on the tracks leading to safety.

'The trucks were packed to the limit,' General Kippenberg recalled, 'and hundreds of men whom they could carry were crammed on to the fighting vehicles. Men were hanging on wherever there was standing room, squeezed inside the gun quods, on the guns themselves, on carriers and anti-tank portees, anywhere imaginable.'[4]

Already German tanks probing for weaknesses were trying to outflank the retreating columns. After passing through an abandoned British position, littered with German dead – '4 Brigade had done tremendous execution with the bayonet', Colonel Hanna leading the men spotted enemy tanks to his front. They came to a halt. Their first vehicle went up in flames, more followed as 'a single shell in some cases went through two or three trucks in line'.

'My recollections are a little vague at this point, but I remember that, with no alternative, we started up and drove straight into the enemy's fire. I can well imagine the feelings of those tank crews when they saw an irresistible tide of vehicles and guns bearing down upon them. Trucks were still exploding in flames, but nothing could have halted that onrush, the product more of instinct than of command. The air was so heavy with dust and smoke that one could do nothing but follow the vehicle in front into the thick blanket ahead. A number of unfortunate men were thrown off motor-cycles or tossed out of trucks. Their death was certain, for vehicles behind had no chance of avoiding them.'[5]

Thus they fled; and in Cairo, the staff began to burn their records in the greatest flap of the war. The Royal Navy fled Alexandria and as the British civilians clambered and fought to get on the packed trains leaving for Palestine, the Egyptians jeered and spat upon them. For now Rommel was coming and they would soon be 'liberated'. The hated English were finished. They were abandoning the 'white man's burden' at last. But they were not just going, they were *running*!

Behind, up in the desert 'at the sharp end', as they fled, the Eighth Army left two divisions of infantry – the 50th and 2nd South African under General Klopper, who had just been promoted to that rank from a staff job and given that post. As we have already seen these two divisions had been prepared to advance and exploit the armoured breakthrough. Now the battle had been lost and the armour was fleeing, leaving them to look after themselves.

The two divisional commanders acted independently. Klopper withdrew hastily into the port of Tobruk, which had held out for most of 1941 against everything which Rommel had been able to fling at it and which had become a kind of symbol of British resistance in the 8th Army. The commander of the 50th did something much more imaginative. He had three alternatives. He could either surrender (unthinkable); follow the rest

Above: **52.** A Sikh patrol of the 14th Army charging a foxhole to kill any Japanese attempting to escape from the phosphorus grenades they had just thrown. (IWM)

Left: **53.** A propaganda poster, issued in 1943, warning British troops of the dire consequences of fraternizing without due care and attention. Troop losses through VD were severe. (IWM)

Opposite above: **54.** Men of the 'Forgotten Army'. These soldiers, from the 23rd Brigade, helped to expel the Japanese from India. (IWM)

51. Men of 'Merrill's Marauders', the first American infantry unit to fight in Burma, clean their rifles while their 'transport' graze behind them. (IWM)

Above: **48.** 19 May 1944: Polish dead being removed from the Cassino battlefield. (IWM)

49. American troops present arms during the liberation ceremonies in the main square of Cherbourg after the port had been captured.

Opposite above: **50.** American infantry moving down the main road to Rome. The soldier lying down is a British artillery signaller of 24th Field Regiment which gave the Americans close support during the advance. (IWM)

46. The American 5th Army landing at Salerno, September 1943. (IWM)

47. British troops clearing a devastated French village on the outskirts of Caen before entering the town itself.

44. Chindit forces preparing to blow up a railway line used by the Japanese in Burma. (IWM)

45. The *Afrikakorps* surrenders, 12 May 1943. Through a tape-marked gap in the minefield, hundreds of prisoners trudge into captivity. (IWM)

Above: **42.** General Wingate (right) with an American Liaison Officer inside a transport Dakota aircraft. It was one of the last photographs ever taken of him. (IWM)

Right: **43.** A Chindit shields his head from the sun with his pack. (IWM)

Above: **40.** General Eisenhower being invested at Algiers with the Grand Cross of the Legion of Honour by General Giraud, Commander-in-Chief of the French Forces in North Africa. The date is 22 May 1943. (IWM)

Left: **41.** General Eisenhower's driver, Kay Summersby. (IWM)

Right: **38.** Guardsmen holding a position in the mud during the attack on Long Stop Hill, Tunisia. Shell fire can be seen exploding on German positions in the background. (IWM)

Below: **39.** 16 March 1943: Gurkhas, khukris drawn, storm a German position in the Tunisian mountains near Medenine. (IWM)

Above: **36.** American troops landing at Surcouf, North Africa, 11 November 1942. (IWM)

Left: **37.** General Slim, the 14th Army Commander. (IWM)

34. General Ritter von Thoma, the defeated Commander of the *Afrikakorps* at El Alamein, saluting General Montgomery outside Montgomery's tent after he had been captured by a British cavalry officer. (IWM)

35. Australian troops attacking an enemy strongpoint through a dense smokescreen. (IWM)

32. July 1942: men of the Scots Guards moving forward in the El Alamein area under the cover of a smokescreen and protected by tanks. (IWM)

33. General Alexander and Lt-General Montgomery, respectively the new Commander-in-Chief, Middle East, and the new Commander of the 8th Army. The photograph was taken on 12 August 1942, the day Montgomery arrived in Cairo to take over his new command. (IWM)

31. By 1942 the emphasis on training had switched from square-bashing to being fit and battle-alert. Here, US Army recruits undergoing basic infantry training limber up with a few calisthenics. (US National Archives)

Above: **28.** British positions in the Western Desert under heavy attack from Stukas, June 1942. In the foreground are Italian troops. (IWM)

Left: **29.** The Commander-in-Chief of the Middle East Forces, Sir Claude Auchinleck (left), in conversion with Lt-General Richie. The photograph was taken on 27 June 1942 at Auchinleck's 8th Army Headquarters. (IWM)

Opposite above: **30.** British prisoners-of-war captured during the battle for Tobruk. (IWM)

26. British prisoners-of-war in Japanese hands after the fall of Hong Kong. (IWM)

27. Japanese troops, headed by Lt-General Sakai and Vice-Admiral Niimi, entering Hong Kong. (IWM)

24. General 'Vinegar' Joe Stilwell during a visit to his men in the front line in northern Burma. He was given his nickname because of his sour disposition. However, as can be seen, he was capable of raising a glimmer of a smile when he wanted to. (IWM)

24. The interior of an officers' hut in a Japanese camp for British prisoners-of-war at Tamuang, Thailand. Each man had 75cm² of space. (IWM)

22. General Yamashita and General Perceval at the surrender ceremony which took place at 7.00 p.m. on 15 February 1942. (IWM)

23. Japanese troops parade through Singapore near Raffles Place to celebrate their victory over the British. (IWM)

Left: **20.** A British Bren-gunner watches for enemy air attacks from a bombed house in Tobruk. (IWM)

Below: **21.** Major-General Morshead (left), the commander of Tobruk, leaving his desert headquarters, 27 October 1941. (IWM)

Above: **18.** A study in determination. General Freyberg VC, the Commander of Allied forces on Crete, gazing over a parapet in the direction of the German advance. (IWM)

Below: **19.** A German transport is hit just after its German parachutists with their equipment have been dropped on Crete. (IWM)

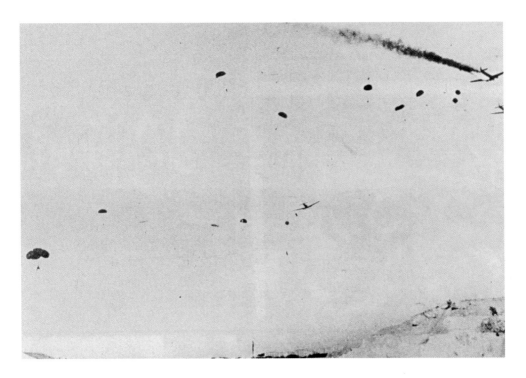

Left: **16.** The inside of Aldershot Detention Barracks. It was this building that gave the nickname 'Glasshouse' to detention barracks because of its glass roof. (*Radio Times* Hulton Library)

Below: **17.** With hands clasped together, the new Commander-in-Chief, Sir Alan Brooke, talks with Allied generals – Polish, Czech and Norwegian – during an exercise somewhere in Britain in 1941. (IWM)

14. Rommel photographed standing beside Major-General Victory Fortune and other British officers after the surrender of the 51st Highland Division. The date is 12 June 1940. (IWM)

15. August 1940: British transport being destroyed to prevent it falling into German hands. (IWM)

12. Men of the 4th Border Regiment, cut off from the main body of the BEF, taking up defensive positions by the roadside. Though infantry, the battalion commandeered vehicles and turned themselves into a motorized unit holding a large sector of the Somme during vital stages of the German advance. (IWM)

13. British and French prisoners-of-war, with arms raised and some carrying white cloths, walk through the hills west of St Valery. Smoke is rising in the background from buildings set alight by the bombardment. (IWM)

12. British troops moving into Belgium across the frontier, 1940. (IWM)

Above: **8.** British, French and Belgian soldiers wait in queues to be taken off from the beaches at Dunkirk. (IWM)

Left: **9.** A British lorry in flames at St Maxent after being hit by a German bomb during the Allied retreat through France. (IWM)

Opposite above: **10.** The face of defeat: exhausted Belgian troops on the Brussels-Louvain road, 14 May 1940. (IWM)

Above: **6.** British infantry, after fighting a rearguard action, move down a street in Dunkirk which was under heavy bombardment. The photograph was taken on 1 June 1940. (IWM)

Below: **7.** On the Dunkirk beaches an infantryman fires at an attacking German plane. (IWM)

Left: **4.** The Commander-in-Chief, Lord Gort, inspecting outpost trenches of the 1st Battalion, Gordon Highlanders, in the front line at Templeuve on 19 October 1939. (IWM)

Below: **5.** The winter of 1940 was one of the coldest on record. Here men from the 2nd Battalion, East Yorkshire Regiment, patrol the Maginot Line in white camouflage smocks. The photograph was taken on 4 February at St Francois. (IWM)

1. Conscripts queuing up to register at Kings Cross, London in 1939. (*Radio Times* Hulton Library)

2. There was even a drill for seeing if your tootsies were sore. Men of the 3rd Battalion, Grenadier Guards, having a foot inspection after a route march in France, September 1939. (IWM)

3. 2nd Battalion, Royal Inniskilling Fusiliers, disembarking from *Royal Sovereign* at Cherbourg, September 1939. (IWM)

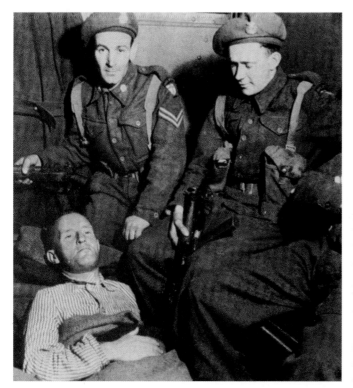

64. 29 May 1945: William Joyce, Lord Haw-Haw, under armed guards before being transported to hospital in an ambulance. He was shot in the thigh at the time of his arrest. (IWM)

65. Fortified caves honey-combed Iwo Jima and they were all full of Japanese prepared to fight to the death. Here a marine covers the entrance to one until a flame-thrower arrives.

62. Men of the 19th Infantry Division recaptured Mandalay Hill, 10 March 1945, a decisive victory in defeating the Japanese. (IWM)

63. The Winning Team.

Left: **60.** German machine-gunners pause for a smoke while moving into territory regained by their counter-offensive in the Ardennes. This photograph was taken from a captured German cine-film. (IWM)

Below: **61.** American infantrymen from the 1st US Army advance cautiously towards a crossroads in Aachen. On their right others clamber over piles of debris to search a guard house.

58. The total devastation of total war. A lone soldier of the 100th Infantry Division, 7th US Army, walks through the ruins of Heilbronn, which was cleared of German troops on 12 April 1944. An important German road and rail centre, it had been blasted by Allied bombers. (IWM)

59. During the last months of the war the infantrymen on both sides became younger and younger. In this poignant photograph a young German girl looks quizzically at a 16-year-old German soldier who, after Lemgo was captured, ran weeping into the American lines. He had been in the Army only 18 days.

56. As the fighting in the Ardennes became more bitter both sides sometimes massacred their prisoners. These American soldiers from the 28th Division were found dead in the snow having had their boots removed. They had all been shot in the head indicating a German atrocity had taken place. (IWM)

57. German servicemen who spoke fluent English were dropped behind the Allied lines during the Ardennes offensive to create confusion. As they were dressed in civilian clothes or in American uniforms they were all treated as spies, and were court-martialled and then shot. (IWM)

55. British troops receive an ecstatic welcome from the people of Brussels, who were liberated on 4 September 1994. (IWM)

fleeing eastwards and probably be cut to ribbons by the panzers; or he could thrust *westwards*!

This the Geordies of the 50th Infantry Division did. They burst through the German lines, leaving Tobruk behind, taking a hundred-to-one chance, making a forced march right into the heart of the enemy! Then they wheeled south right into the heart of the desert before turning east once more and heading for Egypt and safety.

The bold plan stirred the imagination of the cocky little infantrymen from the Tyne-Tees. They went to work with a will as the whole division was split into small groups. Each group was organized by the officers like an old-time Boer commando. Its task was to fight independently, silently and swiftly. Kill and vanish. Rations were strictly rationed, especially water, which was going to be crucial to the success of the adventurous plan. All lights and smoking during the hours of darkness were forbidden. Even talking was prohibited.

The Geordies hit the weakest point in Rommel's front – the Italians. The enemy soldiers were taken as they lay sleeping on the desert. Their attackers seemed here, there and everywhere. An incredible chaos and confusion broke out. Convoys of enemy supply vehicles were ambushed and overwhelmed. Dumps were seized and put to the torch. In the mêlée Italian fired upon Italian. The night sky went wild with a profusion of signal flares as the Italians called for reinforcements, help, enlightenment. But by the time they knew what was really going on, the British had vanished. Days later the 50th Infantry Division reached Egypt, worn and weary but virtually intact. Two years from now the Division of which Montgomery had thought so little would be his leading assault formation for the invasion of Normandy. ...

General Klopper's South Africans were not so lucky. Alan Moorehead, fleeing with the rest through the battered port, didn't like the look of the place one bit. 'On either side of the dusty, dirty land many more lorries and ack-ack guns stood about half-embedded in trenches. The soldiers had rigged up nets and were playing soccer close to the cemetery, now filled with hundreds of white crosses ... A slight sandstorm was blowing and the sand was dirty. A strange sort of atmosphere prevailed over all this ground – a kind of apathy and ugliness one could not describe, but felt very strongly. The very earth was exhausted.'[6]

He wasn't too impressed by the mood of the newcomers either. Moorehead realized that their morale was not improved by the sight of the fleeing 8th Army and the feeling that they were being left in the lurch. But they didn't have the same spirit as the Australians and then the English who had defended the port for month after month the previous year. '*They* believed that they were defending London and their own homes across its scarred, sulphur-coloured plain and the perimeter was as real to them as the cliffs of Dover.

'Now it was altogether different. The new defenders had come as tenants into a strange house, and moreover a house that had fallen somewhat into disrepair. Thousands of them had bundled pell-mell into the fortress at the last moment and they were tired and hungry and embittered from their setbacks of the past five days.' And they were still not digging in, although 'it was hours, not days that counted now.'[7]

On the morning of Saturday 20 June, the blood-red sun colouring the ground mist around Tobruk an unreal ghastly hue, the massed Stukas arrived over the port. One by one they started to fall out of the sky, these black hawks of death, aiming their bombs not at the cowering infantry but at the minefields. Meanwhile German sappers crept forward to clear paths through the fields, while the artillery to their rear thundered.

The first path through the mines was cleared. The jubilant men of the *Afrikakorps* stormed forward, animated not solely to die for 'Folk, Fatherland and Führer', but also by the crowded supply dumps that would be theirs to loot if they succeeded. A small scratch force of British tanks and infantry tried to stop them. They were driven back with heavy losses. The exhausted British infantry fell into German hands in large numbers. All this while the fresh South Africans to the south, south-west and west had not been engaged, save by the bombers and the Germans' guns. Now suddenly fighting started to sound behind them – the hiss of machine guns, the crump of mortars, the snap-and-crackle of a vicious fire-fight. It was the German 90th Light Division coming up from the rear. They were going to be attacked from front and back!

Desperately Klopper radioed Ritchie, 'I will try to fight my way out to the west'. Ritchie had no choice but to accept this. Frantically he waited by his radio for further details. When they came they were of total despair: 'It is too late. Most of my vehicles have been destroyed and it is no longer possible to move. I will continue resistance only long enough to carry out essential demolitions.'[8]

It was the last message to be received from Tobruk. Klopper was going to surrender. ...

When the Coldstreams heard the news, they refused to obey. They fought their way out. Other British officers refused and died fighting. When a huge white flag was hoisted by some native drivers at the HQ of the 6th South African Brigade, 'a sort of cry or moan,' wrote one observer, 'went up from the South African Police. It gave an extraordinary impression of anguish and misery.'[9] After all the heroics of the year before, the cost in human lives, Tobruk had fallen out of the desert war in a matter of hours on a warm summer's day. Some 20,000 men went tamely 'into the bag' and the enemy had won the richest treasure the desert had ever yielded. Now he would be able to re-equip his men with fuel, food and ammunition for the great drive on Egypt and a final solution to the desert war.

In London they called for the dismissal of Churchill, and the Chief of the General Staff, Alan Brooke, wrote in his diary: 'The Middle East situation is about as unhealthy as it can be, and I do not very well see how it can end. ...'[10]

BOOK THREE
1942–1943

Messenger: Prepare you, generals
The enemy comes in in gallant show;
Their bloody sign of battle is hung out,
And something to be done immediately.

Julius Caesar

I

'If we can't stay here, let us stay here dead'

On the same day that General Ritchie launched his ill-fated attack against the *Afrikakorps*, back home 1,500 miles away, a conference of officers was called in the unlikely setting of the Odeon Cinema, Tonbridge. Here before a 'packed house' the Commander of South-Eastern Command, General Montgomery, gave his final assessment on 'Exercise Tiger', an exercise which he regarded as 'a real rough-house'.

He told his weary audience, perched up on the rostrum before the sunken cinema organ, after the usual announcement that there would be 'thirty seconds for coughing. After that no noise, *please* gentlemen', that 'throughout [the exercise, which had lasted 11 days] all troops had only the scale of rations; mobile canteens were forbidden to operate; troops were forbidden to purchase supplies of food or drink from civil stores. Administration under war conditions was thoroughly tested.

'No MT was allowed to be used for the carriage of infantry or other dismounted personnel and most infantry units marched over 150 miles during the course of the exercise. When the operations ceased many infantry soldiers had no soles on their boots! Some infantry units had marched and fought over 250 miles of country when they got back to their normal locations.'

This all meant, according to the perky, brisk little commander, with his high-pitched voice and inability to pronounce his 'r's correctly in the best upper-class manner, that 'a new technique' had been evolved 'on which to base our future training.'[1]

'*Training!*'

Two years after Dunkirk, the great mass of the Army's infantry divisions were still based at home and doing nothing but train. Admittedly it was rough and tough. When two battalions of infantry clashed on an exercise, more often than not, 'Rifles and bayonets would be thrown to the ground,' as one 19-year-old volunteer for the infantry recalled, 'and the men would fight with bare fists, watched by the officers, who remained passive until things showed signs of getting out of hand. These dust-ups resulted in the first-aid men, who were the stretcher-bearers, having some *real* patients to deal with, as well as the imaginary ones labelled by the umpires.'[2]

Men who had volunteered back in 1939, such as the novelist Thomas Firbank of the Coldstream Guards, felt 'a breath of fresh air had come to flutter the cobwebs of Army training' and that now 'the soldier was taught to be a mixture of poacher and gangster, and yet to remain a soldier'.[3] Yet they were still in the UK three years later without ever having heard a single shot fired in action.

Another volunteer of that September, the Canadian Parley Mowat of the 'Hasty Pees', also found the new type of training tough and wearing and felt 'We'll never be readier to fight, God knows!' Yet as 'time slipped by and nothing happened ... wet, cold and dreary, our spirits sank from day to day as we wallowed in the mindless ritual of barrack life. The real war was becoming increasingly chimerical ... something to read about or hear described on the BBC.'[4]

In truth the infantry divisions which would now begin to go overseas to fight would be totally lacking in combat experience, commanded by officers whose last taste of battle (if any at all) had been during the disastrous retreat to Dunkirk. Not *one* single infantry division sent to North Africa in November 1942 to invade in 'Operation Torch' had seen action before. Two years later, of the seven British and one Canadian infantry divisions that would fight the campaign in N.W. Europe, only two would have previous battlefield experience.

Although at this time British and American officers studied the German Army intensively in an attempt to discover what made it so successful, no one seemed to come up with the key to Germany's string of victories over Allied troops. It was simple. Every German formation, however recently formed and poorly trained (in comparison with the Allies), was led by a nucleus of battle-hardened and experienced officers and NCOs. They did not need to *learn* the costly lessons of war in their first engagement. They had already learnt them in Holland, France, Greece, North Africa, Russia. ...

In the *Wehrmacht*, where caste and education did not hold such great sway as they did in the Anglo-American armies, all potential officers served a lengthy period in the ranks, first as a common soldier, then as a corporal, and finally as an 'aspiring officer' (*Offiziersanwärter*) or ensign (*Fähnrich*). Throughout the war, even in those desperate days of 1945, Germany did not produce 'sixty-day wonders', as did the US Army, which could turn out a lieutenant of infantry in that time span. Nor did the fact that a man was a student or university graduate automatically make him eligible to become an officer, as was the case in Britain. Public school boys naturally were – in a class-ridden country such as the United Kingdom – instant officer material. As one commandant of an OCTU told journalist James Hodson that year, 'the 20 best public schools produced the best material of all', though, he added, paying lip-service to democracy, as everyone in the Army was doing now that the men were becoming so 'bolshy', 'the next *so-called* public schools produced men worse than secondary schools'.[5]

The fact that a would-be officer in the German Army held the *Abitur* – a high school diploma – cut no ice in the *Wehrmacht*. First he would have to prove himself in three to six months' service at the front (if he was wounded he was considered automatically eligible to go to officer candidate school). If his nerve didn't break there, then he returned to the *Reich* for attendance at the *Kriegschule*. And in essence the training of sergeants was the same, with NCOs being grouped together for specialized training (unlike the Anglo-American system*) in an NCO school before returning to their units.

Thus, without exception, young German officers and NCOs commanding units, however green and untrained, would be 'old hares' (as the *Wehrmacht* called combat veterans), who knew exactly what battle was about.

This exemplary system of interchange between green and experienced units and between officers and NCOs at the front and those still in training was extended, too, to the establishment of not only new regiments but even to divisions. Thus, for example, when it was decided in 1942 to set up a new SS division – 'the Hitler Youth' – the cadre for the division, which still existed solely on paper, was taken wholesale from another SS division – 'the Adolf Hitler Bodyguard' – currently fighting on the Russian front.

Not only was the new divisional commander, Witt, an experienced combat veteran, but all his regimental commanders, too. His battalion, company and, in some cases, even his platoon commanders all had had battlefield experience. In 1943 (unlike the British Army, where drill would have come first), when this new division was visited by the Army Commander, it still couldn't produce sufficient recruits capable of presenting arms – the cooks had to be pressed into service hastily to do the honours. But at the same time the 'Hitler Youth' was already battleworthy, as the British would soon find out to their cost at Caen. There General Witt's 20,000 'babies' (he didn't allow his teenagers to drink beer; they got milk instead) stopped the men of the British 15th and 49th Infantry Divisions, who had been training for years, *dead*! Even the veterans of the 7th Armoured Division – 'the Desert Rats' of the legend – fared no better against them.

Right throughout the war, in spite of the great stress laid upon training by such commanders as Montgomery and later Eisenhower, there was virtually no attempt to switch officers and NCOs, not to mention battalions

---

* The Americans would adopt the idea in the form of their 'NCOs Academies' *after* the war.

or even companies, between the battlefront and training command. It was the decisive weakness in the Anglo-American concept of training.

In the end, British and American troops would be superbly trained, with their commanders going to extraordinary lengths to ensure that their training was made as realistic as possible. For instance, when a 29-year-old British paratroop colonel was told his objective was to be a gun battery near the French village of Merville on D-Day, he scoured the English countryside to find a stretch of it which resembled the area in question. Finally he found it, had it requisitioned by the War Office (which had to pay £15,000 in compensation for damaged crops) and began to build an exact replica of the Merville Battery. Where the surrounding terrain did not fit with the aerial photographs of the terrain, the young para colonel had the fields and woods bulldozed until it did.

But in the final analysis, all those years of effort between 1940 and 1942 and then later between 1942 and 1944 were simply training. The chief actor in the drama, the German enemy, was absent when 'Red' fought 'Blue'. As R.W. Thompson, the British war correspondent and former infantry officer, noted at the time, during training 'Men did not choke and drown in their own blood, gaps did not open to leave men "naked and alone", spattered with entrails, blood and brains of their friends ... Nor were the coils of wire littered with the obscene offal of war ...'[6]

Invariably the price the British and later the American infantry would pay for this deficiency in their training would be the loss of the best and the bold, those young leaders, officers and NCOs who were prepared to 'have a bash' and would die or be wounded in the attempt. Surprisingly, as we shall see, British and American infantry would tend to go to ground, 'bog down', once these young leaders had been killed, not realizing in battle (for they were not battle-experienced) that to stop during an attack was to be killed. Thereafter the inevitable would follow. The speedy German counter-attack would send them reeling, fleeing to the rear. In that terrible winter of 1944–5, whole companies, battalions, even regiments of the US Army, produced on the conveyor belt system, commanded by senior officers whose last experience of combat had been in the Argonne in 1918, would break and run. ...

A few, a very few, right at the top in the British Army understood the reasons for the series of defeats that the country had suffered since 1939. They knew the men lacked courage and spirit. They knew that even if these deficiencies could be made up for by intensive training, that in a democracy generals were accountable. In the British Army, in which the 'other rankers' could air their grievances to the *Picture Post* and the *Daily Mirror*, there could not be the execution of 10,000 soldiers, as was the case in the German Army during World War Two *pour encourager les autres*. Parliamentary party politics and party interests took precedence over the conduct of the war.

Thus it was that while Britain was fighting for its very existence in this year of 1942, most Labour and Liberal politicians, plus Tory reformers, were more concerned with the 'New Jerusalem' – a better Britain after the war. The 'Beveridge Report' was on everyone's tongue. The socialist Archbishop of Canterbury's (Dr William Temple) *Christianity and the Social Order* sold a staggering 140,000 copies in the year that Singapore and Tobruk fell and Britain lost its Far Eastern empire.

For the CIGS Sir Alan Brooke, that bird-watching Ulster moralist, democracy was 'a great handicap'. Politicians of all shades of opinion were interfering too much in the conduct of the war, and this included Churchill, his political master. That spring, he wrote, 'we have already lost a large proportion of the British Empire and are on the high road to losing a great deal more of it … I have had for the first time since the war started a growing conviction that we are going to lose this war unless we control it very differently and fight it with more determination.

'Furthermore, the interference of the politicians in the attempt to create a new fighting army is made worse by the lack of good military commanders. Half our Corps and Divisional Commanders are totally unfit for their appointments and yet if I were to sack them, I could find no better. They lack clarity, imagination, drive and power of leadership. …'[7]

As he concluded, 'It is all desperately depressing!'

Now to cap it all, there was a grave crisis taking place in the Middle East. The Eighth Army was on the run, with Rommel at their heels. Out there the leadership was discredited and Churchill was howling for heads; the divisional commanders seemed incapable of handling their troops, although some of them had been in combat since the commencement of the desert battles; and the men displayed a woeful lack of spirit and courage. How else could one explain the surrender of 20,000 men at Tobruk, who had allowed themselves to be tamely rounded up by a mere four battalions of infantry, the despised *Italians* at that?

But what was to be done? Who could take over the command of the beaten Eighth Army and stop the rot? For a while the name of 'Strafer' Gott was bantered back and forth as the new commander to replace the disgraced General Ritchie, who had been sacked after Tobruk at Churchill's insistence. '*Defeat* is one thing,' he had growled to Roosevelt in Washington when he had first heard the terrible news, '*Disgrace* is another.'[8] But unfortunately for General Gott, though perhaps fortunately for Britain, the poor General was killed in an aeroplane crash that summer.

Again the Top Brass and Churchill were placed in a quandary, for the latter wanted rid of Auchinleck, who had now taken over temporary command of the 8th Army, as well as being Army Group Commander. In the end, as we all know well, Bernard Law Montgomery, the 'New British Army's' trainer *par excellence*, was sent to take over, and the whole course of British history was changed.

But in the summer of 1942, General Montgomery was an unknown quantity outside the British Army. But aided by his keen perception and his natural, often overweening, vanity, 'Monty', as he would soon be known throughout the Western World, had learnt a lot about the mood of the times in those two years he had spent in the UK since the débâcle at Dunkirk. So far in the war no single general in the whole of the British Army had been able to capture the popular imagination as had Kitchener and Haig in World War I. There has been no 'cult figure', as we would say today, hitherto; and 'Monty' knew that the Briton of the 1940s, brought up to adore film stars, footballers, crooners and the like, needed such a figure. The people and the demoralized Army needed a 'People's General for a People's War'.

Modern wars were fought, he knew, by civilians in uniform. 'Such men are educated,' he wrote later, 'they can think, they can appreciate. They want to know what is going on and what the general wants them to do, and why; they want to see and decide in their own minds what sort of person he recruits is. I have never believed in dealing with soldiers by a process of "remote control"; they are human beings and their lives are precious.'[8] So 'Monty' would let his fighting men see him as often as possible and he would tell them what he wanted them to do. All highly commendable and democratic.

He would make it all too clear by his own appearance that he hated 'bullshit', that bugbear of the civilian soldier. British soldiers would stay washed and cleanly shaven, but there would be no more polishing and blancoing just for the sake of doing so. How could subordinate officers attempt to 'blind the men with bullshit', when their own commander-in-chief wore civilian corduroy trousers, an Aussie's slouch hat, decorated with several different badges, and carried a green 'gamp' at times? Why even the King had 'ticked him off' on account of his irregular sloppy uniform dress!

Here was a 'personality', admired even by the *Daily Mirror*, who had kicked Colonel Blimp squarely in the seat of his ample breeches and propelled him from the scene for good. The past was dead and soon a new 'people's hero' was to be born.

Patton would call him one day 'a silly old fart'. (Patton was two years older than Montgomery incidentally.) Bradley would say of him, 'Montgomery is a third-rate general and he never did anything or won a battle that any other general could not have won as well or better'.[9] Eisenhower confided in writer Cornelius Ryan long after the war that Montgomery 'got so damned personal to make sure that the Americans and me in particular had no credit, had nothing to do with the war, that I eventually stopped communicating with him ... I was just not interested in keeping up communication with a man that just can't tell the truth'.[10]

But all this criticism, however justified, did not matter one iota to the Great British Public and the ordinary British infantryman. A new commander had taken over who was totally different from all those big, beefy, pompous brass hats of the past, who had consistently led them into defeat after defeat. 'It's a general called Montgomery', RSM McMasters described the new commander of the 8th Army enthusiastically to a somewhat blasé Colonel Peniakoff, who had seen new C-in-Cs come and go with alarming regularity. 'A short, wiry fellow with a bee in his bonnet about PT. The first thing he did when he took over was to order half an hour's physical training for Army Headquarters before breakfast. Tubby brigadiers came out in their vests and *ran*! They heaved and they panted, shaking their fat paunches for everyone to see and when they couldn't make the grade they got the sack. Sacked them right and left he did, all the fat bastards!' RSM McMasters chuckled ferociously.

Later the Colonel mused: 'A general who has the courage to sack brigadiers from the Army Staff and who knows how to evoke enthusiastic devotion in the hearts of regular sergeant-majors will, I thought, have no difficulty in defeating Rommel – *or even in winning the war*'.[11]

It was all patently untrue. Montgomery didn't make brigadiers go out for morning runs in the desert, and although he sacked some very quickly after his arrival in the desert, he didn't fire them 'right and left'. But it didn't matter. The 'Monty legend' was starting to be created, and the troops believed it.

Thus it was that on 13 August, 1942, 'Monty', dressed in long shorts to reveal that he certainly hadn't got his 'knees brown' yet, stood on the steps of his predecessor's caravan and addressed his new staff for the first time. Most of them were cynical of his chances of success.

He hadn't 'got sand in his shoes' and he'd be the fourth Army Commander in the last 12 months. What had he to offer? How could he change this dreary series of defeats at the hands of the Germans?

Now, as the desert sun slowly started to slip down on the horizon, his small, foxy, pale face sharp and intent, 'Monty' laid it on the line. As his biographer Nigel Hamilton has called it, it was 'one of the seminal military addresses in British history, as intimately revealing of the general on the verge of greatness as of the man only weeks away from world acclaim'.[12]

'I want first of all to introduce myself to you,' he snapped. 'You do not know me. I do not know you. But we have got to work together; therefore we must understand each other and we must have confidence in each other. I have only been here a few hours. But from what I have seen and heard since I arrived I am prepared to say, here and now, that I have confidence in you. We will then work together as a team and together we will gain the confidence of this great army and go forward to final victory in Africa.

'I believe that one of the first duties of a commander is to create what I call "atmosphere" and in that atmosphere his staff, subordinate commanders and troops will live and work and fight. I do not like the general atmosphere I find here. It is an atmosphere of doubt, of looking back to select the next place to which to withdraw, of loss of confidence in our ability to defeat Rommel, of desperate defence measures by reserves in preparing positions in Cairo and the Delta.

'All that must cease!

'Let us have a new atmosphere …

'What is the use of digging trenches in the Delta? It is quite useless; if we lose this position we lose Egypt; all the fighting troops now in the Delta must come here at once, and will. Here we will stand and fight; there will be no further withdrawal. I have ordered that all plans and instructions dealing with further withdrawal are to be burnt, and at once. We will stand and fight here.

'*If we can't stay here, then let us stay here dead … !*'[13]

The place was El Alamein.

'The Infantry must be
prepared to fight and kill'

Soon the battle would commence – the greatest in Africa in the whole of the twentieth century. For one last time before the British Empire fell apart, all the Imperial infantry were there to spearhead the attack. There were General Dan Pienaar's South Africans, bitter but eager, urgent to erase the smear of Tobruk. The 1st South African Infantry Division would show the rest that they really could fight to the death.

There were Freyberg's New Zealanders, too. By now they were perhaps the best infantrymen of all – God knows they had had enough experience! Freyberg, VC, who had been fighting in wars since Mexico in 1911, was back in command after his most recent wound in July. Now and again he would squeeze his bull-like neck and ease out a piece of wandering shrapnel, which dated back to the old war, when he had been hit winning his VC.

Naturally, Morshead's citizen-soldiers of the 9th Australian Infantry Division, who had held Tobruk for so long, were there as well. They had plenty of old scores to pay off – Greece, Crete, the desert. Ill-disciplined they may have been off duty, but on the battlefield they had a natural discipline – and they were raring to go.

General 'Gertie' Tuker's 4th Indian Division, representing the 'King Raj', was there, too; as was the British 44th Infantry Division, drawn from Kent, Surrey, Sussex, the heartland of England. 'Crasher' Nicols's 50th Infantry Division, the 'Geordies' from the north, made up to strength again after their bold escape from the débâcle of the previous June, waited as well for the order to attack.

But none were more eager than the 'Jocks' of the re-formed 51st Highland Division. They had a score to pay back, the surrender at St Valery two years before, and they had a chip on their shoulder, too. Soon they would be known throughout the British Army as 'the Highway Decorators'. For they would plaster their divisional sign 'HD' everywhere they fought on that year-long trail across nine countries and two continents before finally ceased fighting in Bremerhaven, their honour restored. Under their lanky commander General Wimberley, his hands and legs covered already by desert sores, they were eager for action after two years of training.

Seventeen days before, Montgomery had written: 'Our troops must not think that because we have a good tank and very powerful artillery, the enemy will all surrender. The enemy will not surrender and there will be bitter fighting. The infantry must be prepared to fight and kill ... It is essential to impress on all officers that determined leadership will be vital in this battle ... There have been too many unwounded prisoners taken in this war. We must impress on officers, NCOs and men that when they are cut off or surrounded and there appears no hope of survival, they must organize themselves into a defensive locality and hold out where they are ... *Nothing is hopeless as long as troops have stout hearts.*'[1]

These infantry waiting now for the great battle to commence, which would decide the fate of North Africa, were in stout heart. This time they would not run, surrender, give in. This time they were going to win at last!

Now it was almost time. All day they had lain hidden in the baking hot desert sand. All movement had been forbidden and they crouched in their foxholes, existing on water and hard tack. Now as darkness fell on that day which was to change the history of World War Two, blessed relief came, they were allowed to get out of their holes and stretch their legs. 'Char', 'wads' and dixies full of hot stew were brought up. They slaked their thirst and those who still had an appetite filled their mess-tins with stew. Some could not stop urinating. Others kept looking at their watches every few minutes. A few prayed, but not many. ...

Waiting in the cold white moonlight, General 'Gertie' Evans of the 4th Indian Infantry Division, 'felt a sudden shock of silence. Not a gun nor a rifle fired. The seconds ticked on. Never before had this silence happened.' The General started to grow nervous.[2]

Up front, waiting to direct the traffic, Lieutenants Craig and Howe of the Royal Sussex Regiment also sensed that tension, a strange tingling feeling. 'It was quiet everywhere. There was a full moon but a few fleecy clouds covered it momentarily and dimmed for a while the clarity of the night. The minute of the opening barrage approached ...'[3] Craig felt his heart beginning to beat faster.

Young Charles Barker of the Gordon Highlanders, who had escaped the débâcle of St Valery, read his Bible, and thumbing through it came across the phrase, 'Thou shalt not die but live that thou mayest praise the name of the Lord'. Later in hospital, after being wounded yet again, he 'returned to that same passage and in amazement read the next verse: 'The Lord hath chastened thee sore but He hath not given thee over unto death.'[4] The future brigadier would survive to see the end of the war.

But that was the future. Now as the men sweated, tightened their grips on their weapons with hands that were suddenly damp, the seconds ticked back with electric inexorability. The minute of the opening barrage approached.

'Suddenly, a second before time, a single battery of guns fired a salvo,' Craig, up front, recalled long afterwards. 'It was like a racehorse which, unable to endure the suspense a moment longer, had leapt forward a fraction before the remainder of the field.'[5]

A moment later 'there was a low flickering rumble across the desert and the sky was lit with flash after flash, like sheet lightning illuminating the sand with a ghostly yellow incandescence; the desert rocked and roared from end to end as the western horizon became suffused with the brick-red glow of exploding shells. From out to sea there were flashes from naval vessels as they pounded the shore and bombers droned overhead towards more distant targets.'

Even the generals who had been young subalterns in the trenches in the Old War were impressed by that tremendous 500-gun barrage. To the rear General Freddie de Guingand, Montgomery's Chief of Staff, watched as 'the whole sky was lit up and a roar rent the air ... It was a great and heartening sight. Up and down the desert from north to south the twinkling of the guns could be seen in an unceasing sequence.'[6] They even waxed poetic, like General Evans, who watched as 'wide to the north and south played the swift flickering lightning flashes dead white, as if giants danced a Khuttack war dance whirling their swords above their heads under the moon.'

It was 9.40 on the night of 23 October, 1942. The Battle of El Alamein had commenced. ...

At first came the awesome flickering flashes. Then the noise. A few moments later the moon was blotted out by the whirling smoke, as over the German lines the distress flares sailed into the sky. In an instant, all was confusion and the roar of the guns. But in the occasional pause between the whistle and bursting of the shells, there could be heard the skirl of the pipes. For the Jocks of the Highland Division, advancing in line with the 9th Australians and the 2nd New Zealanders, were being played into their first battle since France by the pipers.

They stumbled on the first line of German wire. It so happened that the leading man with the wire cutters was a regimental barber. 'Get a bloody move on, jock,' an angry voice from the glowing gloom cried, 'You're no cuttin' hair now!'

At last the Germans began to react. Their machine guns broke into frenetic activity. Tracer zipped low over the desert. Men dropped their weapons and clawed the air frantically as if climbing the rungs of an invisible ladder. Others fell flat on their faces without even as much as a soft sigh.

Others dropped, moaning and cursing, hugging their wounded limbs, exhibiting them to those who passed, as if they could not comprehend this awful thing which had just happened to them.

In the van of the Black Watch, Piper McIntyre was hit once, twice and then for the third time as he played his company forward. He went down, still playing. And he continued to play lying in the sand, bleeding to death until he could play no more. When they found him next morning, his stiff fingers were still on the chanter. He was barely twenty.

Up ahead trying to direct the infantry through the gaps in the minefields which stretched the line of the hard-pressed Germans, Lieutenant Craig cowered as the first shell landed close to their position, sending red-hot steel fragments whizzing lethally everywhere. Suddenly he heard a frightened, ghastly whimpering. It was his companion, Howe. 'He was half-kneeling, half-hanging out of the trench, clutching his stomach. A sharp red stain had appeared on his shirt front. He was bending forward, writhing in agony and his eyes were wild with pain and terror, "It's my guts! *Oh, my guts!*" It was a startled hopeless cry like an animal's ...'[7] This night and in the grim, bloody days to come, many young men would die like animals.

Young Charles Barker, trying to find the 5/7th Gordons in the ever increasing confusion, noise and acrid, choking gunsmoke and armed only with a pistol and 18 rounds of ammunition, ran straight 'into hordes of Italian soldiers fully armed. Any one of them could have shot me without trace. I quickly realized there was no point in doing more than encourage as best I could this host of prisoners to follow me down the tape.'[8] But they followed the lone British officer willingly enough. But by the time the shelling from both sides had taken its course, only *seven* of them were left!

Now both sides were taking heavy casualties. The lanes through the minefields, which had now been cleared by brave sappers, were carpeted with British and New Zealand dead, as the defenders started to lay heavy mortar concentrations on the advancing men, turning night into a ghastly glowing day, firing flare after flare into the sky. But the German resistance was beginning to crumble and all the assault divisions were making satisfactory progress.

But still the situation was very confused and no one, whatever his rank, was safe this night. General Wimberley, driving up in his jeep to inspect one of his formations, ran over a mine that hadn't been picked up. Fire erupted beneath the little vehicle and ripped the bottom out of it. The General's driver was killed instantly, while Wimberley himself was flung 20 yards, but without injury.

Later, no less a personage than the acting head of the *Afrikakorps*, General Ritter von Thoma, would be captured in the confusion by a small patrol of the 10th Hussars under the command of Captain Singer. It would be testimony to the gentlemanly character of the fighting in North Africa that when Captain Singer was later killed in action, the stern-faced aristocrat von Thoma would write a letter of condolence to Captain Singer's parents.

But there was nothing gentlemanly about the hard, brutal, bloody slog of the infantry as they battered away at the German front, trying to break open those corridors the tanks would need for their dash through Rommel's lines.

Even before they jumped off, the 7th Battalion the Black Watch had suffered severe casualties, as the Germans shelled their positions mercilessly. Two companies were down to about a hundred men when they charged. 'The enemy was met with in person', as the biographer of the Black Watch puts it delicately.* Bayonets clashed. Men went reeling back, faces smashed in by cruel blows from the brass-shod butts of rifles. Taking and giving casualties all the time, the Black Watch pushed to their objective, a strategic height, the Miteiriya Ridge. Five officers led the surviving 30 men to scale it. Of them one was killed and the other four wounded. In the end the 7th Battalion the Black Watch lost 261 men killed and wounded, 19 of them officers, in two days' fighting – nearly one-third of its strength.

It was no different in the 1st Battalion, the Gordons. Within the first hour one company of the Gordons, consisting of five officers and 102 men, was reduced to one officer and ten men. The 2/13 New Zealand Battalion to their right suffered similarly in the blood bath of the infantry that first day of the Battle of El Alamein. In one company every officer and senior NCO was killed or wounded. In the end what was left of it continued to fight under the command of a young sergeant.

Everywhere the butcher's bill was mounting at a terrible rate. The 6th Green Howards of the 50th Division were lucky in their attack. They broke through the German wire with a handful of casualties. Their fellow Yorkshiremen of the 5th East Yorks weren't. They were stopped dead on the wire with 150 men killed and wounded; a quarter of their strength vanished in a matter of hours.

Watching the ambulances, squat and boxlike, come lurching back from the Australians' sector, infantry officer Neil McCallum noted 'at the back of one, beneath the closed door and down the step, was a trickle of blood'.[9] Not far away, General Wimberley of the Highland Division, watching the tanks come churning back through the sand piled high with the bloodstained bodies of his young Jocks, swore to himself, 'Never again!' Later he was called to the telephone. It was his Corps Commander Oliver Leese. He wanted Wimberley to send the Argylls into the attack once more, in support of the 4th Indian Division.

Strained and irritable, Wimberley moaned, 'Must we really go on attacking like this, sir?'

Leese answered, shocked, 'Surely you of all people are not going to lose heart at this stage.'[10]

---

* Brigadier B. Fergusson.

The Argylls went into the attack, in support of 'Pasha' Russell's Fifth Infantry Brigade. For 'Monty', later to be so parsimonious with the lives of his men, brooked no opposition. Cost what it may, he was going to break through. ...

The Royal Sussex Regiment of the 44th Infantry Division were ordered into the attack. Like many of the young officers who had already fallen in the 51st Highland Division, this was the first battle for young Lieutenant Norman Craig. At first, however, it all seemed so familiar. 'I could scarcely believe this was a real night attack. It was just like an exercise; the routine was so familiar. Yet there was a difference – for there were no umpires and we took liberties which would never have passed in training. The men tramped along in threes, pressing so close behind each other that there was not an inch of space between them, all but the first file fortified by the questionable belief that a shell splinter might hit the front man but those behind would be safe. Every platoon seemed to be squeezed up like this. The officers did not object for it kept the troops together and was the only certain way to avoid losing anyone. In war, if you wanted to chance something, you did so and took the consequences. So we marched bunched together and to Hell with the rules.'[11]

But the reality of the coming battle struck home when the barrage began. 'From a long way to the rear came the smacking roar of the 25-pounders, merging into a continuous rumble, like a hundred gigantic muffled typewriters. The sky was lit with a red unearthly glow. There was a moment's pause before the shells sped overhead in clusters like swarms of angry bees. They were so low that you felt you could reach up and touch them as they raced thicker and faster after each other until they fell, ripping up the sand along our front. The Bofors with their stark, ear-splitting crack sprayed long bursts of fiery tracers down the flanks. A whole battalion of heavy Vickers machine guns began firing right alongside of us, raking the enemy lines, and adding their heavy, saturated chatter to the general din. Altogether it was the most unholy row I had ever heard in my life.'[12]

Now they started to advance into this furious maelstrom, bodies bent, nerves racing electrically, tensed for the first hard burning smack of steel against soft flesh. There was the obscene stonk and belch of an enemy mortar, followed by the high-pitched hiss of the German Spandau machine gun. 'We were being fired upon,' Craig thought with sudden alarm. 'Though this was the very meaning of war, I felt a sense of outrage and betrayal. Someone had blundered. We were some reckless, sacrificial offering to the vanity of the divisional commander. Yet all the major battles of history must have seemed like this, a hopeless shambles to the individual in front, with a coherence only discernible to those in the rear.'[13]

In the end it was the usual bloody shambles. Suddenly and startlingly, as the infantry of the Royal Sussex Regiment were climbing a hill to get to grips with the defenders there was the smack and crack of a single Very flare. It burst and illuminated all below. The German machine gun caught Craig's company completely by surprise.

It sent a 'hail of bullets into the middle of the company. Then there were sharp, single cracks of rifle fire, sounding alarmingly loud and close. Two more white Very lights shot up and after a tantalizing pause burst in a shower overhead. Caught in this pool of light some of the men fell flat on their faces; the rest stood like statues. They were hopeless trapped. The ranks were raked by fire, and after a few moments the company turned and fled back to their slit trenches, dragging the wounded the best they could.'[14]

Another infantry had 'copped a packet'.

The Germans counter-attacked. They ran straight into what was left of a battalion of the Rifle Brigade, a handful of engineers and a battery of anti-tank gunners, 300 men in all. But they were fine men, Regulars mostly, like Sergeant Miles from Southwark, Sergeant Hine from Acton, who had already won the Military Medal, or Sergeant Brown, who was reputed once to have stolen a railway engine and had won an award for bravery, too, the DCM.

Now they waited again this burning morning after repulsing the first massed attack of German and Italian tanks. Before them the surface of the desert rippled and trembled in the heat. Flies were everywhere swarming in black clouds on the dead and wounded and the piles of excreta. On all sides the place was strewn with burning, smoking tanks and British carriers, but the little defending force still had 13 six-pounder anti-tank guns in service, though ammunition was beginning to run out.

Just after midday, eight Italian tanks, accompanied by a self-propelled gun armed with a monstrous long, overhanging 105-mm cannon, rattled within range. As they came into the attack, swirling up the sand in a great brown wake behind them, their turret guns spat fire, raking the waiting infantry with machine-gun bullets. But Colonel Turner, one of the few infantry officers still left alive, ordered the anti-tank gunners to hold their fire until the tanks were within 800 yards range. Now he personally took up his position at one of the six-pounders to act as loader in place of a man just wounded.

The tanks came closer. Now peering through their sights, the number ones could see them quite plainly, neatly bisected by the calibrated glass. Slowly their sweat-damp right hands began to tense over the firing bars, while next to them the loaders braced to heave another shell into the breech.

Then it was time. 'FIRE!' someone yelled desperately. The guns erupted. Flame shot from the muzzles. The guns jerked up and backwards. Their breeches flew open and ejected smoking brass shell cases on to the sand as the crew, half-blinded and buffeted by the blast, instinctively opened their mouths to prevent their ear drums being burst.

One after another the Italian tanks jerked to a stop suddenly, smoke pouring from their turrets, ammunition already beginning to explode, tracer streaking in a crazy zigzag for the burning sky like a monstrous fireworks display. But still there were two left, charging forward, machine guns chattering – and the gunners on the British side were down to exactly two remaining shells.

A rifleman sprang to his feet. He pelted across the sand, with the bullets stitching a lethal pattern at his feet. He swung himself into the seat of a jeep. Going all out, zigzagging crazily, he raced to another gun and frantically loaded a few boxes of six-pounder ammunition into the back. Then he was off again, the Italians now concentrating their fire on the jeep. Bent low over the wheel, he floored the accelerator as enemy bullets tore the jeep to pieces. Ten yards short of the guns it burst into flames, but the rifleman was uninjured.

Hastily the survivors ran out to grab the ammunition, just as a shell splinter sliced through Colonel Turner's helmet and severely wounded him. He keeled over next to the gun.

Sergeant Calistan, a swarthy East-Ender, a Regular who had been a champion boy boxer, took over, as three tanks bore down on his lone gun, which was now silent. They thought obviously that it was going to be easy meat for them. They hadn't reckoned with Calistan. As their slugs pattered on the shield like heavy tropical rain on a tin roof, he took his time, lining them up in his sights, while the others readied themselves with the fresh ammunition. Then he pulled the bar. The six-pounder shot back. Their faces were buffeted by the blast like a slap from a hot, wet hand. Automatically they closed their eyes for an instant. When they opened them again, the first tank was already burning. Moments later the other two were similar burning wrecks. Coolly, Calistan, who would soon be recommended for the VC, turned round and said to the others: 'We haven't had a chance of a brew all morning, but the Eyeties have made us a fire. So let's use it.'

Thereupon he poured some water into a billy can and set it on the bonnet of the burning jeep and proceeded to brew up. As a wounded Colonel Turner recalled later, it was as 'good a cup as I've ever tasted'.[15]

The fight continued, with Turner raising himself now and again to encourage the handful of survivors. Later, however, he began to suffer from hallucinations and believed he was defending a harbour against hostile warships. On seeing a tank, he would cry, 'open fire on that destroyer!'[16]

It was as good an order as any and Sergeant Calistan did his best to oblige. Within the year he would be killed in action ...*

---

* Later he was commissioned as Lieutenant Calistan, DCM and MM (he never got that VC), and was killed in action in Italy.

'KIA'. How easily those three simple letters summed up, neatly packaged, the sudden end of one man's young life. '*Killed-in-action*', stamped behind a man's name in the battalion and regimental rolls as they began to tally up the infantry's dead. For now they had done their job and it was up to the tanks. Of the 13,560 men killed, wounded or posted as missing in the Battle of El Alamein (fifty-eight per cent of them British), the infantry had suffered the most. The 51st Highland Division in its first action had lost 2,827 men (a fifth of its strength). The 9th Australian Infantry Division came next in this terrible score board of death and destruction with 2,495 casualties; while the 2nd New Zealand Division had suffered 2,005 and the South Africans had lost just short of a thousand men. It was a terrible price to pay for the first British victory of World War Two.

The poet Keith Douglas, advancing through what was left of the infantry in his tank, looked carefully at the trenches and stared 'down into the face of a man lying hunched up in a pit. His expression of anger seemed so acute and urgent, his stare so wild and despairing that for a moment I thought him alive. He was like a cleverly posed waxwork, for his position suggested a paroxysm, an orgasm of pain. He seemed to move and writhe. But he was stiff. The dust which powdered his face like an actor's lay on his wide open eyes, whose stare held my gaze like an ancient mariner's. He had tried to cover his wounds with towels against the flies. His haversack, from which he had taken towels and dressings, lay open. His water bottle lay tilted with the cork out. Towels and haversack were dark with dried blood, darker still with the great concourse of flies. This picture, as they say, told a story. It filled me with useless pity.'[17]

A few moments later in this wasteland of death and destruction, which had once been an infantry position, Douglas came across someone who was still alive, a young New Zealand officer. 'His leg was hit in several places below the knee, and covered, like the dead man's wound, with a towel. "The one that got me got my waterbottle," he said. "I've been here for two days. I've had about enough. Can you get me out?" His voice broke and hesitated over the words. He suddenly added, remembering, "Do something for the chap in the next trench," and seeing my face, "Is he dead?"

'"Dead as a doornail," said my voice. ...'[18]

But victory it was. On the night of 4 November, 1942, the BBC announcer in his impeccable upper-class voice, now strangely shaking with excitement, interrupted the programme to warn listeners not to switch off as the 'best news for years' would be given at midnight. Bewildered, excited, wondering what was to come, men and women, by now pale and wan on their wartime rations, who tomorrow would work a 12-hour shift in the war factories (*seven* days a week), stayed up to hear 'the best news for years'.

It was General Alexander's communiqué from Cairo. The Germans were in full retreat in Egypt. The Desert Fox had been beaten at last.

Mr Churchill was in a buoyant mood. Later he would say, 'Before Alamein we never had a victory. After Alamein we never had a defeat.' But when he addressed a meeting of the City of London on the 10th he warned against undue optimism. He growled, thumbs hooked in his waistcoat pockets, 'Now this is not the end. It is not even the beginning of the end. But it is, perhaps, the end of the beginning.'[19]

The infantry had won, after three long bitter years of defeat, their first battle against the Germans. Now the church bells pealed throughout the land, not to announce invasion, but to signal 'Monty's' victory.

There was light at the end of the dark tunnel. ...

III

'Dogs, Indians and British
Soldiers prohibited by law'

On New Year's Eve, 1942, General Eisenhower, the Supreme Commander of all allied forces in North Africa, rose from his sick bed – he had been ill with 'flu most of the day – and dictated a message on the situation in North Africa. 'On the whole,' he remarked, 'I think I keep up my optimism pretty well, although we have suffered some sad disappointments.' He realized, of course, that 'only a sissy indulges in crying and whimpering,' and that the need now was to 'get tougher and tougher', to take losses in one's stride and to 'keep on everlastingly pounding until the other fellow gives way.'[1]

That done, the General, who 'would have given a great deal for the prestige of having been shot at'[2] (for in his thirty-year-long career as an infantryman, rising from second-lieutenant to three-star general he had never once been in action), decided to relax. A small dinner party commenced, his dog Telek 'made water' on the carpet, his chauffeuse-cum-mistress Kay Summerby kissed him at midnight and they all stood up and sang 'Auld Lang Syne'. Thereafter 'Ike' and his cronies played bridge until the small hours, with the Supreme Commander winning. Writing in his journal on New Year's Day, one of those cronies, Harry Butcher, noted: 'I could use some aspirin today.' All the same it had been a 'swell evening' and Ike's success at cards seemed to Butcher to be 'a good omen for the coming year'.[3]

At the front, held by British, French and American troops, it rained: a cold grey drizzle, which, together with the fog on the dripping, heather-covered mountains, made the place look more like Scotland than Africa.

Two months before they had landed so boldly in Morocco and Algeria. The French opposition had been overcome in a matter of 48 hours. Though ironically enough the first American casualties of World War Two in the West (some 500) were caused by the people they thought they had come to 'liberate' – the French! Thereafter the British 1st Army had rushed to seize Tunisia, where they would join up with 'Monty's' 8th Army advancing confidently from Libya. But the mud, the mountains and the Germans had stopped them.

Now the infantry this New Year's Eve camped in the mud of the 'bloody djebels', as they called those hated features which had cost so many good men's lives to capture. Virtually every infantry battalion, which had landed only two short months before, was down to half-strength. The Hampshire Regiment, for instance, had gone into action 800 men strong, and was now down to exactly six officers and 194 men (of whom 100 had not taken part in the bitter December fighting).

It was no different in the Northants. They were virtually immobilized, not only by the mud but by the fact that the Battalion was critically short of officers, who had been the first target of the German snipers and last-ditch machine-gunners; plus the Arabs, who had taken potshots at the Anglo-Americans whenever they felt it was safe to do so. Ironically enough most of the natives sided with the Germans, whom they regarded as their liberators and not the Allied forces. For the latter were suspected of bolstering up the hated French colonial regime.

Now they waited in the mud, which was so bad that for two miles behind the front all supplies had to be brought up by mules and the 250 casualties a day had to be evacuated by the same laborious means. That damned mud, thick, sticky and bottomless, was everywhere. 'The dead were buried in the mud and the living were in it up to their knees. They were wet to the skin all day and all night. They had mud in their hair and mud in their food. When the mud dried, it set like iron and had to be beaten off the boots with a hammer or a rifle-butt.'[4] Thus Alan Moorehead, the war correspondent, wrote from the front that January of the New Year.

But it wasn't only the mud, it was the night cold. They were bitterly cold with snow and frost glittering on the mountain peaks. Young Lieutenant Eric Taylor, who had just come up to the front as a reinforcement for the Northants, recalled 40-odd years later: 'I have never been as cold since that winter of 1942–3. All the infantry had up front was a hole and what they could carry or loot from abandoned French farmhouses. At night we crawled into our holes, wrapped in anything and everything we could find, including rugs and carpets looted from the farms and tarpaulins stolen from the gunners. For a couple of hours one could manage to keep fairly warm, but by two or three in the morning, the biting mountain cold would steal into your very bones and you would be praying for the dawn and first light, trembling like a puppy in your hole, with the stars looking down, icy and unfeeling.'[5]

This New Year's Eve, he was racked with the 'shits', lying awake next to the latrine – a hole straddled by a pole supported by two rations cases – wrapped in an Arab cloak he had found, already feeling the first stirrings of the fleas with which it was infested. Now as this long Thursday night gave way to Friday 1 January, 1942, the 20-year-old officer continued to shiver, while all around him the others snored lustily, and wonder what was going to happen to him in the New Year.

Was it going to be the 'walk-over' they had predicted at the reinforcement camp back in Algiers? The wind-reddened, hollowed-out faces of the infantry didn't seem to indicate that. His new division, the 78th Infantry Division, looked as if it had already taken a hard knock. 'Give me my girl and a ride to the pictures in Manchester in the tram,' one of his new platoon had said wearily the previous evening 'and I'd be fuckingly well happy for life! They can have Africa – and the Army. Let old Jerry have the bloody rotten place.'[6] That had not seemed the talk of men confident of an early victory in Africa. 'Christ, I told myself that awful night of the New Year, what have I let myself in for? I felt, ill, weak, lousy – *and absolutely rotten!*'[7]

A thousand miles away on the other side of Africa, while Ike played his cards, another infantryman was feeling ill and despondent as he lay in his cot that night. He had been in Africa two years now and he was suffering from nausea, fainting fits and dysentery. His face was covered with desert sores. But it wasn't his illnesses which plagued the 'Desert Fox' this night. It was his future and the future of his sadly depleted *Afrikakorps*.

Back in November, he had been told by an irate Hitler, 'Your men threw their weapons away' and fled before Montgomery's troops. When Rommel, had objected, Hitler had snapped 'I don't want to hear any more of that kind of nonsense from your mouth! North Africa will be defended like Stalingrad is being defended. Eisenhower's invasion army must be destroyed at Italy's door, *not* in the Sicilian living-room.'[8]

Well, Stalingrad was now lost with the whole of the 6th Army. But he couldn't let that happen to his *Afrikakorps*. Besides, after two years of being the darling of the German public, with his photograph being sold at kiosks all over the land as if he were a UFA star, it rankled that he might end his career as the 'Desert Fox' a defeated and disgraced commander.

Two days before he had written his New Year's letter to his wife back in Stuttgart stating, 'Our fate is gradually working itself out … It would need a miracle for us to hold out much longer … We will go on fighting as long as it is at all possible.'[9]

Now as he lay on his cot on the last day of 1942, sick with the jaundice which had plagued him for most of the last year, he told himself he needed one final victory, however insignificant strategically, before the inevitable end came in Africa. Montgomery was now too strong for him and the English General knew only too well how Rommel operated. But what about the new boys – the *Amis* – as he called the Americans? So far they had only skirmished with a handful of second-rate German troops. How would they fare in a surprise attack? How …?

Slowly Erwin Rommel, once known as the 'Desert Fox', started to drift off into an uneasy sleep this last night of 1942. Now the only sound was that of the sentries crunching up and down under the harsh silver of the stars, and the 'singing' of the sand – the millions of sand grains contracting in the night cold and rubbing against one another, to give off a strange, haunting melody.

It was the year of decision. It was 1943. ...

Seven thousand miles away another infantry commander brooded about the future this night, General William Slim. Back in the summer of 1942 he had brought home to India what was left of his Burma Corps. In the very nick of time he had saved his infantrymen from falling into the hands of the victorious Japanese. All the same it had been a defeat, and Bill Slim was too much of a realist to try to tell himself anything else.

'Defeat is bitter,' he wrote long afterwards. 'Bitter to the common soldier, but trebly bitter to his general. The soldier may comfort himself with the thought that whatever the result he has done his duty, but the commander has failed in his duty if he has not won victory – for that *is* his duty ... He will go over in his mind the events of the campaign, "Here," he will think, "I went wrong; here I took counsel of my fears when I should have been bold; there I should have waited to gather strength, not struck piecemeal ..." He will recall the look in the eyes of the men who trusted him, "I have failed them," he will say to himself, "and failed my country". He will see himself for what he is – a defeated general. In a dark hour he will turn in upon himself and question the very foundations of his leadership and his manhood.'[10]

Since then he had been able to re-form his troops of the newly created 14th Army, which he now commanded. But there were immense difficulties involved. Behind him the whole of India was in uproar. The Congress Party had launched a large-scale campaign against the British, now that the Japanese were on the frontier of the sub-continent.

Mobs roamed the street, burning, looting, murdering. They cut his signals, destroyed his communications, tried to decapitate his dispatch riders by stretching telegraph wires across the road at night. They tried to encourage his native soldiers to desert at a time when troops were in very short supply. Only a handful were coming from Britain and the only kind of new infantry he could expect from outside were the two divisions to come from West Africa in due course. He had been reduced to the expedient of forming his final and only reserve from the venereal patients in the Calcutta and Barrackpore VD hospitals. In essence, General Slim knew, his was very definitely what his men said it was – *a forgotten army*!

All the same, he was determined to launch a full-scale attack on the Japanese in the Arakan. Somehow he had to take the pressure off India, which in his belief was wide open for civil war and revolution (he already had one whole division – the 70th Infantry – engaged in guarding his rear-line communications). Somehow he had to produce a victory against the Japs and restore public confidence in India and back at home in the Army. But how was he going to do it with the slender resources available to him?

His troops were mainly native, either raw and untrained or demoralized. Every one of them was desperately scared of the Jap, and there had been a 'depressingly large number' of desertions by soldiers being sent up to fight on the new front he would soon open up in the Arakan.

Why should we fight in that bloody wilderness, they asked, for a country like India? The 'wogs' hate our guts – they throw stones at us and spit on us in the streets – and the snooty whites look down upon us. They won't let us into their clubs, cinemas and dance halls. '*Dogs, Indians and British Soldiers prohibited by law*!' they stick notices on the bloody places, just like that. How was he going to do it? Just like Rommel tossing in his sick bed, the big bluff English infantryman pondered what 1943 would bring for him and his 'forgotten army'. ...

It was the same all over the world where man fought against man this first day of the New Year. Young and old, the ones who had already done their share of fighting and were still suffering for it, and those who would fight for the very first time in this year of decision, pondered what fate held in store for them; whether they would survive to see another year begin.

Russell Braddon, the Australian prisoner of the Japanese, had discovered he was very sick. His feet looked 'like purple balloons – the toes mere cocktail sausages attached to them like teats on an udder'.[11] He had contracted beri-beri. Still he had to continue working, with the guards taking an unconcealed interest in his condition. Daily they showed their surprise that he was still alive. They would point to the crop of arms and legs protruding from the washed-out graves beyond his tent and draw a mocking cross on the ground.

Soon he wouldn't be able to walk at all and would be forced to crawl through the mire for a quarter of a mile to find the MO. The latter would ask in irritation what he wanted, pointing out that he, Braddon, was 'extremely unwelcome'. He should stay where he was.

'What out here in the mud?' the sick man would gasp.

The MO would be adamant, but in the end he would throw a jar into the mud in front of the helpless prisoner. It contained Marmite.

'You have beri-beri,' he shouted.

'I know', Braddon replied from the mud.

'Take a spoonful of that a day,' the MO advised.

'Will it do any good?'

'Might,' the MO would reply casually.[12]

It did, and Braddon would survive. ...

A few hundred miles away from where Braddon and his fellow prisoners suffered in worse conditions than existed in many a German concentration camp, another infantryman was on the run from the Japs. Indeed he had been on the run from them on that particular New Year's Day for nearly six months now. Not that that worried Colonel Chapman a great deal. A pre-war explorer, he was used to hardship and loneliness. But for the previous

147

two months he had been very ill. At various times he had suffered from blackwater fever, pneumonia, chronic malaria and tick typhus. Once, all by himself in the jungle, he had been unconscious for seventeen days. Now he had marched barefoot for six days to meet some comrades who were hiding out in the camp of Chinese bandits – 'cheerful and likeable rogues'.

Now he rested among his comrades and the Chinese, who were all heavy opium smokers and were given to raping Malay women by firing over their heads until they stopped and could be taken. Discipline was non-existent. 'The leader, who had no control over his men, had taken the wife of a Chinese he was alleged to have shot, and she ran the camp – in so far as it was run at all. But among these drug-addicts and rapists, the week I spent at this camp was one of the happiest in the jungle.'[13] Colonel Spencer Chapman would be another one who would survive. ...

In Germany, many of the officer prisoners spent the New Year in handcuffs in retaliation for the Canadians' alleged use of handcuffs on their German prisoners taken during the disastrous raid on Dieppe the previous August. In Austria, Elvet Williams of the Welch Regiment, wounded and captured in Crete, spent the afternoon of New Year' Day in his camp's meeting room. There weighty affairs were being attended to. Some precious biscuits had been reported missing. More importantly one of the 'goons', as they called their guards, had been seen going on leave with British chocolate in his possession, and a German woman, who lived opposite their little camp, had somehow come into the possession of a tin of British food. Who was the culprit?

The discussion waxed fast and furious with 'more than a hint of un-British conduct' on the part of the 'accused', until one Stanley Biffin rose to his feet to cool the proceedings. 'Having made it clear what was the purpose of every bar of chocolate and every tin of corned beef, he proceeded to demonstrate, pithily and with dry humour, which threatened to have men collapsing on the floor in stitches, that if a bar of chocolate could procure a weekly roll in the hay with a luscious German blonde, to the physical and mental salvation of the donating prisoner ... then it was a bar of chocolate well spent.'[14]

Not far away in a 'rest camp' for malleable POWs another Canadian infantryman, captured at Dieppe, was getting his 'weekly roll in the hay' without having to pay a bar of chocolate for the favour. His bedmates were being supplied – courtesy the SS. Corporal John Galaher had already spied on his fellow Canadians in return for money and visits to the local whores. Now he was being seduced at the SS's expense into becoming a fighting soldier once more. The SS wanted him to join the new 'British Legion of St George', being set up by John Amery, the profligate son of a former British cabinet minister, who would be duly hanged for his activities. Soon Corporal John Galaher would become *Rottenführer* Galaher, one of the founder members of the first British SS unit.

The morale of the front-line infantryman was always given a boost by the famous 'Jane' strip cartoon.

In due course there would not only be Britons and Canadians serving in the SS in 1943. There would be New Zealanders, Australians, South Africans and Americans, too. Indeed two Englishmen, a former mechanic and an ex-London cabbie, who had been captured by the SS in Greece back in 1941, were already serving on the Russian front with the premier SS division 'the Adolf Hitler Bodyguard'.

All over the Far East young soldiers were locked away in the camps and cages, fighting to survive, eating any kind of scrap that could provide nourishment, yearning for the day when they might be free again. As one of them expressed it 40 years later: 'You don't know the value of freedom because you've never lost it. But those of us who've lost freedom … we know what freedom means. It's wonderful to be able to get up and I can walk outside this house, whereas for five years I was totally enclosed.'[15]

It was no different in Europe. There, too, young men were locked up by the thousands: men who had been behind barbed wire for three years now, some abandoned by their wives long ago and so crazed that they would rush the fence, courting death at the hands of the sentry manning the machine gun in the stork-legged watch tower. And there were others, too, this Friday, 1 January, 1943, who were on the run, with every man against them. In virtually every German-occupied country there were escaped POWs desperately trying to get a ship to Sweden, on to the underground railway through France, over the Alps to link up with the partisans in Jugoslavia, across the Rhine into neutral Switzerland. Everywhere starving hunted young men. …

And in Africa the young infantrymen of America's premier division the First Infantry, known as the 'Big Red One', waited this day for what was to come. Their motto was the proud boast, '*No mission too difficult; no sacrifice too great*'. They were a cocky outfit which had fired the first shots of America's war with Germany back in France in 1917. Now they were going to prove themselves in just the same manner in this new war with the Krauts. Outsiders said of them that they believed their own publicity and they were full of piss and vinegar. 'The First Division,' they said, 'thinks the US Army consists of the "Big Red One – and ten million replacements'. So far they had experienced only one rather nasty brush with the Krauts. Now, however, they were going to experience America's first major defeat at the hands of the German Army. Soon, the Greater German *Wehrmacht* would ensure that the celebrated 'piss and vinegar' of theirs would be knocked out of them for good. …

IV

'It was the first – and only – time
I saw an American army in rout'

On the morning of 12 February, the newly created 4-star General Eisenhower went to the front to visit his troops. The drive was terrible. The drivers of the Army Supply Corps, black and white, hogged the centre of the road, going all out, honking their horns, flashing their lights, in no way impressed by the four stars adorning the hood of Eisenhower's car. Indeed the only person in the Eisenhower convoy to be noticed was his red-headed driver-mistress Kay Summersby, who received wolf whistles and interesting suggestions on what the GIs would like to do to the General's 'white meat'. Eisenhower fumed.

His temper was not improved by what he saw at General Fredendall's HQ. The commander of II Corps, which consisted of the 'Big Red One' and the 1st US armored Division, had located his headquarters in an inaccessible canyon, serviced by a single track. His officers were flustered and tense and really didn't seem to know quite what to do, as the German pressure on the other side of the line started to build up. It was pretty obvious, even without the Ultra intercepts which the Americans were now receiving from the British, that Rommel was about to launch an attack.

Finally Eisenhower left for the VIP tent, where Kay Summersby was already bedded down for the night. He wanted a few hours' sleep before he set off on the long journey back to Algiers. Fully clothed, even wearing a knit cap, he crept into the sleeping bag next to hers and according to her was soon 'snoring like a one-man artillery bombardment'.[1]

Later, when she returned to base, she was confronted by one of 'Ike's' cronies, who told her with a red face, 'there's a lot of gossip about you and the Boss ... They're saying ... well, you sleep together when you go on trips.'

Kay smiled and burst out laughing at the look on the red-faced Colonel's face. 'We did', she exclaimed, leaving him more bewildered and embarrased than ever. 'We did!'[2]

But while they slept on this St Valentine's Day, 1943, the Germans were already moving into the attack. The 10th German Panzer Division, equipped in part with the massive new 60-ton Tigers, were rolling forward to attack Eisenhower's unsuspecting infantry.

The first hit was Major Moore's 2nd Infantry Battalion. After the initial shock, they started to withdraw in columns abreast, almost as if they were on a route march. Moore reasoned that by making no attempt at concealment the Germans might take them for their own men.

They didn't. A lone machine gun opened up on them after they had gone half a mile. It was followed almost instantly by flares and the rapid burr of German burp guns, as the sky above them burst into a blood-red flame. Suddenly they were running, all 600 of them, fear lending speed to their flying feet, disappearing into the desert in groups of two and three, some of the more panicked soldiers throwing away their weapons, even their helmets in their fear.

Moore, for his part, went to ground. There he waited tensely until the volume of fire died away and then stopped altogether. Cautiously he started to search for survivors. In all, he found less than 20. Grimly they resumed their march westwards across the stony desert, without food or drink. They would hike for 36 hours until they found other American troops. Moore would joke, 'The Krauts could have my tin hat, but I wasn't gonna give them my English fleabag – no sir!' And he held up the sleeping bag he had carried with him all the way. A little later his good humour vanished when he discovered that he had lost over half his battalion in their first action. His regimental commander Colonel Drake had fared no better. He, too, had set off for the rear with over 1,000 men and all had gone well until they had bumped into a German tank unit. A German standing in the turret of a Mark IV had challenged the big Colonel, but he had ignored the cry.

At dawn they had been still on their way to the rear when a convoy of lorried infantry caught up with them. They had been spotted this time. Almost immediately a wild fire-fight broke out. The GIs panicked. Several hundred of them ran straight towards the enemy, hands held up in surrender. Others simply threw away their weapons and cowered there in the sand, hands over their ears like small children trying to blot out an unpleasant sound.

Drake managed to rally a few hundred and formed them into a circle, as if they were back in the days of the wagon-trains and were being attacked by Redskins. But these 'Redskins' were driving 30-ton tanks, armed with 75-mm cannon. An armoured car broke through the circle. A German officer waving a huge white flag ordered Drake to surrender. Drake refused. But already tanks were following the armoured car into the circle. Everywhere men were throwing away their weapons and beginning to surrender.

A tank trundled to a halt just yards from the Colonel, whose command was melting away in front of his eyes in their first battle. An officer popped his head out of the turret, rifle levelled: 'Colonel – your surrender!' he yelled.

'You go to hell!' an irate Drake yelled back. He turned his back on the tank, folding his arms across his broad chest, waiting for the impact of the first bullet. None came.

Later Drake was taken to a German colonel, who saluted him and said: 'I want to compliment you on your command for the splendid fight they put up. It was a hopeless thing from the start, but they fought like real soldiers.'[3]

Drake's reply is not recorded. But those few kind words must have served to ease the pain of having lost his regiment in one short day. For on that bloody St Valentine's day in 1943, Drake's 168th Infantry Regiment had been reduced in 24 hours from a strength of 189 officers and 3,720 men to 50 officers and 1,000 soldiers (one battalion was virtually intact, for it had not been engaged in battle), most of whom had surrendered without even having fired a single shot. And there was worse to come. …

Field Marshal Alexander, in charge of all ground operations, ordered in the Guards and the 18th Infantry Regiment of the 'Big Red One' to assist Fredendall's battered retreating infantry. This was the first time he had ever commanded American troops, though in the past he had led troops of all nations, including Russians – *and* Germans; and he didn't like what he saw of them. Soon he would tell General Patton, who was to take over from Fredendall after the defeat, that US soldiers were 'ignorant, ill-trained and rather at a loss, consequently not too happy.' The normally explosive 'Blood an' Guts' Patton listened tamely while the British Field Marshal announced that he found American soldiers to be 'mentally and physically soft and very green'.[4] As for their commander, Fredendall, he would tell Eisenhower, 'Surely you must have better men than that!'[5]

But there was no time for recriminations now. The American front was crumbling everywhere and something had to be done – and done damn soon! At his HQ, visibly shaken by the events of the past 24 hours, Fredendall hastened to appoint Colonel Stark of the Big Red One's 26th Infantry Regiment to take over the command of the vital pass to his front, the one that Rommel would obviously use through which to attack. In that typical slangy, informal manner of speech of his, which caused so many of his orders to be understood, he called Stark that night and said, 'I want you to go to Kasserine [the pass] and pull a Stonewall Jackson. Take over up there.'[6]

Stark was flabbergasted, 'You mean *tonight*, General?'

'Yes – immediately. Stop in at my CP on your way up.'

Stark put down the phone, cursing Fredendall. Then he set about moving his staff and men through the confusion of that terrible, rain-swept night.

Stark and his command were not the only ones moving that night. The Guards and their comrades of the Big Red One trying to move up to the front were finding their progress being slowed increasingly by the counterflow of fleeing American vehicles. Everything with wheels was packed with panicked US troops and they were all moving to the rear.

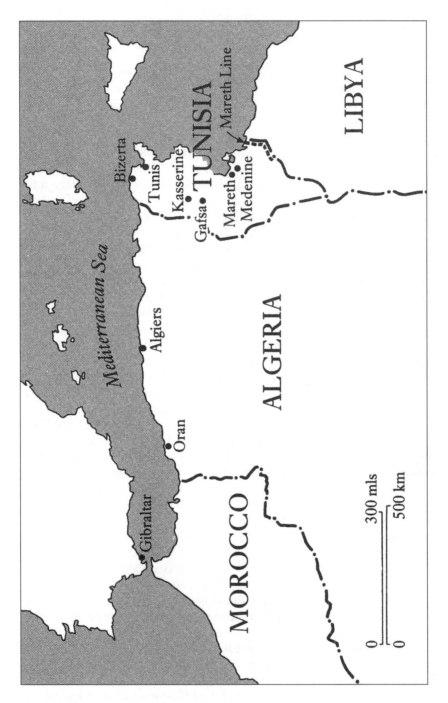

North Africa

Captain Nicolson of the Guards recalled later seeing an American truck crammed with infantrymen fleeing, the GIs leaning out and shrieking at the British, '*He's* right behind us!' And there were no prizes being given away to those who guessed correctly who 'he' was.[7]

Another sergeant of the British 56 Reconnaissance Regiment, leading the way for the armour, also recorded that 'the road was a chaos of retreating Americans and their transport – though not enough transport to carry many of the GIs, who were all in'.[8]

Some stayed and held the position, though the noise of German tanks seemed to be everywhere, as the enemy probed for weak points. 'It was one hell of a long night,' PFC Grimes recalled long afterwards. 'Everybody was jumpy and nervous. Some engineers came up and brought us mines to dig in. We'd never even *seen* a mine before and had no idea how to dig them in and place them in a pattern. But the engineers were not stopping. They were too scared. They took off and let us get on with it, digging them in the best we could in the mud. They never went off later.' But as the rumble of German tanks came closer and men started to tell tall tales about the invincible German Tiger, more and more men 'bugged out'. As Grimes recalled, 'if it had stayed dark much longer we'd have lost the whole goddam company!'[9]

What happened to the Big Red One on that night of 19/20 February, 1943, 'cannot be clearly reconstructed from the record', as the official US history puts it somewhat carefully. But one thing is clear. When Rommel's men hit them, the soldiers of Colonel Stark's command at Kasserine broke. First his 'A' Company was surrounded and its commander captured (though he escaped later). Then as the official history puts it, 'the other companies went out of battalion control. Stragglers reported the situation after daylight.'[10] In essence the first battalion of Stark's 26th Infantry Regiment to be attacked vanished, most of the men tamely surrendering to the triumphant Germans.

The Colonel abandoned his command post. He began to march back the way he had come with his staff. Stragglers came out of the rocks and brush on all sides; some were helmetless, others had thrown away their weapons. White-faced and shocked, they cried the 'Krauts' were only 200 yards behind. Colonel Stark didn't believe them. He slogged on, taking with him a few hundred stragglers. The 26th Infantry Regiment of the proud Big Red One had virtually disappeared. …

That same afternoon as Colonel Stark, a beaten commander without a command, finally reached his own lines, gravel-voiced, barrel-chested General Ernest Harmon was on his way to Fredendall's HQ, at Eisenhower's urgent request, to see if he could sort the mess out. But his progress, like that of the Guards and the 18th Infantry, now fighting a desperate holding action, was painfully slow. Later the General recalled, 'I have never forgotten that harrowing drive … jeeps, trucks, wheeled vehicles of every imaginable sort streamed up the road towards us, sometimes jammed two and even three abreast. It was obvious there was only one thing in the minds of the panic-stricken drivers – to get away from the front, to escape to some place where there was no shooting … It was the first – and only – time I ever saw an American army in rout.'[11]

The retreat was a nightmare. Those who didn't fly panic-stricken for their lives stayed and burned. But most didn't. Millions of dollars' worth of equipment was abandoned. Rommel noted: 'We captured some 20 tanks and 30 armoured troop carriers, most of which were trailing a 75-mm anti-tank gun. The Americans were fantastically well equipped.'[12] But they had simply run, without even attempting to unlimber their guns and tackle the tanks of the 10th Panzer Division.

An evacuating French hospital gave away everything it couldn't carry with it on its flight. A Sergeant Schiavone suddenly found himself the owner of an alarm clock, a silver letter opener, a basket of eggs, three dozen olives and a bottle of peach brandy. A truckload of the fleeing soldiers saw the bottle and started to wave. Shiavone hesitated, then he thought what the hell and gave them the bottle. Happily they passed it from man to man till it was drained and then waved again before they were gone, trailing the rest.

Some waved at the departing Americans. The few French civilians who were being left behind and the handful of local Jews who were now at the mercy of the Muslims. But the latter didn't wave. They were pro-German; they were happy Rommel was coming.

A British infantry battalion, the 2/5th Leicesters, straight off the boat from 'Blighty' were surrounded by German tanks. According to contemporary accounts most of them had never even seen one of their *own* tanks up to now. They surrendered *en masse* as the Germans rasped, 'Come out Englishmen … Hands up! … Surrender to the panzers … you haven't a chance …'

British gunners of one battery fought it out to the last against the tanks. In one day in that single battery they won three Military Medals, a Distinguished Conduct Medal and three Military Crosses. The Lothians were virtually wiped out, but they held their position on the ridge overlooking the site of the Leicesters' surrender. As their CO, Colonel Ffrench-Blake recorded long afterwards, 'It [the battle] was a fine example of the fact that it pays never to give up hope, however desperate the situation …'[13]

In the end the Germans pushed the Americans back 60 miles in seven days. The US 2nd Corps, originally 30,000 strong on that bloody St Valentine's Day, suffered an overwhelming defeat. Nearly a quarter of that force – 6,500 Americans (plus another 4,000 British soldiers who had come to their aid) were killed, wounded, or taken prisoner. With them 400 armoured vehicles, 200 artillery pieces and 500 jeeps and trucks were lost.

So much American equipment was abandoned by the panic-stricken GIs that the 3rd Battalion, the Grenadier Guards, became the first unit in the British Army to become fully equipped with the prized jeeps and half-tracks, all left behind in perfect working order.

Rommel himself thought that the American infantry 'had fought bravely', but that their commanders were 'definitely jittery'.[14] But General Patton who had now taken over 2nd Corps after Fredendall had been 'kicked upstairs', i.e. promoted and sent home to a training command and a hero's reception, thought differently. 'We've pampered and confused our youth,' he growled. 'Now we've got to try to make them attack and kill. God help the United States!'[15]

'Blood an' Guts' sentiments were shared by German Army Intelligence that year. In an assessment of the fighting value and spirit of Allied infantry for the German High Command, the unknown compiler of the detailed study felt that the British Army had finally ironed out most of the problems which had plagued it in the earlier years of the war, though the leadership was 'still heavy-handed.' 'The Canadians have fought well, but those of French-Canadian origin lack the will to fight.' 'The Australians and New Zealanders, in spite of heavy losses, have proved very brave and tough … but their manly bearing lags behind that of the British … The New Zealanders have been shown to be particularly good individual fighters and their strongpoints have often fought to the last man before being overcome.'[16]

This unknown German staff officer was not very complimentary about the troops from other dominions. 'The South Africans have fought in Africa without very much success. Here and there they have attacked bravely, but they lack staying power and their officers have very little value. Their commanders, like those of all the dominion forces, are heavy-handed.' 'The enlarging of the Indian Army has resulted in a strong reduction in its effectiveness. Fighting against the Japanese in Burma the Indians have repeatedly failed to hold their positions … In Africa some of them fought bravely, but it has been noted they were easily inclined to desert and take up arms on our side against their former colonial masters.' [17]

The author concluded that both British and American soldiers could not be compared with those of the Reich. In the final analysis, the German 'infantry soldier's fighting spirit is always much superior to that of the Anglo-Americans.' … In particular, the Anglo-Americans must always have 'full air and artillery support before they will attack. The result is that they do not feel they have to fight to the end if this support is lacking. In addition, the Americans do not feel any great necessity to fight to the end. … Without their superiority in material, their combat value sinks immediately to an appreciable degree …'[18]

The fact that the American infantryman would only fight if he were supported by overwhelming fire-power was a common accusation made by German soldiers in the last three years of the war. It was an argument often used to excuse his own failings. The German soldier was not beaten in a 'fair' fight with American infantry, but by the latter's material superiority. But the Germans conveniently forgot that many of their own victories in Poland, Norway, France and Greece, etc., had been achieved by the same disparity of equipment. The *blitzkrieg*, after all, had been a German invention.

All the same, there was something lacking in the fighting quality of these first American infantrymen to go overseas. One German POW interrogator reported on his prisoners from North Africa: 'Some of them make a curious impression. They were uncommunicative and complained of the personal risk to which each participant in the European war was subjected. They refused to make statements concerning the causes of the war, etc. One could deduct from the conversations with the American POWs that the Americans depended too much upon their abundant material resources, which were supposed to overwhelm the enemy. ... The impression they made upon us was that they were fighting not because of their convictions but for the money they got out of it, carrying out orders in a sober and businesslike way.'[19]

In fact, apart from a handful of men who had served in the tiny pre-war US Regular Army, the average American infantryman of 1943 differed little from the average British infantryman called up in 1939, three years before. Although classified 'A-1', he was not really physically fit in the sense that a German recruit, who had been through four years of the Hitler Youth and six months of the tough 'Labour Service' (*Arbeitsdienst*) by the time he was 18, was. Not only did he not know his right foot from his left (instructors were forced to tie coloured ribbons on awkward recruits' arms and legs so that they could distinguish between the two), but he had little idea which end of the rifle a bullet came from. His German counterpart, on the other hand, had spent years in a para-military force before his call-up and was well familiar already with the average infantry weapons.

But it went deeper than this. By now the British authorities, through propaganda and lectures by earnest young sergeants in the Education Corps, who wore spectacles and had socialist leanings, had convinced the troops that the British cause was worth fighting for. It was not merely a matter of defeating the 'Jerries' and protecting your loved ones back home from their bombs. You were also fighting for a better Britain after the war.

Visiting a battalion of the Argylls in the Tunisian hills that winter of 1943, BBC radio reporter Howard Marshall found them inarticulate but sincere, concerned with the future they were fighting for. 'Did the Atlantic Charter mean anything really, or was it just a lot of catchpenny words?' It had better mean something, they added. They were fighting this war because things had been wrong. They were not very precise about the things which had been wrong. Somehow ordinary people had had a raw deal from the financiers and the politicians. That must not happen again. They would see that it did not happen when they got home. In the meantime they had to smash Germans. They would do that, but it would only be the first part of a much larger job. 'Those owlish parlour pinks and visionaries of a Brave New World had done their job and now the men believed they were really fighting for a "better 'ole'".

Although young American infantrymen, also many of them products of the Depression, were bombarded with similar uplifting propaganda, it had seemingly not worked upon them. Neither had their home country suffered at the hands of the enemy, through the bombs or occupation. Thus it was that many of them – as yet – remained civilians in uniform; 'canteen commandos', as Patton and those of the regular Army called them contemptuously; men who seemingly did not know why they were fighting. They had been drafted and with those 'greetings' that their President had sent them, there was an obligation to serve. No more.

In that February of 1943, as yet unblooded, an 18-year-old PFC in the US 3rd infantry Division (who looked at least four years younger with his handsome, snub-nosed freckled face) waited on the North African coast for his particular call to arms. He was typical of the many; raw, not too well trained, and not particularly fit. More than one of his company commanders had tried to talk him into leaving the rough-tough life of the infantry and transferring to the cooks or company clerks. Once this young Texan volunteer, who had enlisted in the Army as soon as he was old enough, had fainted during close-order drill. Scornfully his Regular Army sergeant had declared: 'How can we win the war with these babies?'[20]

That particular Texan 'baby' was named Audie Murphy. In the next 36 months he would spend 400 days in combat, be wounded three times, and win 33 medals for valour, one of them twice in 48 hours. In the end, when he was still not old enough to vote, the future cowboy movie star would be the most decorated soldier in the whole history of the US Army. Before this war was over, there would be a lot more infantrymen like 20-year-old Second Lieutenant A. Murphy, who had learned to fight, not for any particular creed or political belief, but simply because they were Americans – *and they wanted to survive.* …

V

'Chindit'

At three o'clock on the afternoon of 4 July, 1941, the future general took his temperature and saw it was standing at 104 degrees. To his horror he discovered he had no more atrabin tablets left to dose his raging fever. He panicked. He tried to find his doctor's house. He couldn't. His panic increased. He thought he was losing his memory, going mad.

He staggered back to his bedroom and found his service pistol. But it was dirty, choked with dust and empty of ammunition. He cursed, flung it from him and sought for another weapon to put an end to his misery. He seized the hunting knife which a friend had given him. Staggering over to the mirror, holding the knife in his right hand, he thrust it into the left side of his neck, eyes blazing crazily in the glass. But the effort was almost too much for him.

Suddenly he remembered he had not locked the door behind him properly. With the blood pouring from his neck, he pulled out the knife, staggered to the door and locked it. Now he went back to the mirror and, clenching his teeth, thrust the knife with all his remaining strength into his jugular vein. Moments later he dropped to the floor unconscious, and dying.

But the future General Orde Wingate, overwrought, ill, suffering from fantasies from the overlarge doses of drugs he had been taking, was not fated to die by his own hand this boiling hot day in Cairo. Certainly, he would die violently before the war was out. But not yet. Next door a Colonel Thornhill's siesta was disturbed by the sound of Wingate falling. Later he would comment: 'When I hear a feller lock a door, I don't think anything about it and if I hear a feller fall down, that's his affair, but when I hear a feller lock his door and then fall down – *it's time for action!*'[1]

Now the Colonel sprang into action. He flung his clothes on and tried Wingate's door. It was really locked. He bolted for the lift to find the manager and the master key. Minutes later they were ramming the door with their shoulders until it burst open. As they burst in Wingate regained consciousness for a moment. He remembered after that it seemed to him that he was dead and in hell.

A year later when he had regained his sanity and now had the ear of Churchill and Roosevelt for his bold plans to attack the Japanese in a completely unorthodox way, one of his future column commanders in Burma, Colonel Bernard Fergusson of the Black Watch, saw him as a 'broad-shouldered, uncouth, almost simian officer who used to drift gloomily into the office for two or three days at a time, audibly dream dreams and drift out again'.[2]

Now, however, all of those infantry commanders who craved for action against the vaunted Japanese supermen had fallen under the spell of his almost hypnotic talk and 'had lost the power of distinguishing between the feasible and the fantastic'.[3]

His plan this February 1943, as the great venture prepared to start, was indeed a combination of the two, being both feasible and fantastic at the same time. The wild-eyed General, who wore a tropical helmet and affected something unheard of in the British Army since Victorian times, a full black beard, intended, as he told the highly impressed war correspondent of the *Daily Telegraph* at the time, to introduce into Jap-held Burma, 'Self-contained, mobile fighting units', of mainly British infantry. 'Don't call us guerrillas. One of our functions is to organize Burmese patriots who want to fight with us, but we ourselves aren't guerrillas. I think we can best be described as long-range penetration groups.'[4]

These 'Chindits,' as Wingate called them after the Burmese name for the lion-like figures which stood guard outside their temples to ward off evil, would plunge deep into the heart of the jungle in separate columns, being supplied in a revolutionary new way – for 1943 – by air. Each column would have an RAF unit attached to it to summon up supplies whenever needed. Otherwise the infantry would rely on two of the oldest methods of transport – shanks's pony, with each man carrying a pack and equipment weighing 80 pounds; and mules and buffaloes.

Already the Chindits had had some trouble with the latter, especially the four which supplied milk to Wingate's HQ. One by one these had being dying off during training until there was one left, which Wingate, in desperation, had been dosing with precious Scotch whisky.

In the end, Wingate turned to a local witch doctor for help. He had appeared, heated up some branding irons and then, as another of Wingate's column commanders, Michael Calvert, recalled after the war, 'he shoved the red-hot tip of the iron between her legs. The effect of this particular medicine, as one might expect, was immediate. The shocked animal leapt to her feet and began stamping about. Unperturbed the witch doctor grabbed another branding iron and laid it on the other flank and finally on her shoulder. At each searing touch the buffalo leapt about three feet in the air, but she made no attempt to lash out. Finally, after throwing a pained look at Wingate, she started to graze ...'[5]

So they started out. The men were mostly North Country, between the ages of 28 and 35. Many of them had been previously carrying out rear-line security duties in India, a fairly cushy job in which they had expected they would serve for the rest of the war. Wingate had changed that. Now they were heading into the jungle, marching at night. Elephants carried mortars and heavy machine guns, plodding ahead silent-footed or tearing at the overhanging bamboos or low branches. With the delicate steps of a tight rope walker they picked their way along rocky tracks no wider than their own feet.

Next came the men and mules, laden down – both – with the varied paraphernalia of this strange unit, right down to spare sets of false teeth in case anyone lost his. For the Chindits were going to stay in the jungle behind the Jap lines for at least three months. To the rear came the slower-moving buffaloes and oxen dragging sturdy little carts, again heavily laden. To the observers seeing them off it looked a little like one of the tribal migrations of the Dark Ages.

While they crawled along thus, covering sometimes a mere mile in a whole night, Wingate lectured anyone prepared to listen on the enemy they were soon going to meet, 'The Jap isn't a superman,' he was wont to say. 'I've studied his military manuals and I regard his operational schemes as the product of a third-rate brain. But the individual soldier is a fanatic. Put him in a hole, give him 100 rounds and tell him to die for the Emperor and he will do it. The way to deal with him is to leave him in his hole and go behind him. If this operation of ours is successful, it will save, thousands of lives ...'[6]

The first obstacle to be overcome was the River Chindwin, which was broad and fast flowing and known to be watched by the Japs, who patrolled it at regular intervals and had spies in the riverside villages on the look-out for penetration groups such as Wingate's Chindits. They crossed it at night without casualties, though they did lose some of their mules and one war correspondent thought the crossing was 'more like the seaside on Bank Holiday in England than a military operation in the Burma Jungle ...' with 'naked figures splashing through the shallows and racing over the sands in pursuit of recalcitrant mules'.[7]

Now, however, the Bank Holiday' atmosphere vanished. One day after they crossed, the Japanese became aware of their presence. They sent out a large force 400 men strong, together with elephants, and alerted another 15,000. Wingate set a cracking pace. Each night the men marched 18 to 20 miles deeper and deeper into enemy-held territory. The men grew groggy from the lack of sleep, for even during daytime they got no real rest. They were either busy with military chores or plagued by the insects and flies which left them with no peace.

Once Major Fergusson caught one of his young infantrymen asleep on sentry go. What to do with him? As the Major wrote himself after the war: 'Shooting, thank goodness, is no longer the recognized punishment; to hold a field general court martial and give him penal servitude hardly helps to make him a useful soldier during the next few months ... Yet you cannot let him get away with it lightly; he had all our lives in his hands and put them in pawn.'[8] Major Fergusson did not have the answer. But Wingate did. Soon he would order that serious military offences would be punished by flogging. Not only did he look like a Victorian general, but now he was returning to the punishments employed by the Victorian Army!

A few days later another problem began to plague Wingate, one to which there was no simple solution, however brutal. It was the question of what to do with the seriously wounded. On 6 March, 1943, the point of one of his columns ran into the enemy unexpectedly in a village. There was a short, intense fire-fight in which all of the Japs save one were killed. But the Chindits had suffered casualties, too, including an officer, John Kerr.

Kerr, who had been badly wounded in the leg, was just telling Fergusson what had happened when one of the 'dead' Japs rose and aimed his rifle at the Black Watch Major. His companion was quicker off the mark. He shot the 'dead' Jap and then fired a second bullet into his bleeding body to make sure that he was really dead this time.

Then came the problem of what to do with Kerr and the four other seriously wounded infantrymen. Finally Fergusson took them into the village and left them in the shade of a house with earthen jugs of water. One of them said, 'Thank God, no more walking for a bit.' Another, Corporal Dalr, grinned and said, 'See you make a good job of that bridge' (they had been intending to blow up a nearby bridge), and John Kerr added bravely, 'Don't worry about us, we'll be all right ...'[9]

But there were humorous moments too as they penetrated ever deeper into the jungle, relying ever more on their supplies from the air, leaving most of their transport dead – *or eaten* – behind them, harassing the Japs all the time. One Major, 'Mad Mike' Calvert, attempting to blow up a railway embankment with the enemy within earshot, discovered that he had not prepared the detonators correctly. 'What the hell do we do now?' he whispered urgently to his companion Geoffrey Lockett, in charge of the commando platoon.

The latter was completely unruffled. 'Better light a match and see what we're doing,' he suggested, although the Japs would see the light immediately.

Desperately Calvert looked around for a bush behind which he might conceal the match. But there were no bushes near the embankment. Suddenly 'Mad Mike' had a brainwave. 'Lift up your kilt,' he ordered Geoffrey. Grabbing a handful of detonators and some matches he tugged at the other's kilt.

'Here, be careful!' he protested. 'Watch what you're doing with those things.'

But the thick folds of the kilt held close to the ground proved a first-class blackout curtain, while 'Geoffrey muttered away darkly about suing me for damages'.[10]

Minutes later the time pencils with their explosive charges were planted and the commando platoon was hurrying away into the darkness, with Geoffrey's 'outside plumbing' still intact ...

Major (later Brigadier) 'Mad Mike' Calvert, who would fight as a Chindit long after Wingate was dead and then go on to command an SAS Brigade in Germany, was an old hand at jungle warfare. Of all Wingate's officers he was the most experienced. Once he had been bathing naked in a jungle river when he had come across a Jap officer who was just as naked. They went for each other immediately, although they were both unarmed. 'He knew his jujitsu and the water on his body made him as slippery as an eel, but I was the bigger and stronger. We fought in silence except for the occasional grunt, and struggled and slipped and thrashed around until we were at times waist deep in the swirling river. It was an ungainly fight, almost in slow motion, for it is extraordinarily difficult to keep balance or move quickly and surely two or three feet of water. Our breathing grew heavier and the Jap got more vicious as he jabbed his fingers at my face in an attempt to blind me. I think it was not till then that I fully realized this would have to be a fight to the death.

'I was a trained soldier, taught how to kill with a gun or a bomb, or a bayonet or even a knife in the thick of battle. Somehow this seemed different, more personal, as the two of us, naked as we were, fought in the water. Apart from anything else, I had come to admire this game little Jap. He had all the guts in the world. He could so easily have called up his men and let them fight it out, but he had chosen to protect them by taking me on alone.

'Now he was putting up a tremendous show and I was hard put to it to hold him. I pulled myself together. Brave or not, I had to kill him. Or he would kill me.

'I was thankful for one lesson I had learned: never to take my boots off in the jungle outside camp. Other clothes can be scrambled on in a moment, but boots take time and time can cost lives. Even on this occasion I had stuck to my rule, which was just as well. I managed to grab the Jap's right wrist and force his arm behind his back. And I buried my face in his chest to stop him clawing my eyes. Then as he lashed out with his left arm and both feet I forced him gradually under the water. My boots gave me a firm grip and I shut my eyes and held him under surface. His struggles grew weaker and weaker, flared up again in frantic despair and then he went limp. I held on for a few seconds longer before releasing my grip. Slowly I opened my eyes and for a moment I could see nothing except the eddies of water caused by his final efforts to break free. Then his body emerged on the surface a couple of yards away and floated gently off downstream. ...'[11]

There were not many future brigadiers who had killed an enemy soldier with his bare hands, but Calvert* did. Now he felt his attitude was rubbing off on the average Chindit, as they bumped into ever-increasing Japanese resistance. As he was later to write: 'This ... operation proved that the European soldier, as of old, can shake off the shackles of his civilized neuroses and inhibitions and live and fight as hard as any Asiatic and, because of his intrinsic sounder constitution and basic health due to good feeding, better the Asiatic in overcoming hard conditions. Most soldiers never realized that they could do the things they did and hardly believe it now.'[12] Those who survived.

Now they began slaughtering the mules, which affected some of the Chindits worse than when they were slaughtering the 'Nips'. Because the Japanese were close they were unable to dispatch by bullet the animals to which they had become very attached. Instead they tried the ghastly experiment of slitting their throats, which left the transport officer of No. Five Column 'white faced ... with tears on his cheeks'.[13]

But the mules were the least of No. Five Column's worries. Major Fergusson, leading his men with a grenade in his hand, came across three men squatting on their haunches just outside a small village. At first he took them for Burmese villagers and then, when he was only three yards away from them, he realized they were Japs. 'Resisting a curious instinct which was prompting me to apologize for interrupting them, I pulled the pin out of my grenade, which had suddenly became sticky with sweat, and lobbed it – oh, so neatly – into the fire. I just caught the expression of absolute terror on their faces; they were making no attempt to move; and ran.'[14]

Almost immediately a wild, confused fire fight broke out in the village as the Japanese realized the British were in their midst. The defenders began tossing grenades at the Chindits, but as they were easy to see on account of their glowing fuse, the Chindits caught them and tossed them back. Fergusson was busily engaged doing this when he missed one. He flung himself to the ground. Too late! He felt a sharp pain in the bone of his hip. He yelped with pain and almost lost the monocle which he affected. Next to him one of his officers spotted the Japs who were throwing the grenades and finished them off with a hail of his own bombs. But to make quite sure he went to the 'heap of writhing bodies' and finished them off individually with his rifle, emptying it into them. In the brutal war of the jungle, no quarter was given or expected.

But now Wingate had decided his men were no longer capable of going in much deeper. The time had come to split up into separate groups and

---

* American research on WWII has shown that even in élite formations such us the rangers and paratroopers in action, only 50-odd per cent will fire their weapons at the enemy to kill. Hand-to-hand combat such us above is very rare.

make their way back. Some of the commanders didn't like it. They had wanted to stay on until the monsoon season, but already some men were beginning to drop out of the columns from sheer exhaustion, risking torture and worse at the hands of their enemies (all officers captured by them, wounded or not, were routinely tortured for information by the Japanese). So the ones who disliked the idea of returning gave in reluctantly and set off back for India, with the Japanese now on their heels, and waiting at every one of the rivers they had to cross.

No. Five Column under Fergusson after undergoing a 'nightmarish crossing' of the raging, tremendously swift River Shweli, found to their horror that they hadn't crossed it at all. Their Burmese boatmen had marooned them, either unintentionally or treacherously, on a sandbank, some 100 yards off the far bank. Now in the darkness, with Japanese patrols less than a couple of miles away, the Chindits braved the rest of the river, which was 4ft 6in deep and running at a horrific rate. Every one of them knew that if they lost their footing, they would disappear for ever in the black stream.

'Several times one heard cries for help,' Fergusson wrote later, 'as some unlucky chap lost his footing and went off helplessly downstream. I fear it must have happened to four or five in all. In the inky blackness there was nothing one could do to help. Some parties tried to hold hands all the way over, but it was impossible to maintain one's grip.'[15]

In the end with the headlights of three Jap lorries clearly visible on the road further up the river, there were two score, mostly the smaller men, left on the sandbank who refused to take a chance. Several officers went back to try to convince them to have a go, but weak and frightened as they were, they wouldn't. Now Major Fergusson had to snake the decision, which 'I will have on my conscience for as long as I live'.[16] He decided to leave them to their fate, trying to appease his sorely troubled conscience with the knowledge that most of those left behind were not his best soldiers. Indeed two of them would have been faced with a court-martial had they got out.

Now with his strength reduced to nine officers and 65 men from the original 121 who had started to cross the river, he set off to lead them into the hill country of the Kachins, who were traditionally friendly to the British and where he hoped to find food and shelter for his ragged emaciated survivors, who were now literally starving. There was even talk of eating the column's pet dog Judy (one school of thought was shocked by the thought of what they called cannibalism; the other maintained the dog was too skinny anyway).

Day after day they marched higher into the hills, tormented by the longing for solid, rich food, tortured by an agonized craving for sugar. Once they boiled a kind of grass which looked like asparagus. Another time they swallowed greedily some rich red berries, which left the insides of their mouths shrivelled and as hard as walnuts. Constantly they were on the lookout for bamboo shoots, which were now considered by the starving infantrymen to be the height of culinary delight. But there were none. On one occasion they came across two stray cows, but in their eagerness they shot at them wildly and the cows scuttled away. The men who had missed were treated almost as traitors by the rest.

By now some of the columns had trekked 1,300 miles in the last 88 days and had shed everything save what they stood up in and their weapons. The men were incredibly emaciated, with a body weight loss, on average, of about a third of their original weight. Most of them were glassy-eyed and very, very slow, due to the lack of food. Moving like weary old men, the reason why they had first ventured into the jungle was forgotten now. Their enemy was no longer the 'Nip', though he was still out there somewhere in the steaming hot hell, chasing them. Now the enemy was hunger and fatigue, the desire to simply drop to the soft ground, hug it like a loved one, and never move ever again.

But officers like Wingate, Calvert and Fergusson kept them moving, cajoling them, threatening them, pleading with them, telling themselves repeatedly that they were not (what they really were) a ragged bunch of broken-down fugitives, fleeing for their very lives, but fighting men – soldiers! As Fergusson wrote afterwards, 'I was determined that there should be no nonsense about discipline. I was haunted by what Gunn* had told me of the party from which he had severed himself and took care that the men should hear it. I had in mind what I had read of Captain Scott on his last expedition: how in his tiny tent, shared by three officers and two ratings, he nightly drew a line to represent the boundary between quarter-deck and lower-deck. In like manner I still preserved such state as was possible: officers ate separate from their men and I could be approached only through the proper channels, either through John as second-in-command or through Tommy Blow, now acting as adjutant. We might be in poor shape, but we *were* still soldiers.'[17]

They grew lousy and scratched skinny bodies, already covered with bites and sores, all the time. They got footrot. The boots gave out and men marched in bare feet. Worse still, tea began to run out and it became a major decision each day when and how to have their daily mug of the precious 'char' – before the handful of wet rice or after it, or perhaps with it. Someone discovered a two-ounce tin of cheap cheese at the bottom of his rotting pack and he was looked upon by his awed, envious comrades like the man who had won the football pools in the old days, which now seemed light-years away.

---

* 22-year-old Sergeant Gunn had broken away from a much larger party, commanded by officers, where the discipline of the march had broken down, telling his own section, all older than himself, that they were 'doomed'.

One by one they reached the edges of their last maps, but before them lay the Chindwin, which when they had ventured forth, fit, smart and full of bursting energy, had been held by the British. Was it now? But in the end they didn't care. They just simply had to get across, eat and rest. Nothing else mattered.

But the British *were* still there. So they came back to India. 'Mad Mike' Calvert's column was first. Major Fergusson of the beard and monocle followed six days later. Orde Wingate brought his own column in four days after that. Two men reached India on their own, the last of a party of seven … Lance-corporal 'Sailor' Thompson made it all by himself. …

In the end, of the 3,000 who had sallied forth, 2,182 returned to India. But of these only a mere 600 were fit for further soldiering. Many died shortly after reaching the place of their dreams through those last terrible weeks – India. They hadn't really accomplished very much for the many lives lost and all that suffering – a few hundred Japs killed and a few miles of railway line blown up which could be easily repaired. In spite of the glare of publicity, which suddenly made the name Chindit a household word back in the UK, there was nothing really tangible about their exploits, no important victory or blow to Japan's hopes in the Far East, save this.

It had now been clearly shown that the British infantryman, just average, somewhat over-age men of the King's Regiment, the South Wales Borderers, and the like, could tackle the Japanese and beat him under conditions so terrible that they were virtually unthinkable to the ordinary citizen back home. The Japs were *not* supermen. They had been shown to be soldiers who could be beaten, just like any one soldier. The Chindits had destroyed a legend. …

VI

'Roses, roses all the way'

On the night of Tuesday, 11 May, the same month that the Chindits returned to India, General Eisenhower's HQ announced: 'Organized resistance except by isolated pockets has ceased. General von Arnim, Commander-in-Chief of Axis forces in Tunisia, has been captured. It is estimated that the total number of prisoners captured since 5 May is 150,000 ... Fewer than 1,000 are believed to have succeeded in escaping across the Sicilian Narrows.'[1]

For three and a half years since January 1940, the British had been fighting in Africa, losing 70,000 men in Tunisia alone. Now it was over, with 11 German and 26 Italian divisions wiped out. The war in Africa was over and the *Wehrmacht* had suffered a greater defeat than the one they had suffered in Stalingrad the previous January.

For a while the victorious troops of the 8th Army celebrated while the would-be 'conquerors of Egypt' anxiously offered 50 francs to Arab boatmen to ferry them across to the British to surrender. Alan Moorehead, up ahead to observe the meeting of the 1st and 8th Armies in Tunis, watched the crazy, chaotic confusion of the last moments of the *Afrikakorps*, as 'the French people rushed into the street and they were beside themselves in hysterical delight. Some rushed directly at us, flinging themselves on the running-boards. A girl threw her arms around my driver's neck. An old man took a packet of cigarettes from his pocket and flung them up at us. Someone else brandished a bottle of wine. All the women had flowers that they had hastily plucked from their gardens. A clump of roses hit me full in the mouth!'[2]

There were German soldiers everywhere, rifles slung over their shoulders, watching the amazing scenes open-mouthed with wonder like village yokels. A bren-gun carrier went past full of German prisoners, each one of them stiffly holding a posy of flowers. Hundreds of just liberated British prisoners of the Germans streamed into the streets, yelling and weeping. They had been scheduled to sail for Italy this very day. Now they were free again.

Suddenly sniper fire erupted into the wildly happy scene. Ex-prisoners, liberators, French onlookers, and the new prisoners scattered. Moorehead 'looking up, saw a line of bullets slapping against the brewery wall above us. As each bullet hit, it sent out a little yellow flame and a spray of plaster came down on top of us.'[3] A tank rumbled up and pumped a couple of quick shells into the brewery. An instant later a young, wild-eyed Frenchman, armed with a sten gun he had obtained somewhere or other, rushed in through the door, firing from the hip as he did so in true Wild West fashion.

Then it was all over and the men of the 1st and 8th Armies could celebrate, getting drunk and chasing the local girls, and 'bulling up', too. For this being a British army, there just had to be a victory parade, complete with Winston Churchill, the massed pipe bands of the 51st Highland Division, and the usual hated 'bags of swank'.

But even as the men celebrated their victory, some perceptive reporters noted a sombre mood among the infantry. Asked by one correspondent how he felt to be making history, Sergeant Benson of the 'Big Red One' answered sourly, 'History, Hell! I wish to hell I was back in Iowa running my butcher's shop.' And in Tunisia a British MP, breaking up a traffic jam of American and British trucks, said, 'We're going to keep in a bloody straight line from here to Sicily.'[4]

For at the back of the minds of most of the infantry was the question – *what next*? It was clear to even the dullest of them that now the Germans had been defeated in Africa, Europe would be the next target. By now all of them knew that it was planned to invade France from Britain at some time in the future. That possibility didn't worry them greatly, as long as they could enjoy a stay in their home country. After all many of them had been out in Africa without a home leave since 1940.

Lieutenant Eric Taylor, who in his five months of campaigning with the 1st Army had seen virtually every officer in his battalion, save himself, killed or wounded, recalled over 40 years later, 'The men appeared fit and confident, as brown as berries. They were having time out of war, but not very long, mind you. The CO soon got the old bull going again. That was later. For the time being they were resting after a major campaign, drinking and whoring with the local French girls. But the question uppermost in their minds was is it back to Blighty or was it the start of another bloody hard slog in Italy?'[5]

Another young officer, Neil McCallum, who like Eric Taylor was fated to be wounded in Sicily that July, also noted the same mood, one which turned sour when the men in his infantry battalion learned that they were not going home. 'Discipline, while not breaking down, showed signs of wear and tear. NCOs approached officers with their hands in pockets, cigarettes in mouth. Drunks strode through the battalion lines at night shouting defiance at all and sundry, "Muck the bloody muckers, we're doing no more fighting!" ... At times the camel's back was near breaking and it seemed that mutiny and disorder were a hair's breadth away. Had we been in a country of easy communications, or near a large city, desertions would have been numerous. The situation was handled in the only way such situations can be handled. Licence was tolerated up to a point and for the rest a rigid training programme of exceptional physical severity occupied a fixed number of hours each day ... In a large marquee in the farmer's meadow, a wet canteen was opened and Battalion Orders bore the amazing instruction that all ranks might get drunk, provided they stayed within camp lines.'[6]

That summer as they trained, whored, got drunk and waited, strange rumours abounded in North Africa. It was said that the Mediterranean Fleet was near mutiny; that in one cruiser the stokers had gone on strike and that in another the officers and petty officers had been forced to sail their ship to port, because the ratings wouldn't report for duty. There was talk of a battalion of the Rifle Brigade having mutinied in the desert because they weren't going home. The CO and other officers had apparently walked out on the mutineers and had left the senior NCOs to sort it out. It had taken a weekend of hard talk, threats, and some physical violence to get the riflemen to 'soldier on'.

That same battalion of infantry which had held the German counter-attack at El Alamein so bravely back in 1942 was split up, with 200 of its regulars who had been abroad since 1937 without home leave – *a stagger-ing six years* – going home at last. The remainder were to stay in Africa and fight in the next campaign. Their CO described their mood as 'restless'. It certainly was. They would finally land in Italy, demanding home leave before they would fight.

Rifleman Alex Bowlby, a reinforcement, who had watched the regulars come back to the depot back in the UK, swarming on to the square, swing-ing their belts like clubs and yelling, 'Where's the fucking RSM! Come out and fight, you fuckers!' now in Italy came across 'a great crowd of cheering riflemen charging through the olive grove brandishing sheets of paper and shouting "up the Oicks". The cry was taken up till the whole grove echoed with it. When it stopped there was a great burst of laughter.

'"What on earth's happening?" I asked a rifleman.

'"The lads want home leave before they go into action," he said. "They know they won't get it, but it's their way of showing they haven't forgotten Tunis. They're getting up a round-robin to give to the Company Commander.'[7]

This they did and the company commander received it 'with his usual urbane kindness and D Company got on with the war'.[8]

It was the same with Lieutenant McCallum's Battalion, as serious training for what was to come really got under way. 'As the idea became familiar the attack on Europe fell into place in our minds,' he wrote long afterwards. 'It could be nothing else that we were preparing for, though secrecy enshrouded everything. For all that we were officially told of the future our new battle training might be for no reason but to pass the time. We hated the idea of a new campaign, but it had its eternal fascination. And so the crisis passed and gradually there came a new discipline and almost an enthusiasm.'⁹

But underneath the surface of the Army in Africa the underlying resentment of what was to come remained. If the going got tough, it might well re-emerge again – with a vengeance. But the going was not getting tough. Secret talks were already taking place which would take Italy out of the war – and where would the Germans fight then? They'd have to beat a hasty retreat to their own country. As one barfly confidently told Sergeant Irwin Shaw over a drink in Cairo: 'It is going to be one of the great marches in all military history. A long, narrow, green country, full of handsome people who have been enslaved for 20 years and are now being liberated and know it. You will be greeted like water in the desert, like a circus on the Fourth of July, like Clark Gable at Vassar. The chianti will flow like water and can you imagine,' he speculated, narrowing his eyes dreamily, 'what it will be like to be an American of Italian descent. I can imagine. He would never reach Florence. He would be worn out with hospitality, and would have to be invalided back to the States. *Roses, roses all the way*....'¹⁰

That September day when they prepared to land at Salerno in southern Italy, 100,000 British and 69,000 American infantrymen (photographed incidentally by a certain Major Healey), it seemed it would be just that – roses all the way. For Italy, it had just been announced over the ship's intercom, had surrendered. Spontaneous cheering broke out.' Men danced with each other. Sing-songs were organized. The Americans asked their padres for impromptu services of thanksgiving. British officers drank their whole month's drinks rations in one go. Italy had laid down its arms unconditionally and there would be no fight for the beaches!

That had been on 9 September, 1943. Now, days later, the troops were fighting bitterly on the beaches, not to move inland but to prevent themselves being flung back into the sea. For the Germans had moved in immediately the Italians had surrendered, racing down to the beaches, not only with infantry but with heavy armour. The German panzers had slaughtered the first elements of the British and American infantry, who had no heavy weapons whatsoever with which to defend themselves against the massive frightening Tigers.

Now everyone was in the front line. Generals, cooks, nurses, clerks, wounded, even the dead. For their very burial grounds were under constant enemy fire. Not even the hospital ships attempting to take the wounded back to North Africa were safe. Twice such ships, clearly marked with the Red Cross, were sunk by the *Luftwaffe*. For a crisis had come to Salerno, with the Germans determined, on Hitler's express order, to throw the Anglo-Americans back into the sea. It was going to be another Dunkirk, but this time, as one British officer remarked cynically, 'there'll be no small boats ...'

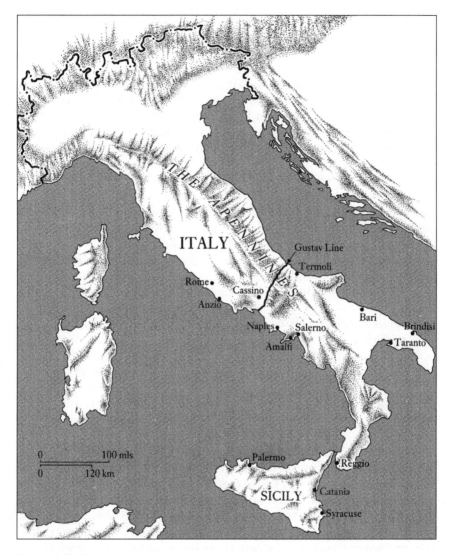

Italy and Sicily

The Germans threw in a massive armoured attack against the 201st Guards Brigade holding a key sector of the front. The anti-tank guns of the Brigade's 9th Royal Fusiliers tried to hold them up, but their shells bounced off the thick hides of the Tigers like glowing golf balls. The CO was killed. The Fusiliers grew jittery. The acting CO told the men, 'Although we are surrounded, we shall not be captured.' Privately he told his officers to destroy all maps and codes.[11]

A few hours later it was all over and most of the surviving Fusiliers surrendered, save those who ran back to the coast, crying in panic, 'Back to the beaches! We're overrun! We've had it! The German tanks are right behind us!'

The Guards, moving up through the shattered remnants of the Fusiliers, were infected by the mood of the latter. Their morale plummeted. The Grenadiers in the van were hit by German armoured cars. One platoon was overrun. A company bolted and fled back the way they had come. Here and there they were stopped by their officers and pushed back into the line forcibly.

As one Guards officer recorded afterwards, 'Nobody will really know what happened and perhaps it is better to gloss over the rest of that day. The morale of the Grenadiers was not high and it is certain that small parties considered the only plan was to return to the beaches as quickly as possible. On their right some Fusiliers … had a similar idea. By mid-afternoon the small roads were full of frightened soldiers, many retiring pell-mell, regardless of officers.'[12]

Young Lieutenant Bulteel of the Coldstream Guards was supervising loading some wounded men into a jeep when another vehicle filled with Grenadiers roared by shouting, 'They're coming! They're through! Get back to the beaches!'

Bulteel reacted correctly. He sprang into the driver's seat, swung the jeep round and effectively blocked the road. Then he pelted towards the HQ of his Company Commander, Major Griffith Jones. The Major, playing the role of the urbane, unflappable Guardee, was on the field telephone and wouldn't let himself be disturbed. Finally he deigned to listen to the excited young officer.

'Mervyn,' Bulteel blurted out, 'some of the Grenadiers have run away. We are to be ready for an immediate counter-attack.'

'Nonsense,' his company commander retorted airily. 'Everything's quite all right. The Grenadiers have attacked again and now they're back where they started. I am going to have a sleep.' Which he proceeded to do.

But everything was not all right. The 201st Guards Brigade was suffering very heavy losses and it seemed they had nothing to stop the German armour pushing right down to the beaches.

It was no better in the American sector of the front. Artillery units of the US 45th Infantry Division were already beginning to pull back without orders and General Clark, the overall US commander back on the island of Sicily, had just received a call from the commander of the US 6th Corps at Salerno saying the situation was critical. When asked what he was going to do about it, the 6th Corps Commander, General Dawley, answered in a resigned manner, 'Nothing, I have no reserves. All I have is prayer.'[13]

It was against this background of a crumbling beachhead that General Alexander, Clark's superior, made his appearance. He told Clark that

Dawley was a 'broken reed' and ordered, 'We stay here and we die here. We do not retreat!'[14]

Now in the midst of this breakdown, with the infantry's morale plummeting, a draft of 1,500 infantrymen, all of them who had been wounded in the fighting in Sicily, were assembled in Tripoli one night and told that three cruisers would be arriving on the following day to return them to their parent units in the 50th and 51st Highland Divisions. Later, after it had all happened, the sergeant-major who made the announcement testified at their trial, 'Up to that time everyone who had gone through that camp had gone to his own unit. That's why I told them they were returning to their own units.'[15]

But they weren't going back to their divisions, for those divisions had already gone or were going back to Britain, earmarked for the Invasion of France. In fact, they were being sent to the battlefront at Salerno as badly needed infantry replacements and the officers who would lead them there knew it. But for security reasons they were not allowed to tell the men, who were overjoyed because they knew from the Army grapevine that return to their units meant they were going back to 'blighty'.

In due course they arrived at Salerno and a handful were sent immediately to reinforce the hard-pressed British 46th and 56th Divisions. The rest, however, received no definite orders. They wandered about aimlessly for four days, being moved on to a further beach when they got in the way.

At last on 20 September, 1943, they were moved into a large field further inland. There they were ordered to march off to join the 46th Infantry Division. About half did so. But some 700 of the infantry staged what they called 'a sit-down strike' and refused to obey their officers' orders. That same afternoon a senior officer told General McCreery, the thin wiry commanding officer of the British X Corps, what had happened to the rear. Hurriedly he swung himself into a jeep and raced to the beach, where he found an appalling situation, now made worse by the crisis at the front.

The men sat on the ground, surrounded by grim-faced, armed redcaps. Already they had been warned of the consequences of mutiny 'in the face of the enemy' and three times they had been ordered to pick up their gear and move off. Stubbornly they had refused to budge. McCreery wondered what he should do. Technically the men had already mutinied. Legally they could be court-martialled and sentenced to at least seven years' penal servitude. In the end he drove his jeep right into the crowd of sullen soldiers and spoke to them.

He told them that as soon as the fighting was over they would be returned to their parent units and if they moved straightaway, the whole incident would be forgotten. But the men were in no mood for appeasement and all the while the Corps Commander spoke he was interrupted by jeers, boos and catcalls. When he was finished McCreery advised the officers in charge to give the men some time to talk it over. They did and most of them agreed to go to the 46th Division. But 192 men refused to do so, including several sergeants. They were placed under immediate close arrest.

They were disarmed and moved down the beach, past a cage holding Germans POWs, who booed them and called them cowards, and placed in a separate cage, where they were guarded by – of all people – Italian soldiers, who had surrendered a few days before and were now classed as 'co-belligerents'. From there they were sent by train to Constantine to be imprisoned; on the way there two of them, Privates Fred Jowett and Archie Newmarch, somehow contrived to miss the train, but hitched a lift in an Arab truck to catch it up!

In the end, though most of them impressed their guards and the prosecution, they were all sentenced to seven years' penal servitude, save the corporals, who received ten years' and the three sergeants, who were ordered to be shot. Thereupon, immediately, their sentences were suspended on condition the men would fight with new units. There would be no 'blighty' for them. Numbly they accepted the condition, but their morale started to sink rapidly. Almost at once, over a dozen men crawled through the wire of their compound and went 'on the trot', i.e. deserted.

Subsequently others deserted before they ever reached the front. Others, when they joined fighting units, refused to go into combat, and were again sentenced to prison. On the troopship taking most of them back to Italy, they were kept on a separate deck. The reason why was soon discovered by the other infantry and they would not speak to them, save to insult them. Their morale sank lower and lower. More deserted as soon as they reached Bari.

The Army naturally hushed up the details of the 'Salerno Mutiny'. But generals such as Wimberley of the 51st Highland Division, to which division most of the 'mutineers' belonged, and Montgomery, in whose army the 51st had been incorporated, of course heard of the incident.

Even before he had left for Britain to command the invasion, Montgomery had ordered, 'We are playing with a very highly explosive material when dealing with the question of formations and personnel returning to UK ... 50 and 51 Divs know they are going home to the UK, they have had their sick and wounded, when fit, sent to Divisions of the 8th Army (i.e. units fighting in Italy). This may have been necessary as an emergency measure, but it is vital that these men be sent back to their Divisions at once – to avoid unrest.'[16]

Now while Wimberley pleaded – unsuccessfully – with the War Office to have the sentences quashed against his former soldiers, Montgomery ordered a senior Army psychiatrist to investigate the matter. The latter came to the conclusion that it was 'a tragedy of errors ... there was a complete absence of clear direction, precise information or firm leadership throughout. There was a total disregard of well-established loyalties in experienced fighting men of previously high morale'.[17]

Colonel Ahrenfeldt, who conducted the investigation, had, of course, produced a whitewash job. The main cause, according to him, was unit loyalty. Nowhere in his report did he state that the real reason for their refusal to serve in Salerno was that they knew that if they were returned to the 50th and 51st Divisions they would be sent home.

For his part Montgomery used the incident in his campaign to denigrate General Alexander and ensure that he was not appointed (instead of Montgomery) to command the Invasion. Some time after the trial and the Ahrenfeldt Report, he wrote to the adjutant-general that he 'should know certain facts about the courts-martial that took place over the refusal of men of 50 Div and 51 Div to serve in other Divisions in Italy'.[18] He placed the blame squarely on the shoulders of Alexander's administrative chief and maintained he was 'unfit to be a Major-General', implying, of course, that Alexander himself was lacking by employing such an incompetent in a key staff position.

But when Montgomery wrote that letter to General Sir Sidney Kirkman, the adjutant-general, in April 1944, he must have been worried in his heart of hearts about the morale and steadfastness of the infantry he would be using in the coming invasion. For the 50th Division would be one of his three assault divisions on D-Day, and the 51st Highland was slated to follow up immediately the beachhead had been consolidated.

Yet over 1,200 men out of the approximately 30,000 men belonging to these two experienced infantry formations had refused to fight – and these were his veterans. How would his other infantry divisions, which had been simply training in Britain for the last four years, fare when they faced shot and shell for the very first time?

Thus it was as D-day came ever closer that Montgomery, on what he called the 'Public Hallowing of the Sword; campaign, made an attempt to make the soldiers realize that the fate of the nation depended upon them and gain public support for the troops going into battle soon. He toured Britain without rest, talking to factory workers, church leaders, trade unionists, trying to inspire them into feeling that soldiers and civilians were in this to the end. His concept was that the men at the sharp end should understand that they were not fighting for their generals because they were ordered to, but for their own people, whatever their politics and class.

He was equally tireless in inspecting his fighting troops, visiting battalion after battalion. Travelling ceaselessly from tented camp to tented camp, he talked to them in their hundreds, their thousands, their hundreds of thousands. Seated on the grass or standing shoulder to shoulder around his jeep, row after row of young upturned serious faces – Americans, Britons, Canadians – they all hung on the words of the little man in the overlarge black beret.

Always he made the same speech. There was no mention of England, no question of hate and revenge. None of the old verities with which generals have always sent soldiers to war. All that 'Monty' spoke of was themselves and the enemy waiting 21 miles away across the water. 'We don't want to forget the German is a good soldier … a very good soldier indeed. But when I look round this morning (or this afternoon or evening) and see some of the magnificent soldiers here … some of the finest soldiers I have seen in my lifetime … I have no doubt about the outcome … Now I have seen you I have complete confidence. And you must have confidence in me …'

There'd be 'three cheers for the General!' Hats would be whipped off and then they'd let go, 'hip … hip … *hurrah*!' Thereafter he might inspect the battalion, gazing up at each young man's tense face, as if he were trying to etch the features on his mind's eye for ever. For a fleeting moment, the soldier would catch a glimpse of that bronzed, beaky face with the fiercely willed mouth and those piercing unwavering blue eyes, then he would be gone.

Sometimes he might stop and ask the battalion commander, 'What's the average age of your battalion, Colonel?'

The officer would reply promptly enough; they all had been well briefed beforehand. 'Twenty-five, *sir*!' he would bark, standing rigidly to attention, cane under his right arm.

'Twenty-five,' Montgomery would muse, repeating the number, as if it had some mystical significance, 'Twenty-five, eh? A good age …'

But some of those young men of 25 had been fighting for five years now and in spite of all Montgomery's effort to improve their morale and 'binge them up', as he called it, they were tired. Would these infantrymen, who had been risking their lives for month after month, year after year, still be prepared to give their all? Had it been wise to bring home veteran formations, such as the 50th and 51st and the 7th Armoured Division, the 'Desert Rats', who had been fighting since December 1939, to bolster up the green formations going into battle for the first time?

One of Montgomery's staff, Brigadier Herbert, felt the 'troops were not altogether right', even as they moved into the embarkation camps. He saw that the troops driving by Montgomery's HQ at Southwick heading for Fareham that May lacked discipline. 'Now two or three people came up to me,' he stated much later, 'and said: Do you realize that these people are out of hand? They were responsible senior fighting soldiers, and they were really worried about it (indiscipline). And I went out and had a look and I agreed. They were not under control – they were forcing people off the road, assing about generally… *in a way that experienced troops going into battle would not behave*! I mean they were the Desert Rats, the most famous division in the British Army, and they were fed up and irresponsible. So that there was some reason to be uncertain as to whether everything was all right or whether it wasn't.'[19]

Now only time and the trial of battle would tell. …

BOOK FOUR
1944–1945

Merry it was to laugh there –
Where death becomes absurd and life absurder.
For power was on us as we slashed bones bare
Not to feel sickness or remorse of murder.

'Apologia Pro Poemate Meo', Wilfred Owen

I

'I have twice had to stand at the end of the track and draw my revolver on retreating men'

Now they were firmly established. The cost had been high. Ten thousand casualties on that first day. At Ouistreham on Sword beach the bodies of the East Yorkshire Regiment had formed a solid khaki carpet from the water's edge to the cliffs. It had been no different at Omaha – 'Bloody Omaha', they called it afterwards – where the men of the 'Big Red One' had been slaughtered in their hundreds. But now they were ashore and moving inland, taking casualties all the time, but still moving, heading towards the key to the whole new front – Caen.

Already, however, the heart-breaking losses and the sheer slog of living rough, eating out of cans, sleeping in holes and every new day expected to batter their way through yet another defensive position, which the Germans had had four years to prepare, were taking their toll. The 2nd East Yorkshires, for example, would fight for 42 days on foot, engaged all the time, losing that June seven officers and 83 other ranks killed, 13 officers and 266 other ranks wounded, plus thirteen missing. That meant *one man in three* had already been killed or wounded; and the figures were no different for most of the other British and Canadian infantry formations. And Caen still stood, uncaptured.

Alan Moorehead, now taking part in his tenth campaign, was there. He noted, that 'there was kind of anarchy in this waste, a thing against which the mind rebelled; an unreasoning and futile violence. We hid in the grey dust and waited for the shelling to stop. There seemed no point in going on. This was the end of the world, the end of the war, the final expression of man's desire to destroy. There was nothing more to see, only more dust.'[1]

A lot of young infantrymen thought pretty much the same by now – 'there seemed no point in going on'. They began to slack, go to ground immediately they came under fire, break off an attack once they were no longer covered by their own artillery barrage, or their officers and senior NCOs were wounded or killed. The fact, too, that the rifle companies were being fleshed out increasingly by reinforcements from England, who were not as well trained and steadfast as the original riflemen didn't help either. Montgomery recognized this too. He wrote to the CIGS; 'The Second Army is very strong; it has in fact reached its peak and can get no stronger. It will in fact get weaker as the manpower situation begins to hit us. Also, the casualties have affected the fighting efficiency of the divisions.'[2]

In particular the 3rd Canadian Division was singled out by senior staff officers as not carrying out its tasks efficiently or with sufficient spirit. One Corps Commander wrote to Montgomery, 'Once the excitement of the initial phase passed, however, the Div lapsed into a very nervy state … reports of enemy activity and their own difficulties were rife; everyone was too quick on the trigger and a general attitude of despondency prevailed … indeed the state of the Div was a reflection of the state of the Commander. He was obviously not standing up to the strain and showed signs of fatigue and nervousness (one almost might say fright) which were patent for us all to see.'[3]

Montgomery himself singled out the 51st Highland Division as being very poor. He signalled London. 'Regret to report that it is the considered opinion of Crocker, Dempsey* and myself that 51 Div is at present NOT repeat NOT battleworthy. It does not fight with determination and has failed in every operation it has been given to do. It cannot fight the Germans successfully.'[4]

He sacked his own protégé General Charles Bullen-Smith from command of the 51st. In his place he appointed 'General Thomas Rennie, who had escaped from St Valery back in 1940, fought all the way through the desert, and had been recently wounded again while commanding the 3rd Infantry Division. Rennie, who now had eight months to live, set about tightening up the Division's morale, which was bad.

Arriving to take over as second-in-command of the Division's 1st Gordons, Major Martin Lindsay was briefed by the new CO. 'They had lost 12 officers, including the Colonel, three company commanders and 200 men in the 35 days since the start of the campaign without achieving very much,' he was told. 'Their last attack had failed miserably.' He (the CO) was rather worried about the morale of the Battalion. The continual shelling had made a number of men 'bomb happy'.[5]

The situation was little different in the Division's 10th Highland Light Infantry – 'Hell's Last Issue'. There a returning CO who had been wounded in a recent attack assembled all his NCOs in a barn for an address. One of them, Sergeant Green, expected they would be praised a little and perhaps lectured a bit on tactics. 'Instead they were treated to a verbal attack on their lack of ability to carry out orders – their cowardly efforts during the attacks which had left so many of them alive. If they had been doing their

---

* A corps and army commander, respectively.

jobs properly, most of them would have been dead or wounded; that they were here at all was proof of their cowardice. The NCOs began to murmur ominously and the RSM had to wave his stick and threaten them.'[6]

Another new officer, Captain Brodie, who was to spend no more than three periods of about six to eight weeks with the Highland Division, during which time, 'I would be wounded not too seriously, have a good time at home as a wounded hero and return fresh to rejoin my braver and tougher friends', didn't like what he saw of his new battalion, the Black Watch. In their last unsuccessful attack they had lost heavily and the few survivors were no help in the re-formed company he now commanded. 'They had been thoroughly frightened and had lost their friends. If I had been more experienced, I would have had them posted.'[7]

But before their next attack, Brodie laid it on the line to the survivors and the 20-year-old replacements who had filled out the gaps in his company. He told them there had been nothing heroic about the old division's surrender back in 1940. Nor should they accept the stuff the newspapers wrote about throwing oneself 'at the mercy of the enemy'. It *was* shameful to surrender!

'So I told them that, while I would not hesitate to shoot anyone who ran away, I expected them to shoot me or any officer or NCO who ordered them to pack in. To my surprise this rather frightened them.'[8]

The net result was that two of the veterans – stretcher-bearers – fled and were never seen again. Hours later Brodie had received his first batch of wounds and was on his way back to 'blighty'. But his company never did run away again, though in view of the appalling casualties they suffered, it would not have been surprising if they had. By the time Caen fell, most of the rifle companies had virtually a 75 per cent turnover in personnel due to casualties. Indeed by the end of the battle in Europe, most British infantry divisions had suffered a 100 per cent casualty rate, while the Canadians had lost up to 200 per cent of their infantry, due to death, wounds, and prisoners. In May 1945, all that most infantry battalions could offer in the way of survivors of the Normandy battle would be a handful of soldiers at battalion HQ and perhaps a single soldier in each rifle company; the rest would be 18-year-old replacements.

While most infantry battalions managed to overcome the shock of the incessant shelling, attacks, and appalling casualties of the Normandy battle and 'soldier on', a few couldn't. There was, for instance, the battalion of the 49th Division which fell completely apart that June.

The battalion had been formed mainly of territorials with a few regular officers and NCOs and had spent the first two years of its war in Iceland, remote from any kind of action. Here it trained and trained, fished, played rugger and won brigade boxing matches. Two more years of training had followed back in the UK. Now after four years these fine young men in their mid-twenties, who had never fired a shot in anger, faced up to the

18-year-olds of the Hitler Youth Division, who were, like them, green-horns, save in one respect – their officers and NCOs (as we have seen) were all veterans of the fighting on the Russian front. In addition, many of these SS teenagers were fanatics; for half of them – 10,000 strong were volunteers straight from the Hitler Youth movement.

The Battalion advanced as they had been taught to advance in these four long years of training, covered by a rolling barrage of four artillery regiments, protected by tanks. But they had not calculated with the Norman terrain – the *bocage*. In a short time they had lost the tanks among the hedges and the barrage had lost them in the same fashion.

Into the woods they went. There was the high-pitched hysterical hiss of the Geman MG 42s firing a thousand rounds a minute. Snipers who had dodged the tanks popped up everywhere, picking off officers and NCOs, easily identifiable because they carried revolvers or wore nicely white-painted stripes and were linked to the radioman. There was the obscene howl and stonk of the German mortars. The 'moaning minnies', their six-barrelled electrically-fired mortar, shrieked into the afternoon sky, dragging long plumes of white smoke behind them. Casualties started to mount. Still the Battalion persisted in its first attack and then they had done it. They had turfed the SS out and were consolidating their position.

Now, however, things began to go wrong for the new boys. They were unable to evacuate their mounting casualties; the only track to the rear was extensively mined. No food could be brought up either and there was nothing to eat but the bitter iron-hard chocolate bar of the 'iron ration'. Snipers started to reappear in the deepest part of the wood, again singling out officers and NCOs. An intensive artillery and mortar barrage descended upon the hard-pressed Yorkshiremen and then the SS came again, yelling and shrieking as if they were drunk or doped, or both. And they were supported by tanks!

The infantry began to give way. Desperately their officers held them together. But there was no stopping that backwards action. Here and there there were brave men who sacrificed themselves to hold the ground they had won at such cost. But it was no use. The leaders – the officers and NCOs – were being killed and wounded all the time and the heart started to go out of the others. In the end they were driven back to where they had started, having lost some 240 men. In their first action after four years of training, they had suffered nearly 30 per cent casualties!

One week later, on Sunday, 25 June, 1944, the 49th Infantry Division was scheduled to attack again. Under a new CO, with its ranks filled out with reinforcements, the Battalion in question moved forward to its start position, plodding up a large slope covered in corn, and criss-crossed with the tracks of many armoured vehicles – German. There was absolutely no cover, but luck was with them – so far at least. They crossed the stream which bordered the field and began to climb the slope beyond. Now some mortar shells began to fall on the infantrymen coming up the slope through the trees, but casualties were light and the officers were optimistic.

They had good reason to be. The Hitler Youth was bleeding to death. It was currently being attacked by one armoured division – the 11th – and two infantry divisions, the 49th and the 15th Scottish. There were simply not enough men to cover the whole front. Hastily, as the Battalion started to dig in at their objective on the top of the height, 'Panzermeyer', as the divisional commander of the Hitler Youth, General Kurt Meyer, was nicknamed, ordered his last reserve, the Reconnaissance Battalion, to go in and do what it could.

The Reconnaissance Battalion was led by an officer after Kurt Meyer's heart, 25-year-old Gert Bremer, who from being a flunkey at Hitler's court before the war, had now seen action in half a dozen countries, winning every decoration for bravery the Third Reich had to offer. Instantly Bremer ordered what was left of his '*jungs*' (as he liked to call his teenagers paternalistically) into action. Although they had not been trained really as infantry and ammunition was short, they moved close to the British positions and set about mortaring them with frightening ferocity.

What happened next was a complete breakdown of the Battalion. The men reacted with hysterics when their comrades were hit, as officer after officer was killed or wounded. Even the firing of their own artillery set them off in a panic. Discipline collapsed. Officers and NCOs began to rip off their badges of rank so that they wouldn't be an obvious target for Bremer's infiltrators. As the battalion commander later reported to Montgomery: 'I have twice had to stand at the end of a track and draw my revolver on retreating men ... Three days running a Major has been killed ... because I have ordered him to help me in effect to stop them running during mortar concentrations.' Then he himself admitted defeat. 'I refused to throw away any more good lives.' His opinion, he stressed, was shared by two fellow commanders.[9]

Montgomery did not accept the colonel's findings. He believed there were no bad troops, just bad officers. Just as in the case of the Salerno Mutiny, he blamed the officers not the men. Forwarding his report on the matter to the War Office, he stated that the Battalion would be broken up as unfit for battle and the survivors returned to the UK. He appended a hand-written note, 'I consider the CO displays a defeatist mentality and is not a "proper chap"'.*[10]

---

* It is difficult to get any further details of this Battalion. Public records are not forthcoming and there seems to be a kind of conspiracy of silence on the matter in the area where the Battalion was recruited.

Thus the rot was stopped and those officers and men who were not 'proper chaps' disappeared into obscurity, in disgrace, or into the 'glass-houses' which were beginning to appear in Normandy now. There again 'soldiers under sentence' would be offered remission of their sentence if they went up the line. Few accepted. They preferred the harshness of the glasshouse to the swift, lethal violence of the front. ...

Now they settled down to the routine of the infantryman's life, a mixture of violent action, set against a background of long hours of relentless foot-slogging, or simply waiting for something to happen, existing in that strange limbo which some have called the 'most exclusive club in the world' – the front. Here they had their own language, their own customs, their own rituals.

They ate 'armoured pig' and 'armoured cow' (spam and corned beef), and soya links, triangular-shaped tinned sausages, bedded in fat, and made of soya beans. If they were American infantrymen, they ate 'shit on a shingle' (chipped beef on bread or toast) and 'Hitler's secret weapon', the ration D-bar, sickly sweet and unappetizing, which had a deadly effect on the bowels. Naturally both Americans and British asked – routinely – when the Compo and K-ration boxes were being opened, '*Hey, sarge, which can has got the cunt in it?*'

'Zigzag' was drunk and 'jig-jig' was to copulate. As the British Army had now been renamed the 'LA' British Army of Liberation), anything stolen, or 'found before it was lost', was now 'liberated'. 'I liberated a French bint last night,' they'd say whenever they could get down to the villages, which was not often, 'for two tins o'bully beef. Could have had her mother for another one!' Naturally with the Army being the way it was, the average infantryman mostly went back on a stretcher. The rear was reserved for the 'feather merchants' and the 'base wallahs'. '*One* man in the line' the GIs cracked, 'and six men to bring up the coca-cola!' But it was to be expected where in the infantry the situation was always either 'SNAFU' – 'situation normal, all fucked up', or 'FUBAR' – 'fucked up beyond all recognition'.

The daily life was simple, hard, very boring if they weren't actually fighting, and had a certain character about it that none of them would ever forget afterwards – those who survived. They 'stood to' at 'first light', that ugly pre-dawn time when the Germans often attacked: the whole battalion under arms and in their waterlogged foxholes that smelt of earth, sweat, shit and human misery. If nothing happened then, if they were British, they 'brewed up' on the hissing little Tommy cookers, petrol-driven cookers that sometimes were as deadly as German mines, for they exploded or caught fire routinely. If they were Americans they made their 'joe' or 'Java' by heating a canteen over the waxed paper that the rations came in. Fried bully or fat bacon, which came out of the tin in long rolls that could be unwound like toilet paper, appeared next; or if they were American the hated cold ham and egg mix or spam. Many a threatening letter was written from the front to Mr Jay C. Hormel, who owned the company in the States which made it.

Thereafter it was the thunderbox to 'take a shit' or in American GI parlance 'a crap'. Simply a pole suspended over a hole, supported by two ration boxes, 'army form blank', i.e. Government-issue lavatory paper, clutched in hand while the lines of squatting men peered into the grey dawn.

If they were not actually fighting, the day would be spent in the hundred and one tasks that the Army thought of to keep idle hands busy. They strung wire, they dug deeper holes, they planned patrols, they cleaned weapons, they cut hair (a tin bowl on the head and the clippers, wielded by an amateur barber, running round its base for the British Army's 'short back and sides'), they washed 'smalls'.

Then came the time to 'shoot the breeze', 'bullshit', 'to have the long awaited spit and a draw', savouring the issue rum, half a mug of it per day per man in the British Army when the infantryman was in the line. The US Army was officially dry, but that didn't stop the average GI. He fought his way across France on blackmarket or looted Calvados or any other kind of hooch he could lay his hands upon. For as the Tommies sang as they marched down those dead-straight, gleaming white French roads to battle that summer, 'Pissed last night, pissed the night before ... gonna get pissed tonight like we've never been pissed before.' They meant it. Many of them were drunk most of the time.

But in the midst of all their crudity, the brutality, the violence of these young men's lives at the front, devoid of home comforts, the presence of women (save whores), a kind of camaraderie, comradeship, developed that none of them would ever experience again. They all knew just how predictably short their lives really were. They all knew, too, that when it did happen and they were dead, they would soon be forgotten. Back home, wherever it as, they would mourn for a while certainly. But the civilians would never be able to comprehend their world in a million years and what it had meant to them to have been an infantryman!

For however much they might moan and groan about their dangerous lot, they knew well their worth. The 'six men who brought up the coca-cola' were worthless in their opinion. They had nothing but contempt for the men in the rear echelon sections, the clerks, the cooks, the bakers, the 'admin wallahs'. Engineers, artillerymen, tankers were respected to a certain extent. But their exposure to danger, just like that of the 'brylcreem boys' (the RAF), was of a limited nature. They had vehicles and tents in which to sleep and they were more behind the front than in it. The infantry was there for good. 'There's only one way out of the infantry, lads,' they said wryly in a bitter mixture of truth and pride, 'and that's *feet first!*'

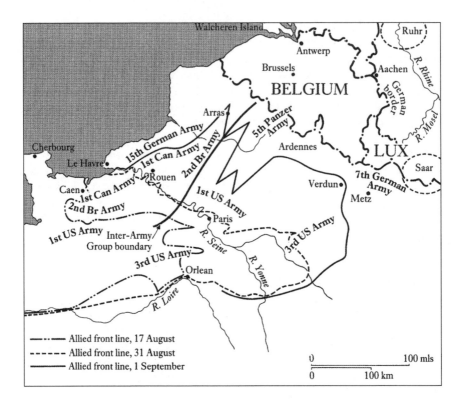

Allied breakout, August/September 1944

Only those who have served in an infantry company in combat can really understand the feeling of togetherness engendered by the common purpose and the common danger. The bliss of a mess-tin full of canned M and V stew, washed down with a mug of 'sarn't-major's char'. The sight of the 'lads' going up, burdened with the usual impedimenta of war, shovels, picks, rifles, packs (with a chipped mug hanging from each one, for the British Army fought on 'char'), and with each man carrying some private treasure looted somewhere or other – a hurricane lamp, a bucket, the odd oil stove, a feathered overlay, which we now call duvets. Clad in their wrinkled khaki, with a leather sleeveless jerkin on top, net camouflage scarves around their necks, their faces reddened and chapped by the wind, more often than not they looked like a straggle of farm labourers setting off for a long day in the fields. The 'real' soldiers were the smartly clad, well-fed and cleanly shaven 'canteen commandos' behind the line. They were just expendable men – the infantry.

As the American writer Paul Fussell, who was wounded in France while leading an infantry section of the US 103rd Division, has put it: 'Those who actually fought in the line during the war, especially if they were wounded, constitute an in-group separate from those who did not. Praise or blame does not attach: rather there is the accidental possession of a special empirical knowledge, a feeling of a mysterious shared ironic awareness manifesting itself in an instinctive scepticism about pretension, publicly enunciated truths, the vanities of learning and the pomp of authority. Those who fought know a secret about themselves' ...[11]

But now Caen fell at last. Now it was Bremer's *'jungs'* of the SS Hitler Youth who were fleeing for their lives, including that dashing General 'Panzermeyer', who would suffer the ignominy of surrendering to a 14-year-old Belgian peasant boy armed with a hunting rifle. The guts and the stubbornness of the infantry, British, Canadian and American, had paid off and the *Wehrmacht* was on the run, a beaten army streaming back to the safety of the Reich.

After them came the infantry, marching to their individual dates with destiny. Behind them they left their dead, their last resting place – in a field, a ditch, behind a barn – marked by an upturned rifle with a bullet-holed helmet hanging from it or a crude cross of boughs. Written on it in pencil or burned into the wood would be their regimental number, a name and rank, followed by those three final overwhelming letters '*KIA*' – killed in action.

Watching them go up against the thunder of the barrage, even veterans such as Wing Commander L. Nickolls of the RAF felt for them and were moved by these doomed young men. As he told the BBC war correspondent at the time: 'I think one of the things I shall never forget is the sight of the British infantry, plodding steadily up those dusty French roads towards the front, single-file, heads bent down against the heavy weight of the kit piled on their backs, armed to the teeth, they were plodding on, slowly and doggedly to the front with the sweat running down their faces and enamel drinking mugs dangling at their hips, never looking back and hardly ever looking to the side – just straight ahead and down a little at the roughness of the road; while the jeeps and the lorries and the tanks and all the other traffic went crowding by, smothering them in great billows and clouds of dust which they never even deigned to notice. That was a sight that somehow caught at your heart. ...'[12]

II

The D-Day dodgers in sunny Italy

We're the D-Day Dodgers out in Italy,
Always drinking vino, always on the spree.
Eighth Army skivers and the Yanks, We laugh at tanks.
For we're the D-Day Dodgers, in sunny Italy …
Looking round the mountains in the mud and rain.
There's lot of little crosses, some which bear no name,
Blood, sweat and toil are gone.
The boys beneath them slumber on.
These are your D-Day Dodgers, who'll stay in Italy. …

This was the bitter song of the infantry in Italy, sung to the tune of *Lili Marlene*; for now that the Army in France were grabbing all the headlines, they felt themselves forgotten men. After nearly a year of bitter fighting up the boot of Italy, they had finally captured Rome, exactly one day *before* D-Day! Its capture had naturally been overshadowed by the landings in Normandy the following day. Now they were back in the mountains once more, fighting a bitter, hard war, where gains at the cost of hundreds of lives might well be measured in a score of yards. 'The soft underbelly', Churchill had called this attack on the southern flank of the Reich, confident that it would permit easy entry into Germany. '*Tough old gut*!' was their cynical comment, as the retreating 'Teds' made them pay for every foot of ground they gained.

Those who had taken part in the original attack in Sicily had long gone, McCallum and Taylor both wounded in Sicily; the Canadian Mowatt of the 'Hasty Pees', who had broken in the South. Even that reluctant soldier Percy Castle of the old 51st Highland Division, who had told his CO he 'would soldier no more', had finally found a way out for himself. At last he had got himself a 'cushy number' – as a swimming instructor at the 8th Army's rest camp at Amalfi.

The infantry losses were terribly high. On average the rifle companies of the British and Canadian divisions had lost 31 per cent of their riflemen by the time they reached Rome. In the American rifle companies the losses were 41 per cent and those of the Poles (who fought so bravely for their hopeless cause, with their country still occupied by the Germans and the Russians, who would never leave it) were even higher – 43 per cent. That meant that nearly every second Polish soldier engaged in combat was killed or wounded!

After the great slaughter of Cassino had ended earlier in that year, they had erected their own memorial over the burial ground of their dead at Point 593. It is still there to this day and the poignancy of its inscription will never fade. It reads:

> We Polish soldiers
> For our freedom and yours
> Have given our souls to God
> Our bodies to the soil of Italy
> And our hearts to Poland ...

But as the veterans died, this forgotten army in Italy was reinforced – sparsely – by new blood from Britain, America, France, New Zealand, South Africa, Greece, even Brazil. Since the days of the Romans themselves there had never been such an army as the Allied one in Italy, with every race, colour and creed represented. In the American Fifth Army there were even Japanese fighting against the Germans in the mountains, in the form of Nisei-Americans, out to prove themselves in spite of the fact that their parents and friends had been treated so cruelly and ruthlessly on the American West Coast by the Californian authorities. In the end the Nisei Regiment would win more awards than any other comparable US outfit.*

Rifleman Bowlby, one of the 'new boys', recollected many years later the feeling of going up to the battlefield, smelling the perfume of the wild flowers on the night air, as it seeped into the three-tonner carrying them. 'Suddenly the smell changed, I got a lungful of decay. Its virulence turned the night. When it reached a pitch that made me want to vomit, the convoy stopped. The smell seeped into the truck. I jumped into the road. Here at least the polluted air had no funnel.'[1]

Now he saw his first dead, dreading the sight, but knowing he needed to see them. 'Two bodies puffed up like Michelin men ... I shot away from them up a lane. On a barbed wire fence hung a vest. Someone had arranged the sleeves in the shape of a cross. The trunk was all bloody and full of holes. The scarecrow, I thought. The Christ. What had the author

---

* In 1942 after Pearl Harbor the property of there humble Japanese farmers had been sized and they had been transported to what were really prison camps in the interior.

intended? To shock? To show man's inhumanity to man? To mock God? The lot perhaps. ...'[2]

But the dead didn't shock the old hands. He found one of them, Baker, raking over the corpses looking for a wristwatch. His face showed his distaste at Baker's cold-bloodedness and the former chuckled, as he continued with his gruesome task. 'Nothing wrong with the dead 'uns,' he growled. 'It's the live 'uns you want to worry about. They do pong a bit though.'[3]

Soon, however, the 'new boy' would become as hard as the rest, shrieking as the British 25-pounders shattered the German positions on the opposite mountain, 'Go on, kill the bastards! ... *Kill them*!' For the infantry soon became hard, even vindictive, in the harsh mountain warfare of northern Italy. Once Bowlby watched as the Germans shelled an Italian chapel, clearly marked with a red cross, which housed the battalion's wounded.'

At first the 'enemy gunners ... fired happily at nothing until a stray shell hit our ADS (advanced dressing station) ... Someone inside began ringing the bell. It drew the attention of the German gunners' observer, but not in the way intended. He simply directed *all* the guns on to the chapel. Dumb with horror we watched it struck again and again. The bell continued to ring. The rate of fire increased. Bits fell of the chapel. It seemed only a matter of time before the whole building collapsed. We listen to that bell as if our lives depended upon it. God and the Devil suddenly seemed very real. When the shelling died down, the bell was still ringing. It continued to ring for minutes after the last shell. We were too moved to say anything. We just grunted and found pieces of kit that needed attention' ...[4]

There were other 'new boys' in Italy by now, too, the men of the 10th US Mountain Division, many of them college boys or members of the National Ski Patrol, plus a handful of German-Austrian refugees, but all of them enthusiastic skiers.

The American mountain infantry that winter completely surprised the Germans and their Austrian allies, who felt they were, naturally, the masters of mountain warfare. Later one captured Austrian mountain division officer said, 'We didn't realize you had really big mountains in the United States and we didn't believe your troops could climb anything quite that awkward' (a peak in the Apennines).[5] But they could and did, moving in total silence across the sheer faces of the steep Apennine peaks, which had been sheared by prehistoric glaciers and then honed down by winter and water, carrying anything from a M1 rifle to an 80-mm mortar.

Whole battalions, 800 men strong, clawed their way up the heights to do battle, with cleated mountain boots and ice-axes distributed sparingly only to the leaders, so that the most heavily laden men could be belayed, if necessary, up the most treacherous spots. The rest, however, had only their rifle butts to belay themselves.

During one such mountain attack, the German defenders were alerted by some noise from below. At a height of 1,500 *vertical* feet, they started to roll down grenades on the attackers, raking their ranks with machine gun fire. One platoon under a young lieutenant named Loose managed to reach their objective in spite of the hail of fire and held out on a peak for 36 hours without food or water and with little ammunition. Just before his radio was shattered by enemy fire Lieutenant Loose called his CO and asked for defensive fire from below.

His CO, Colonel Jackson, asked: 'Do you realize that you are asking for fire exactly on your position?'

The brave young officer replied, 'I do. But if we don't get artillery support soon, you'll have nothing to support.'[6]

Well dug in on the peak now Loose and his men went to ground as the artillery shells thundered up from below and shattered the German counter-attack. In the end Loose fought off seven such attacks and won himself the Distinguished Service Cross for his bravery in this strange battle of the peaks. ...

But there was one group of 'new boys' on the Italian front that winter who caused more controversy than any. They were the infantry who called themselves cynically 'the invisible soldiers', the black men of the US 92nd Infantry Division, a division which was classified by the Army Commander, General Mark Clark, as 'bad', and who felt its record was 'less favourable than any of the white divisions.'[7]

As *Time* magazine wrote after the war: 'It was the hottest potato in the USA ... The 92nd was mostly a Negro outfit and the cynosure of the sensitive Negro press. Its rank and file had the handicap of less-than-average literacy and more than average superstition. The 92nd didn't learn combat discipline easily.' *Newsweek* was even more precise: 'Given the racial climate of the time, the big question was: would the Negro make the grade as a fighting soldier?'

In the event he didn't. When the Germans struck them head on in their first battle, the black men of the 92nd Infantry broke and fled the field. Two months later they were beaten again. But what is more surprising than the fact that a whole American division fled the field at a time when it was clear – even to the Germans – that there was no hope left for Germany is that the black men of the 92nd were even *prepared* to fight for the racist America of the time.

Back 'home' in the States during training the 'invisible soldiers' (called thus because the whites didn't seem to know they were there) had been constantly harassed, abused, humiliated and physically threatened, especially in the Deep South, where most of them were based. Right from the start they were shown, whenever white people deigned to deal with them, that they were third-class citizens, ranking even below the enemy, the Germans.

One sergeant of the 92nd recalled long after the war how on returning from his first leave he passed through El Paso, Texas. There 'the station restaurant was doing rush business with white civilians and German prisoners of war. There sat the so-called enemy comfortably seated, laughing, talking, making friends, with the waitresses at their beck and call. If I had tried to enter that dining-room the ever-present MPs would have busted my skull, a citizen-soldier of the United States. My morale, if I had any left, dipped well below zero.'[8]

It was no different in Italy. White soldiers warned their black 'comrades' to keep away from the white women, threatening emasculation if they caught them with Italian girls. At the same time they spread the rumour among the naive Italian peasants that these black soldiers all had tails – like monkeys. Even the Nisei, who had suffered enough racial prejudice themselves after Pearl Harbor, wanted nothing to do with the men of the 92nd Division.

But in the end they could die just as easily as their white fellow infantry men. That winter black Lieutenant Jefferson Jordan was given the task of recovering the bodies of those who had been killed in battle up on the heights (the Graves Registration teams, as they were called, were mostly black in Italy as well as in north-west Europe). 'We waited till dawn to begin our work,' he recorded much later. 'With the first crack of light I realized that every one of these bodies were black men … Bodies piled upon bodies… The bodies were stacked up in the approaches to the little mountain-top village and in the path of the village. Some were at the entrances to the houses. The British were walking over them so I had my men move them to the side.'[9]

That winter, whatever the infantryman's colour or creed, there were few who escaped their final fate, and the men of the Graves Registration Companies were kept busy at their macabre task. As one of them told a reporter from the US Army's newspaper *The Stars and Stripes*: 'Sure there were a lot of bodies we never identified. You know what a direct hit by a shell does to a guy. Or a mine, or a solid hit with a grenade even. Sometimes all we have left is a leg or a hunk of arm.

'The ones who stink the worst are the guys who got internal wounds and are dead about three weeks with the blood staying inside and rotting, and when you move the body the blood comes out of the nose and mouth. Then some of them bloat up in the sun, they bloat so big that they bust their buttons and then they get blue and the skin peels. They don't all get blue, some of them get black.

'But they all stink. There's only one stink and that's it. You never get used to it either … and after a while the stink gets into your clothes and you can taste it in your mouth. You know what I think? I think that if every civilian in the world could smell this stink, then maybe we wouldn't have any more wars. …'[10]

But the civilians never did smell that particular 'stink of death' and the slaughter went on in Italy, with the mountain tops littered with the dead of a dozen different nationalities, both foe and friend, united now in death. Most were brought down by mule, slung over the saddles of the patient little animals like sacks and herded along the tracks by Algerian muleteers, officered by a mixed group of British and French officers. For the work could not be trusted to the native troops alone. They were afraid of the dead and, if they were not checked by their officers, would often leave the bodies among the shattered rocks and crags to be covered by the snow which was now beginning to fall.

Even the New Zealanders, whom the Germans rated so highly as assault infantry, were beginning to lose heart. Watching his brigade coming out of the line that veteran Brigadier Kippenberger thought he had 'not seen men so exhausted since Flanders. Every man was plastered with wet mud up to his neck and their faces were grey'.[11]

Still he received cheery waves and smiles from his exhausted infantry, save from one platoon. 'The 18 men passed me silently, their faces utterly expressionless, and none replied when I spoke to them. I was startled.'[12]

Later their battalion commander told the Brigadier what had happened. The men were under close arrest because they had refused to go into action. Only the platoon commander and four men had gone in. The remainder had stayed in their blankets and were arrested by the RSM, who found them there, 'Such a thing was unheard of in the Division, 'Kippenberger commented sadly,'and the CO was heartbroken.[13]

But it was not only the 'Teds', the enemy, or the miserable, heartbreaking terrain, it was also the feeling among the troops in Italy that they were a forgotten army, whose exploits received scant attention in the press back home. The infantry, whatever their nationality, felt a sense of waste, loss, purposelessness. What was it all about? Why were they fighting this useless war in Italy, where, after capturing one mountain ridge at great cost, there would be another, already manned by the Germans, who never seemed to give up. Where were they going? And who cared back home?

The French, too, were afflicted by the same malaise. An inquiry into the morale of the First Free French Division, fighting in Italy, found in November 1944, 'that the soldiers of General de Gaulle were regarded [by the civilians] as an alien element, motivated above all by a taste for adventure and that ... the battles in which they had taken part were known only vaguely ... My men were disappointed to find out that no one seemed interested in them nor in what they had done.'[14]

Rifleman Bowlby, after a brief spell in hospital where he had learnt how 'to lie to attention' when the CO made his rounds and had had a brief encounter with a nymphomaniac nurse, now went back up the line with his brigade which had just suffered 220 casualties. His own platoon had been lucky, but now some of his comrades were not taking any further chances. As soon as they heard they were going into action once more, 11 men of his company promptly deserted and fled to the rear.

Later Bowlby, who had volunteered from university for the infantry, wondered if they were not the smart ones after all. For now he started to have 'gory fantasies of lying in the snow bleeding to death', after being shot by one of the snipers who infested his company's area. Once coming back from a fighting patrol and 'sweating like a pig' with the effort of it all, the old cliché flashed into his mind:

And gentlemen in England now abed
Shall hold themselves accurst they were not here.

'Would they, I wondered. Would they?'[15]

Ruefully he concluded *they wouldn't*!

But it was not only the men of the US 5th and the British 8th Armies who felt themselves to be members of 'the forgotten army'. On the other side of the world in Burma, the men of the hard-pressed Fourteenth Army under General Slim experienced the same feeling, as did their comrades of the American Army fighting alongside of them with the Chinese. Many of them had been out in the Far East for three or four years now, without the remotest chance of ever seeing their home countries again till the end of the war.

In the case of the picturesquely named 'Merrill's Marauders', the men were near to mutiny by the summer of 1944. Although Brigadier-General Merrill's men were only in action for a few months that year, they had participated in five major and thirty minor engagements. In the Myitkyina campaign, launched by General 'Vinegar Joe' Stilwell, they were never dry. At times in the constant clashes, the Japanese attackers came within 25 yards of their columns, and their commander, Merrill, suffered a series of heart attacks. His men, too, became victims of a whole range of tropical ailments.

Of the 3,000 volunteers for the Marauders, slightly more than 1,900 became ill. Of these there were 135 cases of total exhaustion and 42 cases of psychoneurosis. In addition there were 424 battle casualties. In essence, virtually every man in the outfit became a campaign statistic.

Somewhere in the course of the campaign 'Vinegar Joe' had promised the Marauders that once they captured the airfield at Myitkyina they would be relieved. But when they did capture the field, Stilwell ordered them to continue fighting. Convalescent soldiers with fevers of well over 100 degrees were ordered out of their sick beds and totally exhausted others were flung back into action.

What happened next was rapidly covered up by the US authorities. But it seems that the men got out of hand, refused orders and wouldn't fight on. The campaign was hurriedly cancelled. Withdrawn to a rest camp, the men became sullen and then violent. The officers lost control.

When they were marched back to the rear 'Vinegar Joe' refused to see them. Nor did he allow his staff to recommend them for any medals (though after the war the Marauders received six Distinguished Service Crosses and 40 Silver Stars). The Marauders were then broken up. A fine all-volunteer unit had fallen victim to the terrible conditions and the remoteness from home of the war they were fighting.

As one observer of them commented, 'The truth of the matter is that no one in the theatre seemed to have the slightest concept as to how to handle combat troops, especially the sick, disgusted, disillusioned, aggressive, overstrained Galahad (the name of the campaign) troops. No doubt 50 pretty little Indian, Chinese or Burmese prostitutes might have been the simplest solution to the whole problem.'[16]

For the Chindits, who were equally as exhausted and diseased as Merrill's Marauders, there was no withdrawing and certainly no 'pretty little Indian, Chinese or Burmese prostitutes' to solve their problems that summer. They had been flown into Burma this time and had been dropped by parachute or by glider to form fortified 'boxes' behind the Japanese lines. Naturally the Japanese had attacked the intruders with all their strength, determined to erase the 'boxes' in case they might form the nuclei for even larger forces. For this time the British were using the old Japanese tactic, which had been so successful before, of penetrating the enemy's rear and forcing him to retreat.

Orde Wingate himself was killed in an air crash on the way to one of the 'boxes' and the hub around which the whole bold enterprise revolved disappeared. No longer could he exert pressure on New Delhi to keep the 'boxes' so well supplied and be given first priority. The Japanese seemed to sense that the days of the Chindits were numbered and they redoubled their efforts. Bitter, almost hand-to-hand fighting followed in which no quarter was given or expected.

The future writer John Masters, then a major in the Gurkha Rifles and commanding one of Wingate's columns, afterwards described a character-istic episode as the fighting reached its climax. 'The enemy began to use his heavy mortar. Its shell weighed about 60 pounds and when it landed on a weapon pit, it saved the need for burial parties ... Every day the padre moved across the Deep sector under sniping, speaking to the men in the trenches, pausing here and there to pick up a handful of yellow earth and sprinkle it over the torn "grave" and say a short prayer.

'The rain now fell steadily. The Deep sector looked like Passchendaele – blasted trees, feet and twisted hands sticking up out of the earth, bloody shirts, ammunition clips, holes half-full of water, each containing two pale, huge-eyed men, trying to keep their rifles out of the mud, and over all the heavy, sweet stench of death from our own bodies and entrails lying unknown in the shattered ground, from Japanese corpses on the wire, or fastened, dead and rotting, in the trees. At night the rain hissed down in total darkness, the trees ran with water, and beyond the devastation, the jungle dripped and crackled.'[17]

Against the background of this lunar landscape the Japanese made their final, all-out assault on his command, men of the Cameronians and the King's Own. First they opened up a hellish bombardment, which made Masters 'ready to vomit', for it 'was more than human flesh could stand'.

Just before the end of the bombardment, as the Japanese massed for the attack, Major Heap of the King's Own stumbled into Masters's dug-out, his face streaked and bloody and exhibiting the strain. 'We've had it, sir,' he said. 'They're destroying all the posts, direct hits all the time ... all machine guns knocked out, crews killed ... I don't think we can hold them if ... the men are ...'

Masters didn't wait to hear what the men were. 'I knew. They were dead, wounded or stunned.' Immediately he ordered another column of the Cameronians to rush over the ridge to take over the Deep.

Soon they were arriving at the double, faces streaked with sweat as they manhandled their weapons and equipment across the high ridge, as a heavy tense silence fell over the position. But still the Japanese did not come. Twilight fell. The survivors of the King's Own were ordered out of their trenches relieved by the panting, harassed Cameronians. Masters watched them file by. 'They staggered, many were wounded, others carried wounded men, their eyes wandered, their mouths drooped open. I wanted to cry but dared not, could only mutter, "Well done ... well done," as they passed.

'The minutes dragged, each one a gift more precious than the first rain,' Masters recalled, as he waited tensely for the Japanese to attack, while his Jocks hastily strung new wire and piled up supplies of ammunition. Two new machine gun posts were set up on the crest of the hill held by the Cameronians. All was ready. *But where were the Japs?*

'With a crash of machine guns and mortars, the battle began. All night the Cameronians and the Japanese 43rd Division fought it out. Our machine guns ripped them from the new position. Twice the Japanese forced into the barbed wire with Bangalore torpedoes and the blasting rain of the mortars wiped them out. At 4 a.m., when they launched their final assault to recover their bodies, we had defeated them ...'[18]

'The Japs were either dead, buried, or had packed up ... it had been a wonderful show'

They were all there now, fighting and beating the Japanese. They weren't particularly fashionable infantry regiments. Not the classy Guards or the Rifle Brigade. Just simple, ordinary run-of-the-mill line battalions: the Royal West Kents, the Worcesters, the DLI, the Royal Scots, the Royal Welch Fusiliers, Dorsets, Norfolks, Cameronians and the like. But now this summer of 1944 they had at last got the measure of the super soldier, the Jap. No longer would they run as the Royal Scots had in what now seemed another age. They stood and dug their heels in and in the end it would be the Jap who would admit defeat – in spite of his vaunted Bushido code of conduct – and run from the battlefield.

This time it was the Japanese infantry who were afraid. Just before his battalion went into action Lieutenant Seisaku Kameyama told his men, 'Keep your heads, keep cool. If you want to find out just how cool you are feeling, put your hands inside your trousers and feel your penis – if it is hanging down, it is good.' The lieutenant promptly tested his own advice 'But it was shrunk up so hard I could hardly grasp it. More than 30 soldiers did the same thing, then looked at me curiously, but I kept a poker-face. I said, "Well mine's down all right. If yours is shrunk up, it's because you're scared."

'Then a young soldier said to me, "Sir, I can't find mine at all. What's happening to it? "With this everyone burst out laughing and I knew I had got the confidence of the men.'[1]

By nightfall only 18 of those 30 young Japanese soldiers would be left.

After the failure of their first daylight attack, the Japanese tried the scare tactics and tricks which had served them so well before during the hours of darkness. Creeping close to the British lines, they cried urgently, 'Hey! Johnny, let me through, let me through. The Japs are after me, they're going to get me!' Then they commenced shouting from all directions, hoping to draw an answering call which would give away the British positions. When this trick failed, they tried another old one; firing single shots with long pauses in between in the hope that some nervous British soldier would fire back. Again their tricks failed to draw fire.

Thereafter they resorted to sniping, which again played on the defenders' nerves; for they felt lone Japs had found gaps in their lines, and where one Jap could go, many could follow.

For most of that first night Captain Arthur Campbell of the Royal West Kents prayed and hoped that none of his company would give away their positions. They didn't, but finally 'they heard the scuffling in the road and knew that the attack was launched. The Japs came in as silently as they could; they wore gym shoes and any part of their equipment that might clink in the darkness was muffled with cloth or removed. But even with the sounds of the shells falling behind them, the men could hear the Japs scrambling up the bank and the loosened stones falling back on the hard surface of the road.'[2]

They attacked in large numbers and for once they were quiet. This time there were none of the blood-curdling yells, the bugles blowing, the shrieks which were their custom in an attack. This time they suddenly appeared out of the glowing darkness, slant-eyed and moon-faced, right in front of the British positions. 'One of them appeared at the end of Scudder's rifle,' Campbell recalled after the battle, 'and he shot him dead. Then came another and another so that Scudder was busy with his rifle and Bobby with his Tommy gun, and Hall left his wireless set to join the fray. All along the top of the bank was a crowd of seething, cursing, sweating men in close combat, killing, maiming, wounding. Then the defenders slowly became aware that there were fewer of the enemy up against them, until there was only one here, who had been left behind, or another there, more determined than his comrades.'[3] The West Kents had beaten them and now 'there was silence in the darkness, except for the groans of the wounded and the rustling of the bushes as the last defeated Jap made his way back through the jungle where he had come from'.[4]

A day later the West Kents counter-attacked the battered ruins of Kohima, in spite of the fact that they, like the rest of the infantry there, had one-third of their men sick or wounded. Indian sappers were pressed into service with them as infantry. For every man capable of holding a rifle was needed in the attack.

As soon as the attack jumped off, two Japanese machine guns on the flank opened up a murderous fire. Men dropped everywhere. The assault began to bog down almost at once, as yet more Japanese joined in, pinning the attacking infantry to a slope. But the Japanese had not reckoned with Lance-Corporal Harman. Quite casually, with the enemy bullets plucking at the dirt around his feet, he advanced, pulling two grenades from his belt and, in real Errol Flynn style, ripping the pins out with his teeth. When he was 30 yards away from the shot-up building from where the machine gun fire was coming, he lobbed both grenades and ran swiftly for the shelter of a wall.

There was a muffled crump, a scream, a yelp of pain and then Harman rushed in. There were two single shots. A few minutes later Lance-Corporal Harman sauntered out of the smoking building with a Japanese machine gun over his shoulder. The attack went on, the men breaking into a great cheer as they doubled forward to the kill. 'In a moment, Lieutenant Wright's Indian sappers were up against the building, blasting at the walls,' Captain Campbell reported afterwards, 'The men streamed in after them, shooting and bayoneting as they went. Then all was confusion, with cursing, sweating, struggling men killing each other in the narrow confines, among the stores and crates and in among the ovens. Donald, who led the attack on the first building, soon cleared it of the enemy and climbed up on the crates so that he could see what was going on around him. One by one he saw the buildings empty as his men came out, smeared with blood, with clothing scorched and torn, all exhausted with the nervous tension of the attack, the horror of the bayoneting and the exertion of hand-to-hand combat.'[5]

But all the Japanese resistance was not broken and again Lance-Corporal Harman went into action without orders, carrying out a one-man war. He ran into the bakery, where the Japanese were hiding in the ovens. Almost immediately he was shot at from two ovens. But luck was still on his side. He dodged the bullets and ran back to fetch some grenades.

Now he worked his way from oven to oven. Pulling out a grenade which had a four-second fuse, he would count to three, lift the oven lid, throw in the grenade and press the lid back closed tight once more. A muffled scream would follow and another Japanese sniper would be torn to shreds in his iron tomb. This he did nine times until all resistance was broken. Then grabbing a badly wounded Japanese under each arm, he staggered outside once more to the wild cheers of his comrades.

The Japs had had enough. The little huts, called *bashas*, in which the remainder were hiding were now blazing fiercely. It was either make a run for it or be burned alive. They decided to take the chance and were shot down one by one ruthlessly by the waiting infantry. One stuck it out to the very last moment as the firing died away and a heavy silence fell over that scene of carnage, broken only by the moans of the wounded. Then he, too, made a run for it. But, as Campbell noted, 'he had stayed too long; his clothes were on fire and, as he ran, he tore at them desperately in jerky, agonized movements. He hurled himself into a small puddle on the ground hoping that the water would put out the fire. But the puddle was too shallow and he lay screaming and scrabbling in the mud until Mathews put a bullet into his body to take away the pain ...'[6]

Thus the cruel slaughter went on, as the Japanese, who had Kohima completely surrounded, now went over to constant shelling and sniping, so that the men had to remain in their slit trenches and dug-outs nearly all the time, eating, fighting, sleeping, defecating – and dying – in their muddy grave-like holes.

The Japanese 'evening hate', as the troops now called the evening bombardment, borrowing the terminology of the old war, for they were now living in conditions just like the Flanders trenches, started punctually every afternoon at four-thirty. Thus it was that the cooks could calculate to the minute when it would be safe to issue the rations to the men in the foxholes; for the Japanese were only 40 yards away from the British perimeter in some places and they needed the cover of the early tropical darkness to avoid being seen.

So they would crawl from position to position dragging with them dixies of stew and potatoes and the most important container of all, that holding the tea. Tea was very precious because of the lack of water and its distribution was supervised by a colour sergeant, who rationed it strictly. There was just enough to allow each man two mouthfuls. Then the cooks would be gone, crawling back the way they had come, hoping they would make it before the evening hate started, leaving the men to last another 24-hours without food or drink.

It was particularly hard on the wounded, who had to remain in their slit trenches (for nowhere was really safe from the Japanese). They were visited by the doctors and padres, but otherwise they lay, fearing they might well be hit again, untended in their holes, with rusty ration cans to be used as their lavatories.

Once Campbell went to visit one of his fellow officers called Bobby, who had been badly wounded and lay next to another pit filled with other rank wounded. He found him reading his Bible, the stench of blood and rotting wounds pervading the area, with a pistol on his chest. Campbell found his friend smiling and cheerful in spite of the fact that he was in bad pain. Before he left he asked Bobby why he kept a pistol on his chest.

Cheerfully the wounded officer replied, as if it were the most obvious thing in the world, 'Oh, that's for me, in case the Japs get in.'[7]

For 13 more days and 13 more nights Bobby would lie there, racked with pain, pistol on chest, waiting for the Japs to come, for now the enemy was making an all-out effort to recapture Kohima. They infiltrated within the shrinking perimeter, pushing in as close as 100 yards of the Royal West Kents' command post. They came even closer to the dressing station, which housed 600 wounded, who were just as likely to be wounded again or killed as the men holding the front. The Indian non-combatants panicked and flooded the dressing station, completely out of control and shouting that the Japanese were right behind them. For an hour or so while British officers restored order, the dressing station, which reeked of blood, stale sweat and festering wounds, was in complete uproar, 'a shambles of wailing wounded, struggling stretcher-bearers, stampeding, fear-struck men in tattered uniforms, a hellish babble of terror and dismay', as Campbell recorded.

But the perimeter held and the panic passed and the battle continued, though for the Royal West Kents there was new hope in the air. Battalion headquarters had received a message that same morning that relief was on the way. Infantry, supported by tanks, was breaking through, driving the enemy back on the road that led to their hard-fought positions.

Yet another brigadier of the British 2nd Infantry Division to which they all belonged was hit, making him the third and last one to be wounded. Indeed of the Division's nine commanders, two had been killed and most of the others wounded, just as a high proportion of the company and platoon commanders had been killed or wounded. But still the Japanese could not break in. Indeed their own resistance was beginning to weaken seriously. Facing the Royal Berkshires and the Royal Welch Fusiliers, the Japs had actually turned and run. All the same they were as cruel in defeat as they had been in victory.

Probing their own front, after the Japs had fled, the men of the Royal Welch Fusiliers found yet another grim reminder of the essential bestiality of the Japanese. Tied to a tree was the dead body of a soldier whose shoulder flashes indicated he belonged to the Royal West Kents. In his battledress there were a dozen rips and slits. The Japanese infantry had used him as a living dummy for their ghoulish bayonet practice!

But the unknown killers had vanished, leaving only their dead behind. As one of the British recorded: 'The Japs were either dead, buried or had packed up ... It had been a wonderful show. All was quiet and someone thrust a bacon sandwich into my hand. I have eaten a lot of bacon sandwiches since then, but no bacon sandwich has ever tasted quite so good again.'[8] So the living rested, ate, and took their time out of war among the dead.

The Dorsets took the district commissioner's tennis court, for which they had been fighting for 16 long, bloody days. They and the Japanese defenders had become personal enemies and at dusk, with the two lines only yards part from each other, the Japanese had taunted them, calling across no-man's land: 'Have you stood to yet?' and the like. Now the Dorsets went to work with a will to kill the last of the Japanese, buried in deep bunkers and holes. They tossed in grenades as they moved from hole to hole or thrust home 25 pounds of explosive, attached to the end of a six-foot-long bamboo stick, slaughtering the defenders one by one without mercy, without even shedding a single thought at the matter. By the summer of 1944 in Burma, for the infantry at least, the only 'good Jap was a dead 'un'.

Now at last there was silence and peace around that tennis court, where before the war the colonial administrators had played gentle tennis and sipped their 'G and Ts', served by attentive white-clad servants; and where most recently two regiments, one British and one Japanese, had fought for the possession of a few square yards of shattered ground. 'Now all that's left is the litter,' the BBC reporter broadcast to the people at home at the time, 'piles of biscuits, dead Japs, black with flies, heaps of Jap ammunition, broken rifles, silver from the District Commissioner's bungalow. And among it, most incongruous of all, there's an official photographer who used to photograph Mayfair lovelies saying: "Move a little to left please." And there's another chap reading an Edgar Wallace thriller in a Sunday newspaper. Yes, today's been a great day for the battalion. Here's hoping they hold the tennis court through the night.'[9]

They did. For the first time in six weeks not a single shot was fired in that part of Kohima. Elsewhere, however, the Japanese were still resisting, though they were critically short of men. The commander of the Japanese 31st Infantry Division threw in anyone capable of bearing arms. Cooks and clerks – they were all shipped up into the crumbling Japanese line now. As one lieutenant of the 31st's 58th Regiment recorded afterwards: 'Even the invalids and the wounded were driven to the front to help supply manpower. Even those with broken legs in splints were herded into battle, malaria cases too. I have seen these going forward with yellow faces, the fever still in their bodies. I saw one man, whose shoulder had been shattered by a bullet, stagger forward to the front. Some of the wounded who were over 40 fondly hoped that they would be sent home, but even they were sent forward.'[10]

But it wasn't only the Japanese who were in a bad way. Most of the Second Division's infantry companies were down to 30 men and some battalions were reduced to 100 men, with losses amounting to a staggering 70 or 80 per cent! Captain Campbell described the relief of the Royal West Kents and the Indian sappers thus: 'The first to leave were the walking wounded, limping along the road in tidy groups, each with a leader ... As they hobbled away the enemy fired on them ... with automatics. Some of the men fell off the road as they were wounded again, but only a few stretcher-bearers stopped to examine the bodies. Some of these were left lying, now dead, others were carried on, among them a young soldier with both legs hanging limp, whom a resourceful orderly loaded into a wheel-barrow.'[11]

Meanwhile the fresh infantry of the Royal Berkshires slipped into the positions still held by the handful of unwounded survivors. The newcomers joked about the appearance of the West Kents, pulled their legs about their straggly beards and torn, stained uniforms. But the West Kents were in no mood for the usual banter of an infantry relief. As Campbell noted, 'They were too tired for humour, they just wanted to get out, back to a good meal and then sleep, sleep, and more sleep ...'[12]

It was nearly over now, as the half-starved Japanese began to pull back towards Imphal. The Durham Light Infantry in the van of the British attack were held up by a pathetic handful of enemy wounded from the nearest hospital. The latter had been ordered to fight to the last man. The Durhams obliged them. They died where they fought – to the last man. Japanese discipline, renowned for its ferocity, where officers slapped sergeants for the slightest offence and the NCOs slapped their private soldiers for having a button undone, started to break down. As a Japanese war correspondent noted: 'At Kohima we were starved and then crushed ... discipline went ... then the troops wavered and we fell into disorder ... The men were barefoot and ragged and threw away everything except canes to help them walk. Their eyes blazed in their lean bodies ... all they had to keep them going was grass and water ... At Kohima we and the enemy were close together for over 50 days and could watch each other's movements, but while they got food, we starved.'[13]

It was the same old song that the once triumphant, arrogant Germans were singing in Italy and north-west Europe, forgetting that back in the great days of victory *they* had had plenty of food and good equipment. In defeat both the Japanese and the Germans blamed their deficiencies, instead of the bravery and drive of the enemy who was beating them. So they retreated steadily, racked by hunger and malaria, eating their horses and mules, just as the Chindits had done in 1943, leaving behind them a trail of bloody faeces (for they all had dysentery) and dead bodies to mark their passing. Curiously enough those who committed suicide in their despair (shooting themselves by placing their rifle the length of their body and pulling the trigger with the big toe or blowing themselves up with a grenade) always laid themselves next to the bodies of others before they did so. It was as if even in death, the Japanese, coming from such a crowded island, needed company.

Lance-Corporal Harman, the hero of the battle of the ovens, was killed in action. Later they would award him a VC. Like most of those earned in Burma, it was given to a soldier who never knew he had been awarded his country's highest decoration for bravery. General Saito, who commanded the division against which he had fought and which finally killed the brave young infantryman, was sacked for his failure to hold the British. Of course, he blamed his disgrace on the stupidity of his army commander. He failed to attribute it to the courage and superior tactics of his enemies, who had chased him out of Kohima.

General Slim, the commander of the 'Forgotten Army', went up front and viewed the rusting and burnt-out tanks he had ordered destroyed in the shameful retreat of his division two and a half years before. Then the Japs had been supermen. Now they had been proven otherwise. His soldiers 'had seen them run. They had smashed for ever the legend of the invincibility of the Japanese Army. Neither our men nor the Japanese soldier himself believed in it any longer.'[14]

Now as the big bluff General walked among the rusting remains of his tanks, resavouring 'in imagination the bitter taste of defeat, I could raise my head. Much had happened since then. Some of what we owed we had paid. Now we were going to pay back the rest – *with interest!*'[15]

In the end, the battle simply petered out, as what was left of the Japanese rearguard vanished into the jungle, leaving over half their number dead on the road to Imphal, which was now completely in British hands. The Japanese had suffered their greatest defeat of the war so far. The shameful disasters of Hong Kong, Malaya, Singapore and Burma back in 1942 had been atoned for. In one of the major battles of World War Two in the Far East, the Japanese had been soundly beaten. They would never march on India again. But the victory left a sour taste in the mouths of those who survived in the 2nd British Infantry Division – the men of the 'Crossed Keys'.*

The media back in India were not allowed to proclaim their triumph, in order not to offend the Indian politicians of the Congress Party. Ever since 1942 they had protested at maintaining a white British formation in India and Burma at the local taxpayers' expense. So the powers that be ordered that the victory at Kohima be attributed to two brigades of the Indian Army which had fought alongside the Second. Objectives captured by British troops were stated to have been taken by Indian soldiers. The censors also forbade any mention being made of the renegade Gandhi Brigade, which had fought for the Japanese and which had been decisively routed. The Gurkas who fought them, lacking the delicate sensibilities of their political masters, back in New Delhi, knew a traitor when they saw one and slaughtered the ones they captured without scruple until they were ordered to be 'nice' to the sepoys of the King Raj who fell into their hands in Japanese uniform.

So they buried their dead, who had paid the price for victory, 1,287 of them, men who would never be returning home now. Each grave had the name, rank and regiment of the dead man, and in due course there would be private memorial plaques set up by sorrowing relatives after the war, ranging from the trite to the moving, 'Our beloved son who died that freedom might live', or 'Good night, Daddy'.

Many who fell have no known grave. They died and rotted and merged into the fetid ground, with nothing to bear witness to the fact that they fought and died in this remote land, so far away from home. Other monuments to the dead were set up by various regiments which had fought there. Mostly they have the regimental insignia above the names of those who fell in the ranks of the regiment: a curiosity now to most of those who chance upon them, as they peer at fading inscriptions in a language they do not understand to regiments which have long ceased to exist.

---

* On account of the divisional insignia.

'We broke our ass for nothing', ex-infantryman Norman Mailer, who, too, fought against the Japanese in the Pacific, makes his disgruntled Sergeant Croft say in the novel *The Naked and the Dead*. Perhaps one can say the same of the infantry of the 2nd British Division, who fought and died at Kohima. Their struggle has been long forgotten, not only by the Burmese in whose earth they lie, but by those at home for whom they fought. Who remembers Lance-Corporal Harman, VC, of the battle of the ovens now or 'Bobby' lying in pain for 13 days and 13 nights with his cocked pistol across his chest, waiting to kill himself if the Japs overran his trench? *Who*?

But at the time they thought they had achieved a great victory. So survivors of the 2nd Infantry had a rough stone monument erected to their dead comrades. On it they had carved those words of Professor Edmonds', which have been carved on monuments to dead British soldiers often enough these last 70-odd years. They are trite and well known, but in 1944 they seemed significant enough, perhaps even moving.

When you go home,
Tell them of us and say
For their tomorrow,
We gave our today ...

IV

Zigzag and jig-jig

The great rush across France and Belgium had stopped. The supply routes stretched back over 200 miles to the beaches. Petrol and ammunition, hauled by truck from Normandy, were in short supply. The weather had finally broken too. At the front it rained, a thin, cold, bitter grey drizzle. The fields where the infantry were dug in turned to mud and swamp; and before them lay the Reich.

The Americans occupied northern France, Belgium and Luxembourg where those countries bordered on Germany. Before them on the brooding wooded heights along the rivers Moselle, Sauer* and Our were the dragons' teeth and pillboxes of the Siegfried Line, on which the Tommies had boasted they would hang their 'dirty washing, mother dear' so long before. The British and the Canadians were further north in that part of Belgium and Holland that is flat and featureless, interspersed with dikes and canals, waterlogged and grey, the slag heaps of the coalmines of the region dominating the bleak horizon.

While the generals fumed because the advance had stopped and the Germans had time to man the Siegfried Line, calling up all available reserves of men and munitions to make up for the débâcle of Normandy, which had virtually destroyed the *Wehrmacht* in the west, the infantry relaxed. They were tired after four months of intensive fighting and their losses had been high. When, for instance, the horsey-looking General Thomas of the British 43rd Infantry Division held a parade to award decorations for bravery to his men, of the 55 men scheduled to be present only 28 appeared. The rest had been killed or severely wounded. As the divisional history recorded, 'the price of victory had indeed been heavy'.[1]

So the British infantry enjoyed their time out of war, while their commanders fumed and tried to make up for the heavy losses they had

---

* 'Sûre' in French.

suffered, flooding the battalions with 18- and 19-year-old reinforcements straight from the depots and men from the 50th, that veteran division of the Desert and Sicily, and the 59th Divisions, which had been broken up to provide replacements. Back home they were now calling up 45-year-olds for the infantry. The barrel was about scraped clean. What 'les Tommies' wanted was 'wallop, bints and good grub' – anything rather than the tinned Compo rations they had been living off these last months. Egg and chips, washed down with fizzy Stella Artois or Jupiter beer – 'real gnat's piss' – were in great demand.

'Wallop and bints' weren't too difficult to find either. In the cities to the rear, Brussels, Loudvain (where Montgomery had once fought so desperately with his 'Iron Division', the 3rd) and Malines there were plenty of 'cafés' where in the back rooms there were peroxided blondes enough, ready for a quick 'jig-jig' – for a price. Along the 'Boul Max' or the Rue Neuve in Brussels and behind the *Gare du Nord*, there were hundreds of whores who the month before had been servicing the *Wehrmacht*, plying their trade. Hard-eyed ladies, lips scarlet and full of fake concupiscence, dressed in wooden, wedge-heeled shoes, short rabbit jackets or coats made out of Army blankets, they stood in every doorway, flashing their torches to illuminate their loins, prepared for a 'jig-jig' there and then.

Naturally the VD rate soared, as more and more whores flooded the big cities behind the line. In Ghent alone, prior to the invasion a quiet, somewhat dreary provincial town, there were 200 registered and 700 unregistered prostitutes by the autumn of 1944; and nearly all of its 146 cafés – 'Cafe Texas', 'Cafe Alaska' and the like – functioned as whorehouses. According to the correspondent of *Newsweek* magazine, who had set up his headquarters in the *Hotel Scribe* with the rest of the accredited journalists, the pavement outside 'had all the better aspects of Custer's last stand'. The street was lined with US Army jeeps, whose embattled drivers were assaulted by battalions of streetwalkers. 'The women of Paris are still very smart,' he recorded. 'They dress fit to kill and make up thickly but on the whole artistically. ... But Chanel No. 5 doesn't smell the same as it did in 1940, although the "feelthy picture man" is still there.'[2]

Most of the young infantrymen had still been in school back in 1940 and Chanel No. 5 didn't interest them one bit. They just wanted to 'get their rocks off' ... 'dip their wick' ... before they went back into the line.

'French girls are easy to get, what with American cigarettes and chocolate and us being heroes in their eyes,' one American infantryman wrote home that autumn, 'so I'm not going to be choosey from now on and get my fun where I can get it while I'm still alive. And to hell with tomorrow – it may never come ... I hear penicillin will cure 95 per cent of VD cases in one day. Do any of your doctors use it yet? But don't worry about me, I'll try to be careful.'[3]

Penicillin did not cure VD in a day. It took eight injections spread over 48 hours to do so. The result was that an infected soldier might well be in 'dock' for nearly a week, and with infantrymen as short as they were, the Army couldn't afford that. Strict procedures were laid down, especially in the British Army, to prevent the disease. Before intercourse a soldier had to sign his name in the book kept by the medical orderlies to certify that he had received a condom, plus a prophylatic kit. After intercourse, complete naturally with 'french letter', he was then supposed to recourse to the nearest 'Green Cross station' – 'pro station' to the Americans – where his organ would be placed in an antiseptic muslin bag. In other centres they used antiseptic fluids, which the soldier, standing at a metal trough, was supposed to squirt into his organ.

Naturally in the heat of the fray many a young soldier forgot the precautions. Often the result was a dose, perhaps even what the British soldier called cynically 'a full house', being both syphilis and gonorrhea – 'siff and guntac'. The punishment was both stiff and painful. The sufferer would be harshly treated in the military hospital to which he was sent. In the 'pox ward', the kid gloves were off. Pumped full of penicillin for 48 or 86 hours, he would then be subjected to the dreaded 'umbrella', a razor-sharp catheter which was inserted into his urethra to clear away any possible lesions. Thereafter he would urinate blood and urine in six different directions and wish he had never even heard the name woman before being sent back up the line; or if he were unlucky to the 'stockade' or 'glasshouse' for 30 days. By then VD was classified as 'a self-inflicted wound' – and there were enough infantrymen already at the front trying to get out of combat by shooting off their little fingers or big toes; or even 'losing' their false teeth. A man who couldn't eat, of course, couldn't fight.

En masse these young infantrymen, British, American, Canadian, were a fairly unprepossessing spectacle as they hurried out of their 'three-tonners' and 'deuce-and-a-halfs' to begin their 36 hours of debauchery in Paris's 'Pig Alley' (*Place Pigalle*) or in Brussels' *Rue Neuve*. Their life at the front had brutalized them. They got drunk. They whored. They fought. They got sick to their stomachs. Their tempers were short. They had lived off their nerves for months now and they were highly strung, quick to take offence.

The Redcaps and the American 'Snowdrops'* were very strict with them. The American military police, in particular, didn't waste words. A club across the back of the head, and the troublemaker was inside the 'paddy wagon', heading for the nearest guard-room. But offenders rarely remained there long. Riflemen were always in short supply and the MPs reasoned that the next battle would soon take the piss and vinegar out of these troublesome young men.

---

* On account of their white-painted helmets.

Some of course deserted, tempted by the life of the big European cities. At one time there were an estimated 20,000 deserters in Paris alone and at the height of the Battle of the Bulge in December 1944, thousands of new deserters flocked to Brussels to live off the black market and whores. But most went 'back up' of their own volition. Pockets empty, head aching, hollow-eyed and wan, morose or blind drunk, silent or talkative, depressed or boastful, they would tumble into the waiting trucks from division and tamely allow themselves to be driven back to the slaughter – the sharp end. Behind them they would leave the 'canteen commandos', the 'staff wallahs', the clerks with the 'cushy billets', the whores, the pimps, the black marketeers, the gracious ladies serving coffee and 'donuts' in the canteens, noting, those who could still see anything, how the people thinned out the closer they got to the front. Until there it was – the silent hills ahead which were Germany, the weary men dug in in the fields and at the sides of the tracks, the boxlike ambulances parked behind barns with that ominous notice, giving them priority, in the windscreens, 'carrying casualties', the waiting guns dug in behind the woods – *the front*!

That autumn before it all started, Captain Robert Merriam of the US 9th Army painted an almost pastoral picture of life at the front. Travelling from Luxembourg to Belgium, where his headquarters were located, he noted, 'All was peaceful, farmers in the fields along the road were ploughing their fields for the winter fallow and some were taking in the last of the summer harvest; cattle were grazing lazily.'[4]

Once his jeep driver stopped along the River Our and pointed to the Siegfried Line on the opposite bank of the tiny river. All was silent and no one fired at the two lone Americans standing there on the narrow valley road. 'Have to be careful at night,' the driver warned. 'Krauts sneak over patrols just to make a social call. Ambushed a jeep in daylight the other day and got a new battalion commander. Hell, he didn't even have a chance to report in! But the only shelling we get is when Jerry goes to the latrine. Seems like they have a machine gun and a mortar there and each one fires a burst – hope they don't get diarrhoea!'[5]

But as the Anglo-Americans started to re-group and prepared to attack into the Reich before the winter clamped his icy grip on that remote frontier, with its fir-clad steep hills and lonely valley villages, the enemy was already ready and waiting for them. In that brief respite when the Allies had been forced to wait for fresh supplies to reach them, the German High Command had done wonders. New 'people's grenadier' divisions had been thrown together from the survivors of the French débâcle and youngsters called hurriedly to the colours. The German war industry had performed miracles, too. In September 1944, German industry produced more tanks, aircraft and guns than they had ever done before, despite the fact that the country's major industries lay shattered and in ruins after nearly two years of intensive Allied bombing.

But the sudden strength of this new German Army, which had appeared shattered for all time to the Allies, was unknown to the public back home – and apparently to the Allied senior commanders, too. They predicted – Eisenhower among them – that the 'boys' would be going home for Christmas. The press proclaimed that Germany was now defended mainly by the *Volkssturm*, the new German Home Guard, 'made up of old men, stomach cases, cripples with glass eyes and wooden legs'.[6] It made a good story and the people at home felt that Hitler's Reich was at last scraping the bottom of the barrel. It wouldn't be long now.

The GIs, who were beginning to probe the first fortifications of the *Westwall*, as the Germans called the Siegfried Line, from south in Trier right up to Aachen on the Dutch–German border, were of a different opinion. 'I don't care if the guy behind the gun,' one of them was quoted as saying, 'is a syphilitic prick who's a hundred years old – he's still sitting behind eight feet of concrete and he's still got enough fingers to press triggers and shoot bullets.'[7] Real estate in Germany suddenly started to get expensive that September.

All along that frontier the defenders began to make the Anglo-Americans pay a high price for their temerity in crossing over on to the 'holy soil of the Reich', as they called it. The last great French city before Germany, Metz held out for three bloody months against Patton and his whole 3rd Army and twice 'Blood an' Guts' had to threaten to sack a corps commander to make him attack again. At the other end of the front, Aachen similarly stopped the US 1st Army for six weeks. It took three whole US divisions, including the famed 'Big Red One', before the single German division defending the old Imperial city withdrew and left Aachen to the Americans.

On 16 November, 1944, the US 1st Army launched its great attack between these two cities, Aachen and Metz, with its objective the Rhine near Cologne. Basically the idea was that if the 1st's division struck hard everywhere, the German defence would crack at one spot or another. There the 1st would break through and drive in full strength for the Rhine.

On that morning, after an 80-minute artillery preparation, 'Operation Q' commenced: the massed bombing attack of nearly 2,000 bombers and lighter-bombers from the US 8th Air Force and 1,188 heavy bombers from the RAF in England. This mighty armada swamped the German rear areas in the Eifel and Rhineland, almost wiping out the cities of Duren and Julich. Then the infantry went into the attack, confident that nothing could stop them after such a massive attack.

In the Hürtgenwald, 50 square miles of rugged, wooded hills south of Aachen, the Germans stopped them dead. Already the American 9th and 28th Infantry Divisions had bled there in what they called 'the death factory' and which would eventually go down in US military history as 'the green hell of the Hürtgen'. For the Germans had prepared their defences well in that remote, inaccessible region. Their cannon had long been zeroed in on all conceivable targets; there were mines and booby traps everywhere; machine gun posts well dug in to cover every trail in the deep forests – and the weather was terrible. Freezing fog or a thin, bitter rain all the time until the snows came late in November, with visibility virtually zero all the time so that Allied air support was nearly impossible. It was the same with the tanks. They could be rarely used in the forests and on steep, muddy trails. In essence this was an infantryman's war: the individual German 'stubble-hopper', as he called himself cynically, and the 'foot-slogger' of the US infantry.

In the Hürtgen, on account of the terrain, the average GI had to do his thinking and fighting without a senior NCO or officer to command and guide him. He had to withstand the freezing misery of his foxhole, the lack of hot food and drink, the fear and worry, the constant depletion of the meagre human resources that he had brought with him from the United States. And time and time again, the values and skills that American society provided, both civilian and military, failed him or proved totally inadequate.

It was not that the average American infantryman was unpatriotic. In general most GIs thought their country far superior to anything they had seen in Europe. Nor was he a coward. There were deeds of great daring and bravery carried out in those grim, dripping forests in the five long months of the Hürtgen fighting. All the same the American infantry turned and ran too often in the battle, not only individuals, but companies, even battalions. The 28th Infantry had done so. Soon it would be the turn of the 4th and 8th Infantry Divisions. Even the élite – 'the Big Red One' – would.

In the end the infantryman's allegiance would be simply to his buddies – not America, not the Army, not even to his Division. But as the infantry battalions now started to fill up with raw replacements, straight from the States, men, who as General Bradley described it 'went into the line at night and perished before the morning' or 'were evacuated as wounded even before they learned the names of their sergeants',[8] then there was trouble, serious trouble, ahead. ...

General 'Tubby' Barton's 4th Infantry Regiment had landed on Utah beach on D-Day. Since then they had fought their way right across France. In theory they were veterans. In practice the rifle battalions were made up of hundreds of green replacements. They went into the line in the dripping rain, scared and cold, stumbling over the still unburied bodies of their predecessors of the 28th Infantry, dropping finally into waterlogged foxholes to wonder what the dawn might bring.

It brought action, plenty of it. For three days the lead regiment, the 12th, tried to regain the positions lost by the 28th Division. By the fourth the 12th was fighting for its very life, with half its number vanished, killed or dead, or stricken down by trenchfoot, and that other malady which would plague the US Army this winter – combat exhaustion.

PFC George Barrette, one of them, recalled how he was affected that November. 'Me and this buddy of mine were in the same hole with only a little brush on top and I remember I was actually bawling. We were both praying to the Lord over and over again to please stop the barrage. We were both shaking and shivering and crying and praying all at the same time. It was our first barrage … When it stopped both of us waited for a while and then we crept out of the hole and I never saw anything like it. All the trees were torn down and the hill was just full of holes. They hit everything, even the battalion aid station. Every officer got hit except one.

'They sent me back to the aid station for a while and I guess they treated me for shock or something. Then they sent me back to my outfit. Everything was just as cold and slimy as it was before and the fog was so thick you couldn't see 15 yards. And it was the same shells, the same god-dam shells. Soon as I got there, the Jerries started laying them down again. They started laying them all over the road and I tried to dig in, and then I started shaking and crying again. I guess I must have banged my head against a tree or something because I lost my senses. I couldn't hear anything. I don't remember exactly what happened, but I was walking down the road and I remember seeing this soldier crawling out of a tank with both arms shot off. I remember helping him and then I don't remember anything more. I guess I must have gone off my nut.'[9]

Combat fatigue!

The 12th Infantry Regiment never came within sight of its objective. Its commanding officer was relieved. Its sister regiment was thrown in. Again they attacked through the German wire against prepared positions. The lead battalion lost 200 men the first morning. It seemed they were walking straight into a solid wall of fire. Men fled. Men went crazy. Men turned into blubbering cowards who evacuated their bowels in their overwhelming fear. Men did impossible things. Young Lieutenant Bernard Ray rushed forward with a bangalore torpedo to blow a hole in the wire which was stopping his company. Just as he reached the wire a mortar shell exploded close by. His body was riddled and ripped cruelly by the razor-sharp shrapnel. Now perhaps he thought he was dying or perhaps he went crazy. No one ever found out. For now Bernard Ray pulled a detonator cap from his pocket, attached it to the primer cord wrapped round his grievously wounded body and fitted it to the Bangalore torpedo. That done, he calmly set off the torpedo, blowing himself and the wire to pieces. But still the 8th Infantry couldn't get through.

The German infantry suffered terribly too. In a diary taken from the dead body of a German soldier, the American Intelligence men found this entry, 'It's Sunday. My God, today is Sunday. With dawn the edge of our forest received a barrage. The earth trembles. The concussion takes our breath. Two wounded are brought to my hole, one with both hands shot off. I am considering whether to cut off the rest of the arm. I'll leave it on. How brave these two are. I hope to God that all this is not in vain. To our left, machine guns begin to chatter – and there comes the Ami.

'In broad waves you can see him across the field. Tanks all around him are firing wildly. Now the American artillery ceases and the tank guns are firing like mad. I can't stick my head out of the hole – finally, here are three German assault guns. With a few shots, we can see several tanks burning once again. The infantry take cover and the attack slows down. It's stopped. It's unbelievable that with this handful of men we hold out against such attacks.'[10]

The 22nd Infantry of the 4th Division under the command of Colonel Buck Lanham, a friend of Hemingway's, were thrown in. They suffered a similar fate to that of their sister regiments. Lanham, normally a very rational man, wrote later of the battle, 'At times my mental anguish was beyond description. My magnificent command had virtually ceased to exist … These men had accomplished miracles … My admiration and respect for them … was transcendental.'[11] After his attack had failed, the small, wiry Colonel started to count the cost. The 22nd Regiment had lost 2,678 men, 500 of these being non-battle casualties. This out of 3,000 men. The 22nd Regiment of Infantry was virtually decimated.

High Command threw in the 8th Infantry Division to take over from the shattered 4th Division. It fared no better, though it, too, was a veteran outfit. But they started out confidently enough. One colonel told his men, 'If you get wounded, you'll get a nice rest in hospital. If you get killed, you won't know anything about it. If neither happens, you will have nothing to worry about. *Let's get going!*'[12]

Desperately the 8th pushed forward, fighting day after day in the advance on the key village of Hurtgen. At the point leading what was left of Company G, which had already lost three commanding officers, Lieutenant Boesch, a burly ex-wrestler, found himself pinned down 100 yards from the German-held village. All day he and his men crouched in their foxholes, risking sudden death every time they put their heads above the rim of their holes. It rained without cease and there was no food. Yet the battalion commander, safe and well to the rear, would not believe that the Germans still held Hürtgen. He insisted that they had retreated and why didn't Boesch 'get off his butt' and move in?

In the end Colonel Kunzig, whom the 220-pound ex-wrestler now hated more than the krauts, sent up two squads of engineers armed with flame-throwers as reinforcements. They were to get Boesch and his battered survivors moving again. They went into the attack at once, but they hadn't gone more than a few paces before two of the engineers were wounded by fire from the nearest house. The rest went to ground immediately.

It started to get dark. The engineers began to grow nervous. The sergeant in charge crawled over to Boesch and whined; 'Lieutenant, isn't it time for us to go back. My men are getting cold in these holes.'

Coldly Boesch said, 'My men have been cold in the same kind of holes for about two weeks now, sergeant. I expect to see you and your men later tonight – you'd better stand by.'

A little later the same sergeant returned and said, 'Lieutenant, I'd like to take my men and return to the company area.'

Boesch could see the engineers had discussed it and the sergeant had been elected to come back to him 'with the verdict'. He said the engineers would stay.

'Well, gee whiz, Lieutenant,' the NCO whined, 'they didn't tell me we were going on a suicide mission.'

'What the hell do you think about the rest of us?' Boesch demanded. 'Don't you think we get a little sick of suicide missions, too?'

'But Lieutenant,' the sergeant said, 'you all are *infantry*!'

Boesch caught himself in time. There was no further use in arguing with him. The man was lily-livered. 'You're goddamed right, *we're infantry*!' he cried proudly. 'As for you, you take your men and your fancy equipment and get the hell back to the rear where you belong.'[13]

Twenty-four hours later they had finally captured Hürtgen, but by that time Lieutenant Boesch was out of the infantry for good. In the usual way – *feet first*. A week later General Stroh, who commanded the 8th and who had already seen his own son killed in action, was relieved and his division was withdrawn. Another division was sent in – the 'Big Red One'.

This time America's premier infantry division was commanded by General Clarence Huebner, after the previous commanding general had been relieved for insubordination. Huebner had entered the Army as a private in 1910. He had been commissioned in the Great War and had held every rank in the 'Big Red One' from private to colonel. He knew his division inside out and believed the 'Big Red One' needed plenty of spit and polish and strict discipline.

Naturally Huebner was not popular with the rank and file of the Division, but he had impressed his will on both the veterans and the greenhorn replacements of the division and it went into battle full of confidence in itself and its ability to master the 'Green Hell of the Hürtgen'. Hemingway, who was up there at the time, visiting his favourite infantry outfit, Colonel Buck Lanham's 22nd Infantry Regiment of the 4th Division, sneered, 'they (the Big Red One) believed their own publicity ... The 1st Infantry Division of the Army of the United States and they and their calypso-singing PRO never let you forget it. He was a nice guy. And it was his job.'[14]

The Division entered the forest at the end of November 1944. The trucks dropped them at the edge of the embattled woods, just as similar trucks had dropped the men of the 28th, 4th and 8th Divisions, who had gone in before them to emerge shattered and decimated. Again the new boys tramped stolidly through the rain, bent like pack animals under the weight of their equipment. In the background was the rumble of the heavy guns and to their front smoke clouds mushroomed above the shell-stripped trees as shells fell. Everywhere there were the dead, American and German, still unburied, some of them hideously burnt and mutilated by phosphorus shells. 'The Hürtgen was the first time I saw roast Kraut being eaten by a Kraut dog,' Hemingway later said in that pseudo-tough manner of his.

The start of their attack was not auspicious. Almost immediately two companies were cut off. The last Huebner heard of them was a whispered radio message, 'There's a Tiger tank coming down the street,' the unknown speaker hissed, 'firing his gun at every house. He's three houses away now!' Silence followed, save for a harsh metallic crackling. Then with sudden electrifying alarm, that made the small hairs stand up on the back of the listening staff officers' necks, the voice cried, '*Here he comes!*[15]

Only one sergeant and 12 men escaped from the massacre. These men were used to guide another company to the attack. It was decimated, too. Thereafter the regimental commander, a Colonel Seitz, declined to attack again. No one seemed to object. The Big Red One was sent into the reserve, having suffered 3,983 battle casualties in a few short days, one-third of its strength.

'The division,' Hemingway wrote in his dispatch for Colliers magazine, 'had not advanced beyond its objective ... No one remembered the separate days any more and history being made each day was never noticed but only merged into the great blur of tiredness and dust, of the smell of dead cattle, the smell of earth new-broken by TNT, the grinding sound of tanks and bulldozers, the sound of automatic rifle and machine gun fire, the interceptive dry tattle of German machine pistol fire, dry as a rattler rattling, and the quick, spurting tap of the German light machine guns – and always waiting for others to come.'[16]

It was poor Hemingway, but it did convey the sounds of the battle, in which the Big Red One like all the other divisions had been fought to a standstill. By the thousand they had come, these young men in khaki, with their red one on their shoulders or the eight or the green sprig of the Fourth, condemned to the slaughter in the dripping forests, and had died violently, leaving the survivors, old men before their time, to trail back through the shattered trees, shoulders bent in defeat.

But the Top Brass who had been battering away at the Hurtgen since late September now were determined not to be cheated of their victory, however pyhrric. Yet another infantry division was brought to the front, the veteran US 2nd Infantry Division. Using the cover of the green 99th Infantry Division, which the Germans would not expect to attack because of its inexperience, the Second would launch an all-out attack on the southern tip of the dreaded Hurtgen Forest. The attack was scheduled to kick off on Saturday, 16 December, 1944, that Saturday which was destined to become the most fateful day in the whole history of the US Army in Europe in World War Two. For the Germans were now no longer just defending, *they were about to attack.* ...

V

'For God's sake, hold ...
we've got to hold!'

Twenty-two-year-old Captain Charles MacDonald of the 2nd US Infantry Division was worried. This was going to be his first battle and now something strange was happening to his front as his company crouched in the snowbound forest, ready to attack into the Hürtgen. The infantry of the green 99th Division were filtering back through the trees, eyes wild with fear, some without rifles and helmets. MacDonald tried to stop them. To no avail! Of the 200 or so he counted moving towards the rear, only two volunteered to stay with him and his men. Up front something big was happening. *What was going on?*

Then it happened. 'Wave after wave of fanatically screaming German infantry stormed the slight tree-covered rise held by the three platoons. A continuous hail of fire exuded from their weapons, answered by volley after volley from the defenders. Germans fell right and left. The few rounds of artillery we did succeed in bringing down caught the attackers in the draw to our front and we could hear their screams of pain when the small arms fire slackened. But they still came on!'[1]

Ammunition started to give out. MacDonald informed Battalion urgently. He was ordered to hold 'at all costs' He wondered whether HQ knew what that meant. 'We must hold until every last man was killed or captured. Company I's last stand! And what is to be gained? Nothing but time. Time born of the bodies of dead men. Time.'[2]

Now the Germans brought up tanks. The great lumbering white-painted Tigers snapped the pines like matchsticks as they rumbled towards the American positions, throwing up flying mud and snow. 'For God's sake, Cap'n,' one of his platoon commanders sobbed over the phone, 'get those tanks down here! Do something for God's sake! These bastards are sitting 75 yards away pumping 88s into our foxholes like we were sitting ducks. *For God's sake.*'[3]

But already the customary 'Tiger phobia' had broken out and the Sherman tanks supporting the infantry had turned tail and were scuttling to the rear as fast as they could go.

'*Hold*!' therefore was the only encouragement MacDonald could offer his platoon commander 'For God's sake, hold … we've got to hold!'[4]

But the time for holding was about over. Now men started to leave their foxholes and drift back 'with vague blank expressions' on their faces. MacDonald jumped from his own hole, ignoring the slugs slapping into the trees all around, and angrily waved them back to their positions. But they wouldn't return. They wandered off, dazed 'and zombie-like'.

Half an hour later the whole company was running for their lives. 'Over the noise of Lopez's machine gun,' MacDonald recorded later, 'I could hear Captain Wilson shouting to withdraw. I wanted to obey, but I was caught in the cross-fire of the heavy machine gun and the attackers. I gritted my teeth and waited for a lull in the firing. None came. I jumped from the hole and ran blindly towards the rear. Bullets snipped at my heels. The tank saw we were running again and opened with renewed vigour, the big shells snapping the tops of the trees around us as if they were matchsticks, but I saw no one fall.'[5]

Dusk was approaching and MacDonald and his survivors knew they wouldn't make their base at the frontier village of Rocherath. So they plunged blindly deeper into the forest. 'I slipped and fell face down in the snow,' MacDonald remembered afterwards. 'I cursed my slick overshoes. I rose and fell again. I found myself not caring if the Germans did fire. My feet were soaked. My clothes were drenched. Perspiration covered my body and my mouth was dry. I wanted a cigarette. I felt like we were helpless little bugs scurrying blindly about now that some monster had lifted the log under which we had been hiding. I wondered if it would not be better to be killed and perhaps that would be an end to everything. …'[6]

Thus was one young American infantryman's initiation into battle that terrible Saturday. But Captain MacDonald would survive to fight on, be wounded and fight again. Many did not. A score of miles from where MacDonald wished he might be dead that dusk, some 16,000 equally green American infantrymen knew the Germans had attacked, but did not know just how serious their own particular position was. For their fate had been virtually sealed already.

They were the men of the 106th US Infantry Division, named the 'Golden Lions' after their divisional patch. They were the newest soldiers of the whole Allied effort on any front throughout the world, having arrived in the line in Belgium exactly *five* days before. They had been told that this was a quiet front where they would be thoroughly trained for battle before actually being sent to fight.

Now suddenly, startlingly, they found themselves in the midst of battle, with German infantry pushing in on both flanks and isolating them on the wooded heights. For them things began to go drastically wrong right from the start. Aware that their flanks were up in the air, the two regimental commanders asked their divisional commander for permission to withdraw. He refused. So they were left on the heights, while to the rear everything broke down, with the men of at least two broken divisions fleeing away from the triumphant Germans.

As Colonel Dupuy, the historian of the ill-fated 106th, would put it later: 'Let's get down to hard facts. Panic, sheer unreasoning panic, flamed the road all day and into the night! Everyone, it seemed, who had any excuse and many who had none was going west that day – west from Schoenberg, west from St Vith, too.* Jeeps, trucks, tanks, guns and great lumbering Corps Artillery, vehicles which took three-quarters of the road – some of them double-banking. Now and again vehicles were weaving into a third line, now and again crashing into ditches. All this on a two-lane highway.'[7]

'The big bug-out', the GIs called it. Caught completely by surprise, they fled in their scores, hundreds and in the end in their thousands. Companies were taken prisoner or wiped out, battalions were lost, a whole regiment of the 28th Infantry was decimated. Soon a whole division – the 106th – would suffer the same awful fate.

Hurriedly the brass scraped together anyone and everyone who could use a rifle in a desperate attempt to hold the crumbling line. One survivor of an improvised company told his story later when it was all over. 'Tom here was a clerk and I'm a mechanic,' he told the *Stars and Stripes'* reporter, 'and neither of us ever held a rifle since way back in basic training.

'So you could have knocked me over with a feather when they gave us rifle and ammo and told us where to stay. There were just a few of us in this house near Staveloo and pretty soon sure enough somebody tells us that we're surrounded and I almost fill up my pants. I say to myself, Consiglio what the hell are you doing here anyway? You're a mechanic not a fighting soldier.

'But that's not the end of it. There's about 35 of us in this house and the Jerries open up with a helluva lot of stuff and some of the guys get knocked off and finally we decide to send somebody out to make contact with some outfit to let them know what the hell's happening up here and for chrissake send reinforcements.

'Yeah, you guessed it, I'm the jerk who volunteered. I'll never forget that as long as I live. Running through the open gates, across the streets down the hill, through the creek. I was going so goddam fast I didn't even feel the water. Then another 80 yards across a field with burp guns opening up all over the place. Then through the woods and over the railroad track. I remember every inch of that trip, to the minute some GI was getting ready to plug me because he thought I was a Jerry.

---

* The HQ of the 106th.

'When I convinced them, though, they did send a tank and get the rest of the guys out of that house. There were only 12 left then …'[8]

Consiglio was one of the fortunate ones. Many didn't survive. They did not escape the advancing panzers and the column after column of eager young soldiers who were emerging from the snowbound hills and heading for the key river – the Meuse. Once across the Meuse, the great plains of northern France and Belgium were wide open. The major allied supply port of Antwerp would be theirs for the taking.

The feelings of the average civilian soldier caught up in this chaotic mess, dumped there by the enormous, impersonal war machine of his country, might best be described in the words of Mel Brooks, the Jewish comic actor. 'Then one day they put us all in trucks, drove us to the railroad station, put us in a locked train with the windows blacked out. We get off the train, we get on a boat. We get off the boat, we get into trucks. We get out of the trucks, we start walking. Suddenly all around us *Wanauhumaahuwaauh!* Sirens! Tigers! We're surrounded by the Germans. It's the Battle of the Bulge! Hands up! "Wait," I say, "we just left Oklahoma. We're Americans. We're supposed to win." Very scarey, but we escaped … And then they start shooting! Incoming mail! Bullshit! Only Burt Lancaster says that. We said "God, oh Christ!" Who knows he might help. He was Jewish, too, "MOTHER!"'[9]

But the joke was on the Americans, not on the Germans. Now over 9,000 men of the 106th Division were wandering around the forest trails and heights on both sides of the Belgian–German frontier, surrounded on all sides by the enemy, who had captured all the roads. Every time they emerged or showed themselves they were plastered by German mortars and artillery.

Already they had abandoned most of their heavy equipment and were marching with what they could carry, plus their wounded.* Although they had done little actual fighting, the men were exhausted by the hard slog up and down the steep hills, all of which promised a way out of the trap, only to find that yet once again the Germans were waiting for them and they had to flee for their lives.

In the end the two colonels leading the trapped regiments decided there was no way out, save surrender. Colonel Descheneaux, a 35-year-old West Pointer, fighting his first battle after 15 years in the army, knew that surrender meant the end of his career. But he felt there was no other step he could take. He gathered his officers together in a forest glade. 'We're being slaughtered', he told them. 'We can't do anything effective.' He hesitated, as if he knew instinctively that his next words

---

* Even today you can follow their progress with the rusting remains of that abandoned equipment.

would mean for the rest of his life. 'It looks as if we'll have to pack it in.'

A Colonel Kelly objected. 'Desch,' he protested, 'you can't surrender!'

The Regimental Commander indicated the mounting pile of dead and wounded next to where they crouched. 'No,' he said.

Kelly hung his head and said no more.

'As far as I am concerned,' Descheneaux then said, 'I'm going to save the lives of as many as I can. *And I don't give damn if I am court-martialled!*'[10]

Not a thousand yards away the other regimental colonel, an older man, Colonel Cavender, who had been in the trenches in the last war but who had never been in action since, had come to the same decision as Descheneaux, though he couldn't bring himself to state it aloud. He told his officers, 'I was a GI in World War One, and I want to see things from their standpoint. No man in this outfit has eaten all day, and we haven't had water since early morning.' There was no reaction from his officers. Cavender was a man reluctant to take responsibility; he was the kind of old soldier who was happier when he was given an order to do something. But now there was no one there to do so. It was up to him. Out it came then, that shocking suggestion which, he knew, would mean the end of his military career, too. 'Now what's your attitude on surrendering?'[11]

It was to be the largest mass surrender of American troops of the war in the West and the second largest surrender of US soldiers since the Civil War. Some 10,000 men went into the bag that day, enthusiastically filmed by the German newsreel photographers to delight the audiences back home. In a letter taken from the dead body of a young German grenadier, he wrote enthusiastically of these miserable young 'Golden Lions' as they were brought out of the forest, hands in the air, 'Endless columns of prisoners pass; at first, about 100 of them, half of them Negroes … American soldiers have little spirit for fighting. Most of them said: *"What do we want here? At home we can have everything much better!"*'[12]

Marching down with his men Colonel Descheneaux was accosted by one of his unshaven riflemen, 'I've got a message for you, colonel,' the man said. Descheneaux looked at him dully, still wrapped up in his own miserable thoughts. Thereupon the man stuck out his tongue and gave him a raspberry – the Bronx cheer. Descheneaux had saved his life and thus had ruined his career and lost his honour. This was his reward.

But it really didn't matter any more. Colonel Descheneaux and the many thousands who went into captivity with him would have a lifetime to ponder over that 19 December, 1944. Some like 'Desch' would live to regret the decisions made that day. Others like 19-year-old PFC Kurt Vonnegut would find it a decisive experience. It would fuel his anti-war stance and would lead to the creation of his famous novel *Slaughterhouse Five*.

A wave of self-inflicted wounds now broke out, as the infantry's casualties steadily mounted. Medic Leslie Atwell, attached to an infantry division in the line, noted in his diary that month, 'Time after time men were carried into the aid station from nearby houses wincing with pain, shot through the foot. Each swore it had been an accident, "I was cleaning my rifle" sometimes the wounded man would say, pointing to a friend, "He can tell you. He was in the room with me". And often on the face of the friend there would be a look of duplicity as he backed up the story.'[13]

But there were plenty of genuine casualties, too. One day a buddy of Atwell's was brought into the dressing station, grinning all over his face and saying his good-byes. 'Where are you going?' Atwell asked him.

'Home, I hope,' his friend answered. 'I have a pair of winners here. Two frozen feet.'

'Lucky bastard!' one of his company commented. 'And there I was sticking them in the water, trying everything. They wouldn't freeze!'[14]

But trenchfoot or frozen feet which might get them out of the line for a while could also end more drastically, as PFC Gardener told the reporter of the *Stars and Stripes*. After two weeks in the line he found his feet were dead. So he took off his boots – for the first time in a fortnight – and found his feet 'looked blue and frozen. I started to rub them but I was too tired and I fell asleep. When I got up the next morning, my feet were like balloons and red and swollen so I couldn't put my shoes on ... They kept me in hospital for about 90 days before they let me go. Some guys had big black blisters – and a couple of guys had their feet cut off!'[15]

Rapidly, however, the men who were surviving the bitter clashes in the snowbound forests were becoming different from the easy-going GIs of the summer. *They* had always been well supplied and looked after, knowing that their superior air forces and armour would always get them out of any mess that they might land in. In the Ardennes and Vogges Forests, there was little that air and armour could do to help the hard-pressed infantry.

The easy optimism of the summer, the belief that the Germans were about beaten, had been replaced by a stubborn bitterness, an anger at the fact that they had been caught off guard and that the Germans were actually winning again. Even 'Blood an' Guts' Patton, so bold and brash, confided to his diary, 'we can still lose this war'. Those GIs who had not 'bugged out', broken down and given in to 'nerves'; those who had not meekly surrendered to the enemy; those who had seen their comrades overrun by the massive Tigers and slaughtered so cruelly; those who had not gone 'over the hill' at the first sign of danger and deserted to the big cities of the rear – they all became vicious, relentless, and sometimes cold-blooded killers.

That surprise attack of December 1944 is always associated with the 'Malmedy Massacre', the alleged slaughter of nearly 100 US prisoners by the SS at the crossroads near Malmedy, Belgium. But unreported in the Press at the time were the several instances when American infantry killed German prisoners. Captain MacDonald reported afterwards how his company captured a German who had just been blinded in action. The poor miserable German asked for a cigarette and one of MacDonald's men exploded with rage. He aimed a savage kick at the German, crying, '*Why you Nazi sonafabitch*! Of all the goddam nerve! If it wasn't for you and all your kind, all of us would be smoking now.'

Hurriedly MacDonald stepped in and ordered two men to take the blind prisoner back to HQ. But the escort returned surprisingly quickly. I MacDonald was suspicious. Did you get him back to HQ?' he asked.

'Yessir,' they replied promptly and seemed in a hurry to get to their section.

'But MacDonald stopped them and asked them again. One of the two looked at his feet in the scuffed dirty snow and said, 'To tell you the truth, Cap'n, we didn't get to A Company. The sonofabitch tried to make a run for it.' He raised his head and looked the young officer straight in the face. 'Know what I mean?'

'Oh,' MacDonald said, nodding his head slowly, 'I see …'[15]

Snipers were routinely shot as were other German soldiers who held out a little too long. After the 'Malmedy Massacre', some regimental commanders officially ordered prisoners from the SS and paratroopers to be shot, although this, of course, was against the Rules of Land Warfare.

The inexperienced American 11th Division, after taking 60 German prisoners at the village of Chenogne, led them out into the woods. Volunteers were called for. Minutes later the prisoners were shot down in cold blood, just as an officer came running up, yelling, 'There's been a mistake. We're supposed to take prisoners, not shoot them!'[16]

They were learning a lot these infantrymen fighting on the frontier, things that the German *Landser* had learned long before in the snowy wastes of the Russian tundra. They had learnt how to fight in knee-deep snow during the coldest winter in Europe within living memory – and survive. Medics found out that by tucking the frozen morphine syrettes under their armpits, they could defreeze them and plunge their contents into the arms of wounded infantrymen, giving them the boon of blessed oblivion. Plasma could be kept from freezing by placing the bottles under the bonnets of jeeps, next to the engines.

They were learning to combat frostbite and trench-foot, too, which were still causing more casualties than the Germans. They made themselves 'tootsie-warmers', bits cut from blankets abandoned by dead or wounded comrades and used like a foot-muff, in the same manner that German soldiers bound their feet in their 'foot-rags' rather than wear socks. They knew by now that a too-tight boot restricts circulation and leads rapidly to trench-foot. So, if they didn't have overshoes, which were now being introduced to stop the complaint, they chose a boot two sizes too large for them and stuffed the inside with old newspapers.

Instead of the issue overcoat which always got soaked to the thighs in the snow and then froze at night, they wore two GI woollen shirts, one on top of the other. These were changed each day because the one closer to the body was always wet with sweat. Or they simply sawed or cut the tail and made a thigh-length jacket of the greatcoat (unthinkable in the British Army, where this would have been regarded as a heinous crime, i.e. as damage to 'Government property', a punishable offence).

The infantry learned how to heat food over a bottle filled with gasoline, using a twist of rag as a wick. They also used the old British trick of the desert war in order to 'brew-up' – the can filled with a porridge of earth and petrol. And they learnt *not* to eat snow, no matter how thirsty they were. For snow brought on diarrhoea. Alcohol was out for the sensible fighting soldier, too. It resulted in an initial glow, which was followed by a deadly cooling off of the body temperature afterwards.

But most of all the American infantry learned how to kill, without remorse or pity. For finally they had learnt how to shed one of Western society's strictest taboos – that killing one's fellow men is wrong. All his previous life – at home, in school, outside in the working world – the boy and then the young man had been taught that aggression and attack on others was unacceptable; he had absorbed it virtually with his mother's milk. Always he had been admonished to be 'a good boy'. As the military historian of the US Forces in World War Two, Brigadier-General H.A. Marshal, revealed after the war, most American soldiers, even in élite units such as marines and paratroopers, never actually attempted to fight the enemy in combat. 'Only about a quarter of the fighting soldiers will fire their weapons against the enemy,' he wrote.[17]

By 11 January, 1945, when the frontier battles started slowly to come to an end and the German invaders commenced their bitter fighting retreat back the way they had come, their progress marked by purple, frozen dead bodies and their bloody faeces in the snow, the Americans' casualties were 55,421, of whom 18,418 were missing: the population of an average-sized small town vanished in a single month. The American Army, so confident, so full of its own victories, had been caught completely by surprise and had been given, as Montgomery, who had been called in to clear up the mess, chortled gleefully, 'a bloody nose'.

But the Ardennes surprise attack had taught the Americans something else. How to fight and kill – and that they were mortal, killed as quickly and as easily as anyone else. As Paul Fussell, a platoon commander with the 103rd Infantry Division recalled long afterwards: 'And now those who had fought have grown much older, we must wonder at the frantic avidity with which we struggled then to avoid death, digging our foxholes like madmen, running from danger with burning lungs and pounding hearts. What, really, were we so frightened of? Sometimes now the feeling comes over us that Housman's lines, which in our boyhood we thought attractively cynical, are just:

Life to be sure, is nothing much to lose;
But young men think it is and we were young ...[18]

VI

'These men of the British Infantry are heroes. These are the men, who with their flesh and blood, buy victory'

Now it was the turn of Montgomery's infantry. Two and a half divisions of them had gone to help the Americans in the Ardennes and they had lost nearly 2,000 men in that battle. But the great majority of Monty's men had spent that terrible December patrolling or skirmishing and trying to get 'their feet under the table', as they called it, with some nice comfortable Dutch family behind the line; or even better with some plump jolly Dutch farmgirl, but modest and virginal – at first.

Now on 16 January, 1945, he attacked the Siegfried Line, or at least the 20-mile-long Heinsberg salient, defended by three main lines of fortifications, which were an off-shoot of the *Westwall*. This formidable position was held by two infantry divisions, supported by 156 guns and 18 mobile assault guns.

It was not an easy nut to crack. But Montgomery was confident he could do it. He had one armoured division, two infantry divisions, and a commando brigade at his disposal. His one infantry division – the 43rd – had been in action since Normandy, but the other, which was going to bear the main burden of the attack, was relatively inexperienced. The 52nd Lowland Division had spent most of the war in Britain training. First it had trained as a mountain division for nearly three years, earmarked for action in Norway. Then it had been transformed into an air-landing division, as the back-up for a para attack. In the end, in October 1944, it had gone into action assaulting – ironically enough – the lowest point in Europe, the Dutch coast at Walcheren!

This division, which was the only infantry division in Europe which still had a high proportion of its original officers and NCOs from 1939 within its ranks, now went into the assault. The attack went in at seven-thirty that winter's morning. The infantry advanced through a thick, milky white fog, bayonets fixed, wading through its silent waves, waiting for the high-pitched screech of a Spandau, bodies tensed for the first impact of hot steel.

It came soon enough. As the 4/5th Royal Scots Fusiliers began to cross the first stream and scramble up the opposite bank, protected by barbed wire and mines, German machine guns opened up from the houses to their front. Suddenly they were galvanized into violent action. They doubled forward, bent low, as if against heavy rain, as the first men started to go down, howling with pain, clutching their shattered limbs, or pitching silent the wet earth, dead before they reached it.

Among them was Fusilier Dennis Donnini. Nineteen years old, he was the son of an Italian ice-cream seller from northern England, who had never been naturalized. Donnini had already lost his brother killed in action. Now, after seven months in the Army, he was struck in the head and fell to the ground badly wounded. But he regained consciousness after a few minutes. Struggling to his feet, bleeding heavily he staggered 30 yards down a little road to lob a grenade through the nearest house from which fire was coming. The Germans fled.

Together with a few survivors of his decimated company the young infantryman ran to the cover of a barn, all the while under intensive fire. There, while the others sought cover frantically, Donnini doubled into a shell-pocked field, swept by enemy bullets, to bring in a wounded comrade. Still he wasn't done, though he was weakening visibly. Animated by that crazy, irrational energy and courage of the battlefield, he seized a bren gun and charged the German trenches firing from the hip. He was hit again. He dropped to one knee, still firing.

Somehow he managed to get up again and, weaving and swaying like a battered boxer, refusing to go down for a count of ten, he staggered on until a German stick grenade flung at him when he was less than ten yards from the German trenches exploded immediately in front of him. This time he went down for good. The bren gun dropped from suddenly nerveless fingers and his legs collapsed beneath him like those of a newborn foal. Later he was awarded his country's highest honour, the Victoria Cross – posthumously.

Apart from the Victoria Cross, the reputation of no decoration is more scrupulously safeguarded than that of the Distinguished Conduct Medal. To earn it, a soldier has to display not only tremendous courage but also outstanding initiative. No DCM was ever better earned than the one awarded during this battle by Lance-Corporal Leitch of the 4th King's Own Scottish Borderers.

His company was caught out in the open by a tremendous and well-aimed German mortar barrage. Within minutes his CO was badly wounded, the communications with the rear went dead. The gunners standing by to support the KOSBs with their fire stared blankly at the field telephones, wondering what had happened, fearing the worst.

Abruptly a clear Scottish voice came over the radio, breaking through the metallic chatter of the chaotic traffic on the air waves. It was Lance-Corporal Alexander Leitch, effectively beginning to direct the fire of the guns on the enemy mortars. Some time later when help arrived and the stretcher-bearers doubled forward to pick up the moaning wounded and take them to the waiting ambulance jeeps, Leitch asked if they were coming back 'Why do you ask', they said. He replied quietly from his slit trench, 'I think I have been wounded in both legs.' In fact one leg had been severed and the other badly wounded and mangled before he had called up the guns. He well deserved his medal. ...

Not all were brave, however. R. Wingfield of the Queen's had been buried alive in his trench and had developed a very high temperature, so that he had been evacuated to rearline hospital. Here he found himself in a wardful of malingerers who were faking illnesses in order to dodge being sent back up the line. They initiated the bemused rifleman in the use of toothpaste, cordite, and cotton-wool in order to simulate sickness.

One of them explained. 'They're temperature happy here. They'd take the temperature of a bloody stiff before they'd accept it as genuine. You ain't got a temperature. You want one. Easy! As soon as you come in 'ere, you take your toothpaste, squeezes a nice dose on the 'andle and you shoves the paste as far back under your tongue as you can. Don't move your tongue. Now, what's the effect of brushing your teeth? It feels hot, don't it. Well, this little lot under your tongue froths like hell. When the thermometer goes under your tongue, Bob's your uncle. Oh! One point. When they pulls out the thermometer, keep your lips tightly closed. That wipes any trace of the toothpaste off. The medics know what's going on but they can't prove a damned thing. It ain't an offence in the Army to clean your teeth. The MO's doing his nut!'[1]

Others told Wingfield how they had chewed bits of cordite from shells, which 'makes the old ticker bang like a belt-fed 88. *Nearly blew the MO's head off!*'[2] Some trying to 'get their ticket' favoured swallowing cotton balls. These were allowed to work their way through the body's passages for a couple of days until they showed up as duodenal ulcers on the X-rays. As Wingfield commented later: 'These lads received the France–Germany Star* for gallantry in the face of the RAMC. They fought to the last and were discharged at the end of the war, passing to the higher service of 'doing' civvy doctors. That may explain the present state of the National Health Service ...'[3]

But just like Wingfield, who would soon be wounded in an infantry assault, the great majority of the ordinary soldiers kept on doggedly until their time came; for in the battle for Germany up to the Rhine, an infantry subaltern's life was limited to four short weeks and that of his men not much longer. Montgomery was in a hurry to reach the great river, Germany's last natural barrier of any significance, and he brooked no

---

* The decoration awarded to all who took part in the campaign.

delay. He urged on his infantry with unaccustomed harshness – for him – and although his supply of infantry was running out rapidly, he was prepared to take high casualties to break through the Reichswald Forest, which barred the way to the Rhine.

Fighting next to the 52nd, the 51st – 'the Highway Decorators' – were now urged to capture their objectives rapidly so that the tanks could break out. In the van was the 1st Gordons commanded by Colonel Martin Lindsay. He was given the order to capture a vital road by dawn. His company commanders objected, including Dany of the lead company, who preferred to wait for the light. But Lindsay told him, after the former had preferred to wait for the light. But Lindsay told him, after the former had said, 'it's going to be a horrible show', 'I don't care a bit. We've got to take this position now, cost what it may! Get all the bren-guns up in line. Fire rapid for one minute and make as much noise as possible. I don't believe the sods will put up much of a show once they realize we are right behind them. As soon as the brens stop firing we'll rush the place.'

The attack was a surprising success, the wild, cheering Jocks winkling out a company of German infantry, all crying '*Kamerad*' and then set off again up the road they had captured to link up with the Camerons of Canada, their two pipers playing the regimental march.

Suddenly their progress in the bright moonlight was stopped by a loud bang and Dany fell with a groan. 'Everybody stand still exactly where you are,' Lindsay shouted urgently and then he called for the Canadians to hurry up with sappers to plot a way through the minefield into which they had walked and stretcher-bearers to move Dany, who was badly injured in the foot.

With forced cheerfulness, Lindsay, who was standing on one foot, cried, 'Never mind Dany. The moonlight's lovely and I'll get you a bar to your MC for this day's work, you mark my words.'[5]

Suddenly there was another huge bang. One of the Canadian stretcher-bearers had walked on a mine, too. In the end a Canadian sapper sergeant went in, prodding for mines the whole way and the wounded were brought out. Lindsay followed, placing his feet delicately, as if walking on eggshells directly in his footsteps.

Later Lindsay recorded, 'By this time Macpherson ... had been evacuated so D Company had lost all its four officers in the course of the day. I formed up the company and marched them back. I was dead-tired and felt none of the elation to which I was entitled when I reported to Brigade that the road was clear.'[6]

Now the 1st Gordons were down to some 300 men out of the 600 who had landed in Normandy. By the time it was all over they would lose 75 officers and 986 men in battle, a staggering 150 per cent casualty rate! As usual the poor bloody infantry were paying the butcher's bill. ...

By now Montgomery's infantry had reached the peak of their efficiency, although their ranks were fleshed out by 18-year-old boys and 'six-week killers', as they were mocked, men culled from the artillery to serve as infantry. Many of their brigadiers were in their mid-thirties while the battalion commanders were ten years younger. By now all their officers were experienced, except of course the replacements who were now becoming increasingly younger, some subalterns being barely 18. Now social position counted for little in most battalions, save perhaps in the Guards. Many of them were from state schools. Before the war three-quarters of them had been from public schools.

Discipline, however, was fair but still strict. Whenever possible in the line the men had to shave and their hair was cut short. Unlike their German opponents they were not thus infected with lice. A watch was kept on hard spirits among the men (although officers and NCOs got a monthly ration). Each man received a half-mug of rum when in the line and now and again there was an issue of beer. But always when they weren't fighting the men were training and by now every division had its battle school, where reinforcements were given a brief course of training under realistic conditions by battle-experienced infantry officers. In the 43rd Division, for example, replacements were ordered to dig in and then to their surprise they were mortared by the mortarmen, who landed bombs within 60 yards of the startled young soldiers' positions. As the battleschool instructors cracked: 'Death'll come as a happy release to you lads after this!'

On average the assault infantry were aged between 18 and 22, that age when young men are most aggressive, unburdened by the ties of marriage and children. According to the experts these young infantrymen were supposed to 'wear out after 200–300 days of combat, if they were American, and 400 days if they were British. Thereafter, *if they survived*, they would break down and succumb to that bane of the American commanders, 'combat fatigue' or go 'bomb-happy', as the British had it.

Montgomery took good care that this did not happen too much in his armies. He set up rest camps for likely cases just behind the line, where the men were drugged for a couple of days so that they slept and slept. Afterwards they were fed well and entertained for a further couple of days before being sent up the line again. This kind of treatment worked and over 70 per cent of them returned, fit for duty, unlike the staggering 300,000 American soldiers who had to be sent back to the States during the war for battle fatigue and other psychoneuroses. For in spite of the fact that they came from the world's greatest democracy, many American officers seemed to show little interest in their men's welfare. Once the American infantry were in the line, they appeared to be regarded as cannon fodder, highly expendable, therefore not worth wasting too much care or time on. British officers checked their men's feet, their food and their morale. American

232

officers, mostly, didn't. The result was that discipline went, efficiency went and in the end morale, too. ...

Still the infantry battered away in the forest trying to break through down to the Rhine. Major Brodie, back again with the 51st Highland Division, ready for another attack, briefed his men on how to carry out house-to-house fighting once they came close to their objective, the Rhenish town of Goch. 'Explore the ground floor, throwing grenades ... into each room or spray it with a Sten,' he told them. 'Then dash to the far end and turn about. Don't fix bayonets because it will make the rifles too long and clumsy. If there's a hole in the ceiling, look out for bombs being dropped down. Occupy rooms facing forward and to the flanks. But don't stare straight out of the window. Hide behind the wall at the side and look out diagonally ... Two men, one on each side of the window, if possible. Oh, and watch the stairs in case they rush down or roll grenades down them ...'[8]

Lecture over and they were off, with the same old dread background music to war thundering in their ears. They captured their first prisoners and one of the veteran sergeants asked Brodie, 'Can't we have 'em sir?' Brodie asked what the sergeant meant and he pointed to some of the younger soldiers who hadn't killed a German yet. They wanted to kill the prisoners! A shocked Brodie said they couldn't. They ran into machine gun fire and Brodie knew he had to impress his men. He sauntered almost casually across the street and wasn't even touched. The man behind him did the same and ran straight into a burst, which killed him. Later Brodie recorded, 'I was thoroughly ashamed of myself. I should have told him what to do or not to do. He is the one man for whose death I reproach myself.'[9]

They captured a wounded German colonel lying on a stretcher. Brodie passed the word that his men must salute the German as he was borne away into captivity. This they did, with the result that lots of other German soldiers emerged from the various shattered houses with their hands up. Civilized behaviour had paid dividends.

Brodie was wounded again. There was a lot of hand-to-hand fighting, and one officer bayoneted a German officer, who in his turn shot him through the jaw. Brodie found himself in the middle of a lot of Germans. '*Gib doch eine Antwort*,' someone called petulantly. Hastily Brodie, assuming his best Bavarian accent, said, '*Ich bin der Otto*'. Then he let fly with his pistol and ran for his life, followed by a platoon of his jocks.

But as was customary for Brodie his luck was already beginning to run out. He was hit in the throat by a piece of a grenade, 'which tickled a bit'. Then leading a charge firing from the hip he was hit again. 'I was hit in the leg and one or two other places ... nothing very serious. However, being hit does sting a lot at the time and is rather a shock, and what with the bitter cold ... I was getting a bit delirious and shouting at the soldiers.' So he was carted off, but as he was going across a field, he was hit once again in the foot. He looked so bad that the CO decided he could have his own jeep to take him back to the dressing station. Yet his problems were still not over. The jeep skidded and deposited him in a ditch full of icy water, which he concluded wryly 'probably did my foot good'.[10] Hours later he was back in hospital in Birmingham. But he'd be back in the line again before it was all over. ...

Yes, even in the midst of the tragedy and cruelty of war there were these moments of grim, gallows humour. Wingfield, now back with the infantry, and commanding a section not a dozen miles away from where Major Brodie was wounded, found himself preparing to attack a fixed German position, or so he thought. 'All was ready,' he wrote afterwards. 'There was only one thing left to do. No one wanted to give the order. I gulped and turning to my section shouted, "*Fix bayonets!*" That seemed to bring us all to life. I heard the nasty snick of the bayonets locking home. I pulled out the safety of my Sten and stood up. Men to left and right stood up.

'No one moved. We all stared at the ditch ahead. This was a bayonet charge. We had practised it before, stupid men in training trying to raise an empty scream while prodding a sandbag. This thing was no practice. It was the dread problem of "Him or Me"; that problem which had never arisen yet and which we assumed would never arise. These men in the ditch were not going to give up easily. Oh God, let it be *him*!'[11]

Off they went, running all out, screaming their heads off, ready for the kill. Suddenly, when they were a hundred yards away from the 'enemy', they saw the lip of the ditch was lined with bits of waving white paper. Carried away by the unreasoning atavistic blood-lust of combat, the charging infantry yelled, 'So you're trying to pack up now, you bastards! It's too bloody late'... 'I sprayed a burst at the paper. It went down. Fifty yards ... forty yards ... thirty ... twenty ... and with a wild yell I was over and in.'[12]

Wingfield, pushing down the trench, saw the familiar grey-green clad figures. Germans! He pressed the trigger of his Sten. Nothing happened! It had jammed. Hastily he fumbled with the little automatic, as a voice cried suddenly from behind the Germans, 'What the fuck do you lot think you're doing?'

They had charged their own B Company, who held the trench with an assortment of Germans, ranging from the very dead to those petrified with fright!

Soon thereafter the comedy turned into near tragedy for Wingfield. Wounded, he and several comrades, dead and wounded, were left behind in a shell-cratered field as the battalion was forced to withdraw. Now there were Germans everywhere. '*Tod* (dead)', one of them grunted as he stepped on Wingfield's badly wounded abdomen. Somehow the lance-corporal managed to keep quiet, as to the rear a British Vickers machine gun opened fire and tracer cut the air just above the wounded man's head. On all sides the Germans were going down. 'A horrid sound, midway between a cough and a belch, and a body fell heavily across my legs, quivered, thrashed and lay still. His Schmeisser toppled over my shoulders and clouted me over the ear.'[13]

What was left of the Germans withdrew. Now a walking barrage started to creep forward to cover the advancing British infantry. Unfortunately, it fell on the British wounded as well as the retreating Germans. Wingfield, with the rest, screamed for mercy, his nerve broken at last, crying to God and demanding, 'No more ... no more!' A shell landed right among the wounded and then another and another. 'Their concussion threw me this way and that, forward and backward. The earth heaved. It shook. I seemed to bounce like a ball. I turned a complete somersault and landed on my knees with a crash. I buried my face in the ground. I closed my eyes. I daren't look any more.'[14]

But in the end the barrage passed over them and stopped. Then there was the welcome sound of British voices and one of Wingfield's mates bent over him, 'Glad to see you're out of it, Corps,' he said and then added greedily, 'Can I have that tin of soup you've got clasped to your manly bosom?'[15]

Wingfield laughed and gave him it. Later, after he was bandaged up, he was carried out to a carrier which would transport him to the rear for treatment. To his great alarm, in it already sat the Padre, complete with steel helmet. The chaplain saw the fearful expression on the wounded man's face and said hastily, 'Don't worry, boy. I'm not with you in case you die on the way, I'm just going down to the CCC* to see the rest of the boys. You're our last customer.'

Wingfield relaxed at last. He had been lying out in no-man's land for seven long hours with two tracer bullets through his hips. Now he was being borne to the rear 'on a moving feather bed'. He knew he was finished as an infantryman. He was leaving his battalion for good. 'I was out!'[16]

The Germans flooded the whole low-lying area of the battlefield isolating themselves and the attackers on small patches of high ground or in the villages. Now the Canadians who were cut off from the rear for four days called themselves 'the water rats' (a pun on the 8th Army's nickname, 'the Desert Rats'). They were supplied by Buffaloes, amphibious armoured troop carriers which sailed from 'island' to 'island' bringing with them ammunition and great heaps of self-heating soup, the only warm food available, though the tins had to be treated carefully. They were liable to go off like a bomb if not handled correctly.

Sergeant Audrey Cousins won the Canadian Army's first Victoria Cross to be gained in Germany. But it cost him his life. A day later another Canadian, Major Tiltson of the Essex Scottish, won the same high award

---

* Casualty Clearing Centre.

and survived. But it still cost him both his legs. Horror upon horror, but still the infantry kept pressing on, despite the casualties, which in the end would amount to 16,000 men killed alone and three times that number wounded.

Watching yet another infantry attack that January, former infantry officer and *Sunday Times* war correspondent R.W. Thompson, felt a 'kind of wonder' and 'a sense of despair'. 'Here is one with a heavy mortar tube on his shoulder,' he wrote for his readers back home, who never in a million years would ever be able to visualize the life these young men led. 'Another with a bren over his shoulder. They pause and wait and plod on, ready to fight, ready to charge with bayonets fixed, ready to die. ... This 24 hours has made me know a fact we all know: these men of the British infantry are heroes. These are the men, who with their flesh and blood, buy victory. You can smash from the air, pound to rubble with artillery, thrust through with armour, but always these men on foot, the men with the rifles and bayonets and the steady slogging courage, must go on. Without them, all else is in vain.'[17]

As a gunner told the bespectacled correspondent, watching yet another company of fresh-faced boys commanded by a teenage subaltern, who would be dead within the hour, going up, 'Compared with them, it's a picnic for the rest of us. They're the bloody heroes ...'[18]

VII

'The troops have done us damn well'

In reconquering Burma and the Pacific islands from the Japanese, who were now totally on the defensive, the Allied commanders were faced with the same problems as those conquering Germany. It was a matter of securing crossings over the great waterways which faced them. In the Pacific it was the bloody business of 'island hopping', getting ever closer to mainland Japan itself. In Burma General Slim had already crossed the Chindwin and secured firm bridgeheads. Now there remained the broad Irrawaddy – the Rhine of Burma, so to speak.

So his infantry toiled up the Tiddim road, which was given the nickname of 'the chocolate staircase'. Here it climbed 3,000 feet in seven miles, with 38 hairpin bends and an average gradient of one in twelve. As its surface was earth the thousands of men and animals who had toiled up had churned it into ankle-deep grey, clinging mud. But that wasn't the only problem. Constantly the mountain-side was being washed away by the torrential rains. There'd be an ominous rumble, a sudden rending sound and the whole mountain-side would begin to slide down at a tremendous rate, burying animals and men alike if they didn't get out of the way in time. Then weary or not, the infantry, men and *officers*, would have to recourse to pick and shovel to clear the track yet once again. As Field Marshal Lord Slim was to write after the war, 'No soldier who marched up the Chocolate Staircase is ever likely to forget the name of the place.'[1]

But not only was the going heartbreaking and exceedingly tough, the enemy was too. For just as the marines were finding during the 'island hopping' campaign in the Pacific, the Japanese were past masters at digging themselves in and resisting fanatically to the very end. Their morale was no longer what it had been back in 1942, but just as the German paras fighting Montgomery's Canadians and British in the Rhineland, the Japanese made the British infantry pay bitterly for every inch of ground they gained.

It was a highly dangerous and skilled job to winkle out the individual Japanese, a mere handful of whom might hold up a whole battalion for hours. Flame-throwers, tanks, bangalore torpedoes, high-explosive – all were employed against the fanatical Japanese rearguards. In the last resort, the infantry whistled up bulldozers, which had now been armoured. These simply raced for the Japanese positions, tearing and piling up earth in front of them as they advanced, which they then deposited in front of the entrance to the enemy dug-out, effectively burying the defenders alive.

But even then the Japanese were dangerous, digging out other exits, popping up to shoot unsuspecting soldiers, who thought all resistance had been long overcome. Masters, the future novelist, leading his men to victory on the top of Mandalay Hill, which dominated the Burmese city of that name, knew there were still scores of Japanese beneath the surface of the hill in mysterious chambers beneath the temples which crowned the place. So he commenced a gruesome campaign of extermination among these temples, which were the most sacred places of the Buddhist faith.

'Sikh machine gunners sat all day on the flat roofs, their guns aimed down the hill on either side of the covered stairway. Every now and then a Japanese put out his head and fired a quick upward shot. A Sikh got a bullet through his brain five yards from me. Our engineers brought up beehive charges, blew holes through the concrete, poured in petrol and fired Very light down the holes. The sullen explosions rocked the buildings and the Japanese rolled out into the open, but firing. Our machine-gunners pressed their thumbpieces. The Japanese fell, burning. We blew in huge steel doors with Piats, rolled in kegs of petrol or oil and set them on fire with tracer bullets. Our infantry fought into the tunnels behind a hail of grenades and licking sheets of fire from the flame-throwers. Grimly, under the stench of burning bodies and the growing pall of decay, past the equally repellent Buddhist statuary (showing famine, pestilence, men eaten by vultures) the battalions fought their way down the ridge to the southern foot – to face the moat and the 30-foot-thick walls of Fort Dufferin.'[2]

The British thought they might have to assault the place like medieval warriors attacking an enemy castle. There was talk of scaling ladders and ropes. Fortunately, however, a municipal employee was found who knew the Fort's sewer system. He showed the commanders an exit sewer and immediately they set about preparing an infantry assault down the great, evil smelling drain; while the rest fought on in the brick and stone rubble of the burning shattered town, 'among the corpses of children and dead dogs.'[3] Fortunately that night the Japanese withdrew and the potentially lethal sewer assault was not launched. But again the cost had been high and the infantry losses were severe. The rows of upturned rifles, with slouched jungle hats hanging from them, or crude white crosses were becoming ever larger.

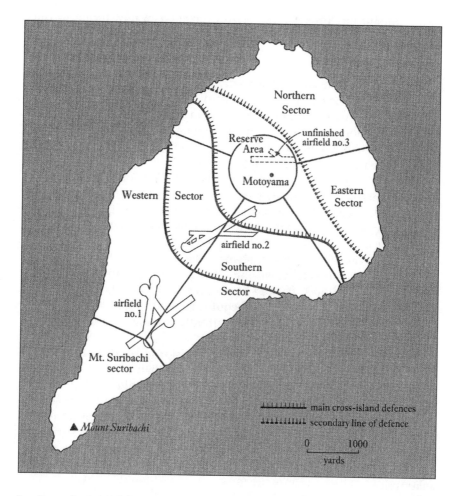

Iwo Jima – Japanese defences

Slim called on the native Karen guerillas to rise in revolt to hasten his drive towards Rangoon, for the monsoon was due in six weeks. The Karens, who had been brutally treated by the Japanese went to work with a will, massacring their forage parties, shooting up staff cars, killing sentries, guarding vital bridges. But the brunt of the battle was still being borne by the poor bloody infantry, who were sweltering in the pre-monsoon heat and very weary. But all the same they were elated at their success. As Major B. Ditmas said at the time, 'we were weary in body but exhilarated in spirit, for from the slow-moving jungle war forcing our way inch by inch forward against some of the finest infantry in the world, we had now gone over to the pursuit, occupying three or four positions a day, trying to catch up with a demoralized enemy and kill him before he escaped from the roads and villages of the Irrawaddy valley into the misty Yomas on our left. [4]

Now, too, the Japanese were actually beginning to surrender, including even an officer who called out to the British from the far side of a stream: 'Do not shoot. I am not a combatant. I am an artillery officer.'[5] This caused a lot of jokes about their own artillery among the advancing British and Indian troops. But whether they surrendered or fled, the Japanese in Burma were now about beaten at last. ...

Thus while Slim pushed his way towards Rangoon, the Americans, several thousand miles away, were assaulting island after island in the chain that led across the Pacific: islands such as Tarawa, Okinawa, Iwo Jima, exotic-sounding names which would become part of American folk history.

Iwo Jima was an ugly place, shaped like a lopsided pear, with black beaches of volcanic ash, measuring some five by two miles and packed with 22,000 Jap soldiers. Its only importance to the Americans was that it was exactly half way to Tokyo and equipped with a fighter base that took heavy toll of the American bombers currently waging a massive bombing campaign against the Japanese homeland.

On 18 February, 1945, three Marine divisions assaulted those black beaches, which were soon going to run red with their blood. The Japanese were waiting for them, of course. They had been told by their officers that the Marines would cut off the left forearm of every Japanese prisoner and carve it into a letter opener to be sent to President Roosevelt. If that didn't suffice to make them fight to the end and not surrender, they were told, too, that the Marines were fond of cutting off prisoners' heads, boiling off the flesh, and turning the skulls into souvenir ashtrays!

Tense and anxious the Marines, clad in their camouflaged uniforms, heavily laden with equipment, crouched in their assault craft as the boats raced for the beach and waiting enemy. The barrage had now ended – 8,000 shells pumped at the beach by the Navy in 30 minutes – and the place was wreathed in smoke. But the Marines had no illusions. They knew just how hard the Japs had fought at Leyte and Luzon, all winter; they'd heard just how deep the enemy dug himself in to survive all aerial and artillery bombardments. But here and there there was still some young men who retained a bitter sense of humour, such as Sergeant Goldblatt, who rasped at his men just before they hit the beach, 'I'll kill the first sonofabitch who says this is it!' No one did. The John Wayne kind of histrionics were out in Sergeant Goldblatt's platoon.

Thirty thousand Marines swarmed ashore, firing from the hip as they did so, running straight into the minefields and the withering fire from the Japanese bunkers and deep caves which were everywhere. Men went down screaming and writhing, littering the black sand with their bodies, dead and dying before they could fire even a single shot in retaliation. Others were attempting to climb the 10-foot terraces which faced them, slipping and sliding as if they were climbing a waterfall.

The corpsmen were everywhere as the cries for help and succour started to come from all sides, bent double with the weight of the wounded, braving the bullets and shells as they hurried back to the beach and the waiting boats. Most of the wounded Marines were too deep in shock or had already been drugged by buddies to scream or moan. But 'one of them gripped his stretcher poles,' a correspondent noted, 'sat up straight, stared at the sky and screamed and screamed and screamed, the shells coming in closer all around him, the black cinders flying in his face. His screaming was an almost inhuman animal sound, sometimes gurgling and sickening, but so loud pitched that it reached into the guts of everyone in the area, the sound scraping at their souls until some of them openly wished, "*Why doesn't he die?*"

And finally he fell slowly on to his shoulder, rolled over on his back and lay still.'[6]

Now the assault had broken up into small teams of men, backed up by tanks and assault engineers, armed with explosives and flame-throwers: brave men whose ranks grew steadily thinner as they attacked pillbox after pillbox. The technique was simple and brutal. The tanks would blast away with their guns, trying to keep the defenders away from their firing slits. Under this cover, the infantry and engineers would dart forward, zigzagging crazily, braving the fire coming from other pillboxes. An engineer would stop, press the trigger of his terrible weapon, and a sheet of blue-yellow flame would blurt out like the forked tongue of some dreadful primeval monster. Fire would wreathe the pillbox for a moment, and if the attackers were lucky they'd reach the wall and begin lobbing grenades through the various slits and holes. If they weren't, the Japanese would concentrate their fire on the engineer with the flame-thrower – an obvious target because of the heavy fuel pack on his bent shoulder – and suddenly he would be a pitiful, shrieking, human torch himself ...

The front was everywhere. After eight days of murderous combat, Radio Tokyo announced that the American portion of the island was 'not more than the size of the forehead of a cat';[7] and the radio station had it about right. Seventy thousand Americans and their equipment were packed in the couple of square miles which made up the waist of the island, their every movement clearly visible to the Japanese staff who directed the battle from the mustard-coloured Mount Suribachi. Whenever a man showed his head above ground, one Marine battalion commander testified afterwards, it was certain death. When a marine wanted to drink or urinate a man lay on his side in his hole. If he wanted to defecate, he did it in the same place.

One bitter young Marine, Martin Culpepper, told a correspondent how he had been surprised by a shell burst. 'It caught me off guard, you know … and I just jumped without thinking. Well I hit the side of the thing and slid down on my right side. I was moving fast … Well I started to climb back out … There it was … the crap was as fresh as hell. And I put my hand on it before I knew what happened.'[8]

Another Marine said hotly, 'There ought to be the death penalty on that sort of thing. It takes a worthless, selfish one-way sonofabitch with ingrown hairs to do something like that.'

'You know,' Culpepper said, 'they oughta make a movie showing war like it is. It would be sensational. People falling in crap, parts of people lying around, bodies flung about, people getting shot while they were trying to take a crap … And they could throw in a little crap in the air conditioning so that when you come out, you'd know how it felt.'[9]

But for many of the men on Iwo Jima there would be no post-war movies, with or without the odour of 'crap'. After the initial loss of 600 dead and 2,000 wounded on the first day, for the next 26 days there would be more than 1,000 casualties each day. But the fighting was too intense to collect most of the dead. They just lay where they had fallen and rotted away. This caused a plague of flies. They were huge blue beasts, which didn't buzz or hover, but simply swamped the corpses, staying there till they were thick, fat and full like overripe plums.

The Marines' chief doctor solved the problem in the end, however. He ordered planes to spray the whole island with DDT, the dead, the living, the Americans – *and the Japanese*! One had to stay healthy in order to fight a war.

'Among the Americans who served on Iwo Island,' Admiral Nimitz, the US Naval commander said, 'uncommon valor was a common virtue'. In spite of the horrific casualties and the brutality of this close-quarter fighting, there were many Marines who lived up to the Corps motto. Take Sergeant William Harrell, for instance. A grenade tore off his left hand and broke his thigh, so he lay in his hole helpless. Suddenly a Japanese officer appeared with a drawn sabre, towering above him. Harrell wasn't beaten, however. He shot the Jap with his right hand and as the latter reeled back, he collapsed with exhaustion. Another Jap appeared and shoved a grenade under the Sergeant's head. That revived him … He killed the enemy soldier and pushed the grenade as far away from him as possible. Next moment the grenade blew up and carried away his other hand. At dawn the brave Sergeant was carried away, still alive.

Another Marine rushed out to help a wounded comrade. Just as he reached the place where the wounded man was sheltering, a sniper shot him three times in the stomach. Ignoring his own wounds, the man tended the Marine, gave first aid to another casualty and headed back to have his own wounds treated. He didn't make it. He was shot and killed by yet another sniper.

Thus the killing went on and on. In the end it turned out to be the most, costly battle in the Marine Corps' 168-year history, with twice as many Marines dying in that four-week battle than in the whole of World War One. As someone commented, 'It was the most expensive piece of real estate the United States had ever bought – 550 dead and 2,500 wounded for every square mile of the place!'

Many of the dead were barely recognizable, just pieces of human flesh like offal in a butcher's shop. Once a foot was found in a boot which had the Marine's serial number on the tongue. Solemnly the dead Marine's boot, complete with foot, was buried in the black sand. Then came urgent orders to have the foot exhumed. Its owner was still alive, albeit without his foot, in a military hospital in Saipan!

In the end, the 28th Marine Regiment under the command of 'Harry the Horse' Liversedge captured the key site Mount Suribachi with a six-man patrol, together with a Marine photographer, reaching the summit at the end of the four-day battle for the feature. Here the photographer asked the patrol to pose, raising a small ship's flag at the end of a piece of Japanese piping. One of the six refused, saying the others 'was Hollywood Marines!' The others obliged and to make it more Tinseltown-like, in that very same instant, two Japanese raced out of a nearby cave, waving swords. A Marine shot one while the other threw a grenade and disappeared. The camera was smashed and the photographer thought his historic photograph was damaged or useless. It wasn't. Not that it mattered. The Marine Corps had its eye, as always, on gaining maximum publicity. Already another patrol with yet another and much larger flag and another photographer were on their way. His picture of the second raising of the Stars and Stripes over Iwo Jima would become world famous, featured in every high school textbook on American history.

People like a larger flag.

Four days later it was over. The battle of Iwo Jima, which had lasted 26 days, had entered the history books. Yet even as it ended, the top brass were completing their plans for the invasion of yet another island, Okinawa. It would take two months to capture at the cost of 100,000 casualties, with the Japanese naval commander Admiral Minoru Ota ceremonially slitting his throat in a cave at the end and the American Commander General Buckner being killed in action one day afterwards. And there was still Japan to be invaded. ...

In Europe the battle flared up fiercely for one last time, even though there was no hope for Nazi Germany now. In Italy the American 5th Army and the British 8th Army fought a desperate, retreating 10th German Army; while the partisans of the north harassed the smaller German units ruthlessly, rarely taking prisoners. Just like the *Goums* of the French Army, which was also fighting in these last battles, the partisans tended to kill the prisoners.

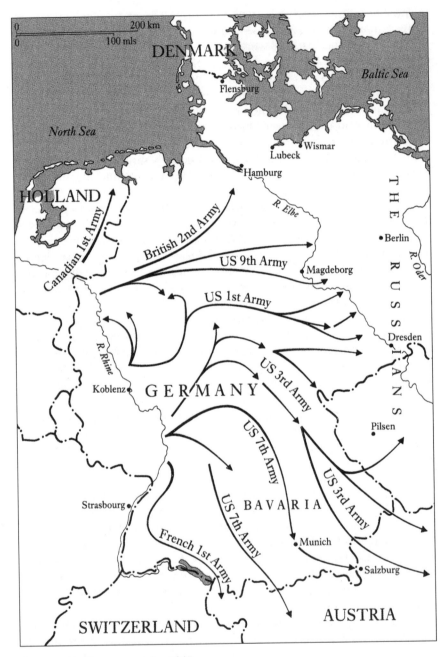

Overrunning Germany, spring 1945.

Unlike the 'Moors', as the Italians called them, the partisans did *not* first bugger their prisoners before killing and emasculating them. No wonder the *Goums* and the Gurkhas were the most feared soldiers in Italy.

New Zealand Intelligence officer Geoffrey Cox had asked a group of typical partisans to bring him in some Germans suspected of hiding in the local area. 'Any prisoners you can get will be valuable,' he told them. '*Si, si prigionieri*' their leader agreed happily. A half an hour later Cox heard three shots, and the partisans appeared without prisoners but with the paybook of one of them, an SS officer, covered with blood.

Curiously Cox flicked through it, noting the campaigns the dead man had fought, in the good days of victory after victory for Nazi Germany: 'Medal for the *Einmarsch* into Austria; medal for the *Einmarsch* into Czechoslovakia; medal for the Polish campaign; Iron Cross Second Class in France ...' Now it was all over for him and nearly for Germany, too.

Cox stared at the dead man's pictures, officers and storm troopers, 'with the same relentless faces' and mused: 'This was the type Hitler had loosed on Europe, brave, desperate, efficient. And now he had come to his end in an Italian field, shot down by an Italian farmer's boy with a Sten gun, shot in the back, I learned later as he crouched in hiding ...'[10]

In Germany itself they were over the Rhine by now and were swarming to north, south and east, long fingers of armour followed up the infantry, who were suddenly finding they were no longer needed so much. The 'great swan', as the British called it, ('the rat race' for the Americans), was for the armour, covering 20, even 30 miles a day into the heart of the Reich.

It was crazy time. Ten million former slave workers were on the move. A couple of million Germans were fleeing from the Russians. Society was breaking down. Women were raped and were impatient of being raped. A sergeant of the 52nd Division's infantry was shot in the buttocks while 'on the job', carried out of a factory where he had been engaged in intercourse with a Russian girl, face down on a stretcher, bleeding from a wound in his rump. After the war he was awarded a Dutch decoration for having been one of the men of the Division wounded three times. In due course, his section would rib him with, 'When yer grandkids ask, how did ye get yer medal, sarge, *what are ya gonna tell em?*'[11] In Koblenz the American medic with the infantry, Lester Atwell, watched how drunken GIs rutted with 'frauleins' in the gutter under shellfire and other 'frauleins', 'impatient of rape', chased after the men even when they were going into the attack.

William Bohlenberger, taking a 'piss stop' during the great 'rat race', suddenly looked around 'as if in a dream and then [he was] running like somebody gone crazy, running to a little house off the road and yelling, 'Mom ... Mom ...'

'To make it more Hollywood,' the chronicler of the incident from the *Stars and Stripes* noted, 'his mother was washing dishes in the kitchen and his brother was in the living room, still wearing his German uniform. It had been 15 years since they had all seen each other and the American soldier and his German mother were incoherently crying the way you'd expect them to cry. But the American soldier and his German soldier-brother didn't say a word to each other.'[12]

But as the armour surged forward and the infantry broke up Germany into little pieces behind them, there were still men being killed violently, ambushed by teenage fanatics in short pants, machine-gunned mercilessly by a handful of last-ditch SS men from half the countries of Occupied Europe, who had nothing more to lose. And the sudden merciless slaughter, some might even say minor massacres, were not all one-sided.

During the advance of General LeClerc's Free French division crossing Bavaria in the dying hours of the Reich, his men bumped into a small group of other French soldiers, a score of bedraggled teenagers in the field grey of the SS. They were members of the *Charlemagne SS Division*, all volunteers who had fought for two years in Russia. LeClerc inspected them personally and there is a photograph of him extant, *kepi* set squarely on his hard head, eyeing them with a mixture of contempt and disbelief as they lined up against a wall. Then he turned. His men shot the lot without mercy. Their graves are still to be found in the cemetery of the nearby village.

Photographer Walter Rosenblum was in Munich when the infantry of Patton's 42nd Division – 'the Rainbow Division' – slugged it out with a handful of desperate SS men in Munich. 'There was a fire fight between Americans and SS troops in a square. It looked as though it were a Wild West movie scenario. Only it was real ... The Americans were taking a tremendous beating. But they were battle-hardened, had lost a lot of guys, and were not to be trifled with. The SS surrendered.' Walter Rosenblum had been with various infantry outfits since D-Day, but even he was startled by what happened next. 'It was in the back of a courtyard. I sat down on a long bench against the wall. It was like a stage set. They put the Germans against the wall. I was sitting with a single-lens Eimo up near my eye. There were about three or four Americans with Tommy sub-machine guns. They killed all the Germans. Shot 'em all. I filmed the whole sequence. I still wasn't that battle-hardened and I thought they did the wrong thing. The Germans were quite brave. They sensed what was happening and they just stood there.'[13]

Now in the twilight hours of the Reich, which Hitler had once boasted would last a thousand years, it was dangerous – even lethal – to be an SS trooper. The troops were wild, almost out of control in some cases (in April the US Army arraigned 500 men for rape in Germany, and those were the ones who were caught); they had itchy trigger fingers. Some of the SS accepted their fate stoically, even heroically. Others panicked, tried to burn the tell-tale SS blood grouping tattooed on the inside of their upper arm with heated teaspoons or remove it altogether with knives. But it availed them little. Brave or coward, they were condemned men.

In the confusion of the time, some 2,000 SS men of the beaten 6th Mountain Division, trying to sneak through Patton's lines, captured an American field hospital. They remained there one night and then fled again, taking with them what transport and food they could find, leaving patients and staff unharmed. Due to the nature of the 'rat race', rumours spread quicker than fact. It was said that the SS had raped the American female nurses and then killed the male staff. The men of the US 5th Infantry Division believed the rumours and, without orders from above, decided to take no further SS men prisoner that week. Some 500 of the SS Mountain Division were slaughtered before the killing was stopped. The village chronicles of the Hesse and Wurttemberg, from whence the forebears of so many of these American soldiers came (including their commanding general Eisenhower), are full of the grisly stories of *Amis* slaughtering SS men.

It was no different on the British front. After infantry of the 53rd Division had been shot in cold blood on capture at the small German town of Rethel by young SS men of the Hitler Youth's depot battalion, the word went out among the infantry: take no prisoners from the Hitler Youth! Wherever officers had a tight control of their men, this did not happen. It was different where sections were acting independently and being commanded by NCOs.

Such was the case at the tiny village of Vahrendorf just south of the besieged port of Hamburg. Here on the morning of 26 April, 1945, the young SS from the depot, most of them 17- and 18-year-olds, launched a final attack on the infantry of the most experienced division in the British Army, the 7th Armoured – 'the Desert Rats'.

The fighting was heavy. But in the end the British positions in and around the one-street village were restored and the SS fled, leaving 60 dead in the surrounding fields and some 70 prisoners in the hands of the various sections of the two battalions of infantry which had defended Vahrendorf. What happened next was no advertisement for the British Army, but then the SS had been killing British prisoners right back to 1940.

Two NCOs took a dozen youngsters out to a gravel pit just north of the village. 'We saw them go,' remembers an old lady, who was young then, 'with the Tommies prodding them with their bayonets and kicking them. Some time later there was rattle of shots and the Tommies came back without them. After they, the Tommies, had gone, we dug the bodies out of the gravel and buried them in the local cemetery.'[14] And there they, too, rest to this day, another sad monument to man's inhumanity to man. ...

On Sunday, 29 April, the 15th Scottish Division made its third assault across a major river, the Seine, the Rhine and now the Elbe. Under the cover of a typical Montgomery barrage they made the crossing with only slight loss and began to fan out to the west and north. But not for long. At dawn an officer patrol of the Cameronians bumped into the van of a hastily thrown-together German infantry division. Hurriedly they fled to report their findings, just as the Germans hit the Cameronians' positions.

The Jocks called down a terrific artillery barrage. The German infantry, old men and fanatical young boys, dug in right under the British positions and began to slog it out. Here and there their suicidal determination was too much for the Cameronians. They were forced to retreat.

Brigadier Villiers, the commander of the brigade to which the Cameronians belonged, was worried. This was a full-scale attack and as long as the Germans held the small wood to the Cameronians' front, his breakout to the north would be stopped. Also Montgomery was breathing down his neck. He wanted his troops to reach the Baltic in the Lubeck area before the Russians. If the latter beat the British, they could sweep on into Denmark placing the mouth of the Baltic under their control. He ordered up the Seaforths. They were to clear the wood – and clear it fast!

The Seaforths advanced across the fields in a thin rain. It had grown strangely quiet. Now they were about 100 yards from the dark fir wood, which seemed to exude danger. Still no sign of the enemy. Fifty yards! A young subaltern raised his hand. It was as if the movement signified something to the tense men crouched there, waiting. There was a single pistol shot. In an instant the whole front edge of the wood crackled with small arms fire.

The Seaforths were galvanized into violent action. An officer waved his arm. Sergeants bellowed orders and, with a wild roar, they were running for the wood, rifles clasped tightly to their right hips in sweat-damp hands.

It took four hours. When it was all over and the slaughter had ceased, there were only four Germans left alive, and the Seaforths were exhausted, the barrels of their brens gleaming with the heat, piles of gleaming cartridge cases everywhere. The way north was free. The 15th Scottish, the 6th Airborne, the 5th Division and their comrades of the 11th Armoured would beat the Russians to the coast. Twenty miles away that same day, a man who had once written, 'As a young man of pure British descent, some of whose forefathers have held high positions in the British Army, I have always been desirous of devoting what little capability and energy I may possess to the country which I love so dearly'[15] staggered into the underground studios of Radio Hamburg, which would surrender soon.

The little man with his nose jammed on his face at an odd angle and a deep-set scar which ran from right ear to mouth, might have been exhausted or drunk. The two German radio technicians didn't know or care now. The renegade broadcaster's career was over. This was to be his last broadcast to England before they came for him and hanged him.

So William Joyce, alias 'Lord Haw Haw', spoke to England for one last time. He said his piece with obstinate dignity, then ended with six carefully phrased sentences in that nasal voice of his which had sent shivers of fear and rage down the spines of his listeners for so many years, 'Britain's victories are barren,' he intoned; 'they leave her poor and they leave her people hungry; they leave her bereft of markets and the wealth she possessed six years ago. But above all they leave her with an immensely greater problem than she had then.

'We are nearing the end of one phase in Europe's history, but the next will be no happier. It will be grimmer, harder and perhaps bloodier. ...'[16]

Slowly the little man who was to prove a better prophet than many a British cabinet minister in this moment of victory for the Empire – at so much cost – rubbed his eyes wearily, then staggered out the way he had come. ...

Now it was virtually over. Some got drunk. Some grew moody. Some were tearful. The last British troops to be in contact with the defeated Germans were the 4th Battalion of the Dorsets of the 43rd Infantry Division. They waited dourly for the end to come. Back in the autumn, virtually the whole battalion had been lost trying to help the trapped 1st Airborne Division at Arnhem. They were taking no chances with the Germans.

At five on the morning of the cease-fire, they stood to for the last time in World War Two, relaxing for the first time since they had crossed the Rhine back in March. R. W. Thompson, the war correspondent, up front to witness the event, felt 'there was no mood for celebration, only for thankfulness.'[17] An officer found a flagstaff in the small village of Kunstedt, which they had captured after heavy fighting the day before, and raised the Union Jack. Then everyone sat down to the usual breakfast, 'char' and 'soya links'. As they sat there a lone German officer wandered through the village. No one cared. There was a slight hubbub outside. Some Germans had come in to surrender. No one knew quite what to do with them. 'Oh Lord', a company commander commented, 'You really can't take prisoners now!'[18]

Further back, General Thomas, the divisional commander, was briefing his officers on the day's business when the message was brought to him that the war was now officially over. He frowned at it, as if he simply couldn't take it in. Finally he folded his frayed canvas map case and without a word walked outside the caravan to the waiting armoured car. Just before he clambered in, he turned to Brigadier Essame and broke his heavy brooding silence. *'The troops have done us damned well!'* he barked and then he was gone, as the Very lights started to sail up in the air above the front in crazy, multi-coloured profusion to celebrate the great victory.

On the Baltic coast, paratrooper James Byrom, who had dropped first in Normandy on D-Day, was on duty at the great hospital in Wismar, full of German wounded, the day they celebrated. Most of his friends had sworn long ago they would get blind drunk this day. Those who had survived the long struggle from Normandy through the Ardennes and the second drop over the Rhine were now doing so. He, however, remained 'as sober as a judge'.

Now he stood at the window of the hospital watching the magnificent sunset of this day of victory. 'On the ward below the wounded Germans talked quietly. Presently, as the glow of their cigarettes confirmed that it was dark, the victory celebrations began. Up from the British lines came brilliant flares, singly and in clusters, but without pattern or prodigality, as if one soldier in each platoon had been given an official coloured hat and told to fling it in the air. But further away in the Russian lines the glow of bonfires steadily lit the sky. Distance subdued the flickering static cones that were slightly blurred by smoke or mist; and I could fancy that they were ghost fires of other historic triumphs, so strongly did I feel then, as a symbol of the unreality of victory in relation to the recurring failure to keep peace ...'[19]

On the other side of the world three months later Russell Braddon, newly released by the bomb of Hiroshima and sailing home after all those years of awful Japanese captivity, experienced similar sentiments in this moment of victory, 'Then the sense of loneliness returned. All those blokes – Pommies and Australians – gone. ... For us and for the undefeated Japanese soldiers all over South-East Asia, the war hadn't ended. It had just, momentarily, stopped. ... So, for those of us who had suffered under them, and for the Nipponese themselves, this was just an interlude – the Hiroshima Incident, probably, they would call it. But the war itself, that of Asia against the white man, that – under one guise or another; in one place or another – still has ... years to go. The trouble was, of course, that no one at home would believe it ...'[20]

'*Ofer*,' the small, humorous-looking middle-aged German said, as he stopped Lester Atwell, the infantry medic, and a fellow infantryman in the cobbled street of the small German town, 'War *ofer. Gut* friends?' The German stretched out his hand and Atwell's friend took it automatically. 'Now', said the German with his old codger's grin, '*togedder we fight the Russian, no?*'[21]

Envoi

Life, to be sure, is nothing much to lose;
But young men think it is, and we were young.

Housman

By the end of the 11-month campaign in north-west Europe, nearly five million servicemen had come to continental Europe. While the fighting troops, the infantry and the tankmen, had made up only 20 per cent of this huge force, they had absorbed 70 per cent of the casualties. The final butcher's bill for the British, Canadian and American armies engaged in the campaign came to 782,374 men killed, wounded or reported missing: the population of a large city vanished in less than a year. No one, it seems, has ever assessed the total losses of the troops fighting in Italy and Burma. The 8th in Italy and the 14th in Burma remained 'forgotten armies' right to the end.

But, in truth, who today remembers any one of them, wherever they fought? Who recalls that dying Grenadier Guardsman at Dunkirk with his 'permission to fall out, sir?'; or Piper McIntyre of the Black Watch playing his pipes at El Alamein till he died of his wounds, barely 20; or Lance Corporal Harman at Kohima, fighting his one-man 'battle of the ovens', emerging with a 'Jap' beneath each arm; or the son of the Italian ice-cream merchant Fusilier Donnini winning the VC in the *Reichswald* and dying in the attempt, aged 19? All that effort, all that sacrifice? Who remembers? As Norman Mailer makes his fictional infantry NCO Sergeant Crofts say in *The Naked and the Dead* – 'We broke our ass for nothing!'

Right from the start they had been doomed. Those mostly working-class young men were sent to their deaths ill-armed and ill-prepared by their countries. In Britain before the war Major Attlee's Labour Party, riddled by pacifism, had – from 1929 onwards – systematically opposed the national government's measures to re-arm. Anyone calling for more defence, in the light of the looming menace of the Axis powers, was denounced as a war-monger. In the very year that Hitler invaded Czechoslovakia, the

Labour Party conference voted not only to reduce the RAF, but to abolish it altogether! Four short months before the outbreak of war in 1939 the party of *Major* Attlee, as he was fond of entitling himself, voted against conscription.

The situation had been little better in the United States. There public parsimony and the strong isolationist lobby – 'the America Firsters' – denied the US Forces money and support. Thus it was that the break-neck, tremendous expansion of the US Army between 1940 and 1942 meant that its soldiers went overseas inadequately trained for battle, led by average senior officers who should have been pensioned off years before, or callow '60-day wonders' who had never heard a shot fired in anger.

In the end, I suppose, it mattered little. The dead never did learn that they had died for virtually nothing. Their enemies of then are now allies and more powerful – economically – than ever; and rightly so. The Empire that the British fought and died for has vanished. What price the Chindits, the Battle of Kohima and that long, epic struggle in the jungle?

As for those who survived the infantryman's war, they had learnt a lot about themselves, their fellow men, the Army and organized society. As one veteran infantryman recalled 40 years later: 'To me there were two different wars. There was the war of the guy on the front line. You don't come off until you're wounded, killed, or, if lucky, relieved. Then there was the support personnel. Their view of war was different than mine. The man up front puts his life on the line day after day.'[1]

Another American infantryman realized many years later that his seven months of combat had completely transformed his attitude to 'civilized' society. 'My experience in the war was ironic because my innocence had prepared me to encounter in it something like the same reasonableness that governed prewar life. This, after all, was the tone dominating the American relation to the war: talk of the "Future", allotments and bond purchases carefully sent home, hopeful fantasies of the "postwar world". I assumed, in short, that everyone would behave according to the clear advantages offered by reason. I had assumed that in war, like chess, when you were beaten you "resigned"; that when you were outnumbered and outgunned, you retreated; that when you were surrounded, you surrendered. I found out differently and with a vengeance.

What I found was people obeying fatuous and murderous "orders" for no reason I could understand, killing themselves because someone "told them to", prolonging the war when it was hopelessly lost because – because it was unreasonable to do so. It was my introduction to the shakiness of society. It was my first experience of the profoundly irrational element and it made ridiculous all talk of plans and preparations for the future and goodwill and intelligent arrangements.'[2]

Another idealistic young infantryman, who would survive his six months of combat to become a clergyman, wrote in his first letter home after his initiation into combat, 'Things have been pretty hot for us in the past two weeks and I haven't been able to get a letter off. My mind is absolutely stripped of any traces of reason for war – if there was any in the first place. Maybe the overall picture justifies what goes on up here, but from the infantryman's point of view it is hard to see. A lot of my friends are not here any more, which is a terrible reminder of the evil of war. Every once in a while, I have to stop and justify what goes on here by thinking of the great cause we are fighting for.'[3]

Perhaps that 'great cause' didn't really matter very much even then. The average infantryman was fighting to save his own skin and that of his comrades. It certainly has absolutely no significance today. I doubt if many of those who laid their lives 'on the line' are proud of having done so today. For in the end nothing came out of their victory save new wars, new oppressions, new injustices. What was perhaps of real importance to them, when they come to consider it today, was that they learnt something of themselves, found their true selves.

As Alan Moorehead, the Australian war correspondent who had been watching allied soldiers in combat from 1939 right to the end in 1945, wrote at the time: 'You could almost watch him [the soldier] grow from month to month in the early days. He was suddenly projected out of the shallow and materialistic world into a world where there were real possibilities of touching the heights and here and there a man found greatness in himself ... And at those moments there was a surpassing satisfaction, a sense of purity, the confused adolescent dreams of greatness come true. Not all the cynicism, not all the ugliness and fatigue in the world will take that moment away from people who experienced it.'[4]

Almost universally, especially among thinking American ex-infantrymen, there is a feeling that for the very first – and only – time in their lives they were living in a non-competitive society. There at the front everyone was in the same boat, not competing with each other, surviving on the same basic material and same human resources. Almost universally, too, these white-haired, balding and paunchy old ex-infantrymen remember the comradeship of the line; how everyone depended upon his 'buddy' or 'mate' for his very life.

'I was somebody,' one of them recalled 40-odd years later, 'I was in an organization, sometimes I'd get mad, sometimes I didn't. 'Cause I was kind of a rebellious guy ... Anyway I was with people I trusted, that I had confidence in. Most of the time I woulda gone to the moon with these guys. Jeez, I don't wanna get tearful.'[5] So many years later the survivors can still remember the names, the peculiar habits, the odd quirks of men who are long dead – could be their grandsons today. *Buddies!* ...

Ending his account of the activities of his battalion of the KOSB in north-west Europe during the 1944–45 campaign, in which the battalion had had a 100 per cent turnover of officers and men due to battle injuries, Captain Robert Woollcombe wrote, 'Some remain in the Fields they won … The others, I suppose, are ordinary human beings again.'[6]

But were – are – they? Could they ever forget what it was like? Going up in the rain, leather jerkins slick and gleaming, the inevitable enamel mug bouncing up and down on the pack, shoulders bent under their load, faces strained and serious, with the lowering of the guns behind; passing the waiting ambulances, the drivers smoking and pretending not to see them, but seeing them all the same. The sudden clatter of the machine guns like someone running an iron bar along a length of iron railings.

Then some of them would come back. Running perhaps, shouting, eyes wide and wild with unreasoning fear; or hobbling and hopping, one arm outstretched like a blind man feeling his way or slung over the front of a muddy jeep with the ugly yellow shell dressing, already turning scarlet, clapped over their wounds; or doubling back the terrified prisoners, faces red and flushed, helmets pushed back to reveal the puckered red marks on the white forehead, cursing and threatening, prodding their prisoners with the bayonet when they seemed to be slowing down. '*Mak Schnell*, you Jerry buggers … *Mak schnell!*'

The still, khaki-clad bodies in the fields, all boots, forlorn, abandoned, the price of victory. Their comrades plodding on to their inevitable fate, a few cocky with helmets tilted to one side, fag ends stuck behind their ears. But most of them sombre, intent, knowing, grey ghosts vanishing into brown drifting gunsmoke of that time, boots soundless, the thunder of the guns muted, the cries of rage, surprise, pain, triumph softened, almost gone, echoing down the tunnel of time into the past. Germans, Americans, Britons, Canadians, Australians, New Zealanders, South Africans, friend and foe alike, united in death or memory.

Ordinary human beings? No, just the Poor Bloody Infantry.

Notes

BOOK ONE

Chapter 1

1   D. Flowers and J. Reeves, *The Taste of Courage* (Harper & Brothers, 1960)
2   S. Mays, *No More Soldiering For Me* (Eyre & Spottiswoode, 1971)
3   Ibid.
4   R. Lewin, *Freedom's Battle* (Arrow, 1972)
5   T. Firbank, *I Bought a Star* (Sidgwick & Jackson, 1951)
6   *The Taste of Courage*, op. cit.
7   F. Mowat, *And No Birds Sang* (Cassell, 1979)
8   R. Atkin, *Dieppe 42* (Macmillan, 1980)
9   Private communication to author

Chapter 2

1   M. Hamilton, *Monty* vol. 1 (Coronet, 1985)
2   N. Longmate, *How We Lived Then* (Arrow, 1973)
3   *I Bought A Star*, op. cit.
4   Ed. R. Lewin, *The War On Land* (Hutchinson, 1969)
5   Personal communication to the author
6   R. Grant, *The 51st Division at War* (Ian Allen, 1977)
7   Gunbuster, *Battle Dress* (Hodder & Stoughton, 1941)

Chapter 3

1   Edited, *Youth at War* (Batsford, 1944)
2   Ibid.
3   *51st Highland Division*, loc. cit.
4   J. Hodson, *Through a Dark Night* (Gollancz, 1941)
5   Monty Vol. 1, loc. cit.

6   Ibid.
7   Ibid.
8   Ibid.
9   Ibid.
10   *The War On Land*, loc. cit.
11   G. Aris, The Fifth British Division (Divisional Benevolent Fund, 1959)
12   *Through a Dark Night*, loc. cit.
13   M. Ansell, *Soldier On* (Peter Davies, 1973)
14   Ibid.
15   *Through a Dark Night*, loc. cit.
16   R. Collier, *1940 The World in Flames* (Penguin, 1979)
17   Ibid.
18   *Through a Dark Night*, loc. cit.

Chapter 4

1   *Youth at War*, loc. cit.
2   Ibid.
3   Quoted in R. Collier, *1940 The World in Flames* (Penguin, 1979)
4   G. Instone, *Freedom is the Spur* (Pan, 1956)
5   *Battle Dress*, loc. cit.
6   B. Horrocks, *A Full Life* (Leo Cooper, 1974)
7   *History of Third Division*, op. cit.
8   Ibid.
9   *The World in Flames*, op. cit.
10   Ibid.
11   *Youth at War*, op. cit.
12   Ibid.
13   *Through a Dark Night*, loc. cit.
14   Ibid.
15   *A Full Life*, op. cit.

Chapter 5

1   *Daily Telegraph* 17 Nov, 1936
2   This account is based on L. Aitken, *Massacre on the Road to Dunkirk* (Kimber, 1977)
3   Quoted in *The War on Land*, loc. cit.
4   *The Full Life*, loc. cit.
5   *Monty*, Vol. 1, loc. cit.
6   *War on Land*, op. cit.
7   Ibid.
8   M. Glover, *The Fight for the Channel Ports* (Leo Cooper, 1985)
9   A. Vincent, *The Long Road Home* (N.E.L., 1956)
10   Ibid.

11 *Freedom is the Spur*, loc. cit.
12 Ibid.
13 A. Neave, *The Flames of Calais* (Coronet, 1972)
14 Ibid.
15 Ibid.

Chapter 6

1 *Battle Dress*, loc. cit.
2 Ibid.
3 *Infantry Officer*, loc. cit.
4 Ibid.
5 *1940*, loc. cit.
6 R. Collier, *The Sands of Dunkirk* (Dell, 1961)
7 Ibid.
8 *History of Third Division*, loc. cit.
9 *Battle Dress*, loc. cit.
10 *Daily Telegraph* 11 July, 1940
11 Ibid.
12 N. Nicolson, *Alex* (Pan, 1973)
13 Ibid.
14 *The Sands of Dunkirk*, op. cit.

Chapter 7

1 L. Hart, *The Rommel Papers* (Arrow, 1984)
2 E. Linklater, *The Highland Division* (HMSO, 1942)
3 Ibid.
4 Ibid.
5 Personal communication to the author
6 R. Grant, *The 51st Highland Division at War* (Ian Allen, 1977)
7 Personal communication to the author
8 Ibid.
9 *Radio Times* 1985
10 *The Highland Division*, op. cit.
11 Personal communication to the author
12 *How We Lived Then*, loc. cit.
13 *Monty* Vol. 1, loc. cit.
14 Ibid.
15 Ibid.
16 Edited, *Annals of the King's Royal Rifle Corps* (Gale and Polden, 1962)

BOOK TWO

Chapter 1

1 Quoted in *Taste of Courage*, loc. cit.
2 *1940*, loc. cit.
3 J. Frost, *A Drop Too Many* (Sphere, 1980)
4 Ibid.
5 *Monty* Vol. II, loc. cit.
6 Ibid.
7 *And No Birds Sang*, loc. cit.
8 N. Craig, *The Broken Plume* (Imperial War Museum, 1985)
9 *I Bought a Star*, loc. cit.
10 *People in Glass Houses*, Military Prison Staff Corps paper, Colchester
11 Ibid.
12 Lt. Z, *Penguin New Writing* 31 March, 1947
13 J. Hodson, *The Home Front* (Victor Gollancz, 1944)
14 *The Picture Post*, July 1943
15 *Daily Mirror*, 13 May, 1943
16 Ibid.
17 *Monty*, op. cit.
18 Ibid.
19 *A Drop Too Many*, op. cit.

Chapter 2

1 H. Kippenberger, *Infantry Brigadier* (OUP, 1952)
2 *A Taste of Courage*, loc. cit.
3 Ibid.
4 E. W. Underhill, *The Royal Leicestershire Regt.* (Glen Parav Barracks, S. Wigston, Leics. Privately published, 1955)
5 *Infantry Brigadier*, op. cit.
6 *Taste of Courage*, op. cit.
7 *The War on Land*, loc. cit.
8 *Infantry Brigadier*, op. cit.
9 Ibid.
10 *Taste of Courage*, op. cit.
11 *Infantry Brigadier*, op. cit.
12 Ibid.
13 E. Williams, *Arbeitskommando* (Gollancz , 1975)
14 *Infantry Brigadier*, op. cit.
15 Ibid.
16 Personal communication to the author
17 *The War on Land*, op. cit.

18 *Infantry Brigadier*, op. cit.
19 Ibid.
20 G. Clifton, *The Happy Hunted* (Cassell, 1952)

Chapter 3

1 Edited, *Alamein and the Desert War (Sunday Times*, 1967)
2 *Taste of Courage*, loc. cit.
3 J. Costello, *Love Sex and War* (Collins, 1985)
4 Ibid.
5 Personal communication to the author
6 *Taste of Courage*, loc. cit.
7 Ibid.
8 B. Fergusson, *The Black Watch* (Collins, 1950)
9 Ibid.
10 *The Happy Hunted*, op. cit.
11 Ibid.
12 A. Moorehead, *African Trilogy* (Hamish Hamilton, 1944)

Chapter 4

1 T. Carew, *Hostages to Fortune* (Coronet, 1971)
2 Ibid.
3 *The War on Land*, loc. cit.
4 Ibid.
5 Ibid.
6 Ibid.
7 N. Barber, *A Sinister Twilight* (Collins, 1968)
8 Ibid.
9 Ibid.

Chapter 5

1 *A Sinister Twilight*, loc. cit.
2 Ibid.
3 Ibid.
4 Ibid
5 Personal communication to the author
6 *A Sinister Twilight*, op. cit.
7 *Taste of Courage*, loc. cit.
8 Ibid.
9 Ibid.
10 Ibid.
11 *The Times* 2 Feb., 1942
12 Peter Lewis, *A People's War* (Channel Four Books, 1986)

13 J. Kennedy, *The Business of War* (Hutchinson, 1957)
14 Ibid.
15 Ibid.
16 *A People's War*, op. cit.
17 J.F. Kennedy, *Why England Slept* (Funk N.Y., 1962)

Chapter 6

1 *Taste of Courage*, loc. cit.
2 J. and C. Blair, *Return from the River Kwai* (Futura, 1980)
3 R. Braddon, *The Naked Island* (Werner Laurie, 1950)
4 *Hostages to Fortune*, loc. cit.
5 *Return from the River Kwai*, op. cit.
6 *The War on Land*, loc. cit.
7 W. Slim, *Defeat into Victory* (Cassell, 1956)
8 Ibid.
9 *Taste of Courage*, op. cit.

Chapter 7

1 A. Moorehead, *A Year of Battle* (Hamilton, 1944)
2 Ibid.
3 Ibid.
4 *Taste of Courage*, loc. cit.
5 Ibid.
6 *A Year of Battle*, op. cit.
7 Ibid.
8 *The War on Land*, loc. cit.
9 *Taste of Courage*, op. cit.
10 Ibid.

BOOK THREE

Chapter 1

1 *Monty*, loc. cit.
2 D. Anderson, *Three Cheers for the Next Man to Die* (Hale, 1983)
3 *I Bought a Star*, loc. cit.
4 *And No Birds Sang*, loc. cit.
5 N. Hodson, *Home Front* (Gollancz, 1944)
6 R. Thompson, *D-Day* (Pan/Ballantine, 1970)
7 *Monty*, loc. cit.
8 *A People's War*, loc. cit.
9 Montgomery, *A Path to Leadership* (Collins, 1961)
10 O. Bradley, *A General's Story* (Simon & Schuster, 1983)

11 C. Ryan, *A Bridge Too Far* (Popular Library, 1968)
12 *The War on Land*, loc. cit.
13 *Monty*, op. cit.
14 Ibid.

Chapter 2

1 *Monty*, op. cit.
2 *The War on Land*, loc. cit.
3 *The Broken Plume*, loc. cit.
4 *The 51st Highland Division*, loc. cit.
5 *The Broken Plume*, op. cit.
6 F. de Guingand, *Operation Victory* (Hodder & Stoughton, 1947)
7 *The Broken Plume*, op. cit.
8 *The 51st Highland Division*, op. cit.
9 N. McCallum, *Journey with a Pistol* (Gollancz, 1959)
10 L. Phillips, *Alamein* (Pan, 1962)
11 *The Broken Plume*, op. cit.
12 Ibid.
13 Ibid.
14 Ibid.
15 *Alamein*, loc. cit.
16 Ibid.
17 *The War on Land* , op. cit.
18 Ibid.
19 *A People's War*, loc. cit.

Chapter 3

1 D. Eisenhower, *Crusade in Europe* (Doubleday, 1948)
2 *Sunday Times* 6 December 1986
3 H. Butcher, *My Three Years with Eisenhower* (Doubleday, 1946)
4 A. Moorehead, *The African Trilogy* (Four Square, 1947)
5 Personal communication to the author
6 Ibid.
7 Ibid.
8 *The Rommel Papers*, loc. cit.
9 Ibid.
10 W. Slim, *Defeat into Victory* (Cassell, 1950)
11 *The Naked Island*, loc. cit.
12 Ibid.
13 S. Chapman, *The Jungle is Neutral* (Chatto and Windus, 1950)
14 *Arbeitskommando*, loc. cit.
15 Personal communication to the author

Chapter 4

1 K. Summersby, (Collins, 1982)
2 Ibid.
3 M. Blumenson, *Kasserine* (Dell, 1963)
4 *Alex*, loc. cit.
5 Ibid.
6 *Kasserine*, loc. cit.
7 *Alex*, op. cit.
8 Ibid.
9 R. Martin, *The GI War* (Little Brown, 1962)
10 Kasserine, op. cit.
11 E. Harmon, *Combat Commander* (Prentice Hall, 1975)
12 *The Rommel Papers*, loc. cit.
13 F. Blake, *The 17/21 Lancers* (Leo Cooper, 1968)
14 *The Rommel Papers*, op. cit.
15 L. Farago, *Patton* (Oblensky Press, 1966)
16 Unknown, *Study of Allied Fighting Spirit* (1943)
17 Ibid.
18 Ibid.
19 V. Hickson, *The American Fighting Man* (Collier-Macmillan, 1969)
20 Private communication from Murchy family to the author

Chapter 5

1 C. Sykes, *Orde Wingate* (Collins, 1965)
2 B. Fergusson, *Beyond the Chindwin* (Fontana, 1955)
3 Ibid.
4 *Daily Telegraph* 20 Feb., 1943
5 *The War on Land*, loc. cit.
6 *Daily Telegraph*, op. cit.
7 Ibid.
8 *Beyond the Chindwin*, op. cit.
9 Ibid.
10 *War on Land*, loc. cit.
11 Ibid.
12 M. Calvert, *Prisoners of Hope* (Cape, 1952)
13 *Beyond the Chindwin*, op. cit.
14 Ibid.
15 Ibid.
16 Ibid.
17 Ibid.

NOTES

Chapter 6

1 *African Trilogy*, loc. cit.
2 Ibid.
3 Ibid.
4 *The GI War*, loc. cit.
5 Personal communication to the author
6 *Journey with a Pistol*, loc. cit.
7 A. Bowlby, *Recollections of Rifleman Bowlby* (Leo Cooper, 1972)
8 Ibid.
9 *Journey with a Pistol*, op. cit.
10 *The GI War*, op. cit.
11 H. Pond, *Salerno* (Pan, 1968)
12 Ibid.
13 M. Blumenson, *General Mark Clark* (Cape, 1985)
14 Ibid.
15 Alan Patient, *Mutiny at Salerno, Listener* 25 Feb., 1982
16 *Monty*, loc. cit.
17 *Salerno*, op. cit.
18 *Monty*, op. cit.
19 Ibid.

BOOK FOUR

Chapter 1

1 A. Moorehead, *Eclipse* (Collins, 1945)
2 *Monty*, loc. cit.
3 Ibid.
4 Ibid.
5 M. Lindsay, *So Few Got Through* (Arrow, 1950)
6 A. McKee, *Caen* (Papermac, 1964)
7 *The 51st Highland Division*, loc. cit.
8 Ibid.
9 D. Irving, *War Between the Generals* (Gogdon and Weed, 1981)
10 Ibid.
11 P. Fussell, *The Boy Scout's Handbook* (Oxford, 1982)
12 Edited, BBC War Report (Collins, 1945)

Chapter 2

1 *Recollections of Rifleman Bowlby*, loc. cit.
2 Ibid.
3 Ibid.
4 Ibid.

5 H. Burton, *The Ski Troops* (Simon and Schuster, 1971)
6 Ibid.
7 M. Clark, *Calculated Risk* (Harrap, 1951)
8 M. Motley, *The Invisible Soldier* (Wayne State University Press, 1975)
9 Ibid.
10 *The Stars and Stripes*, November, 1944
11 *The War On Land*, loc. cit.
12 Ibid.
13 Ibid.
14 J. Ellis, *Cassino* (Deutsch, 1983)
15 *Recollections of Rifleman Bowlby*, loc. cit.
16 V. Hicken, *The American Fighting Man* (Collins, 1969)
17 J. Masters, *The Road Past Mandalay* (Joseph, 1970)
18 Ibid.

Chapter 3

1 A. Swinson, *Kohima* (Arrow, 1966)
2 *The Taste of Courage*, loc. cit.
3 Ibid.
4 Ibid.
5 Ibid.
6 Ibid.
7 Ibid.
8 *Kohima*, op. cit.
9 BBC War Report, loc. cit.
10 *Kohima*, op. cit.
11 *The Taste of Courage*, op. cit.
12 Ibid.
13 *Kohima*, op. cit.
14 *Defeat into Victory*, loc. cit.
15 Ibid.

Chapter 4

1 H. Essame, *The 43rd Wessex Division at War* (Clowes, 1952)
2 J. Costello, *Love Sex and War* (Collins, 1985)
3 Ibid.
4 R. Meriam, *Dark December* (Ballantine, 1947)
5 Ibid.
6 *The GI War*, loc. cit.
7 Ibid.
8 *A General's Story*, loc. cit.
9 *The GI War*, loc. cit.
10 C. MacDonald, *The Battle of the Hürtgen Forest* (Prentice Hall, 1956)
11 E. Hemingway, *Colliers* (December, 1944)

12 *The Battle of the Hürtgen Forest,* op. cit.
13 P. Boesch, *Road to Hürtgen Forest in Hell* (Gulf, 1962)
14 *Colliers,* op. cit.
15 *The Battle of the Hürtgen Forest,* op. cit.
16 *Colliers,* op. cit.

Chapter 5

1   C. MacDonald, *Company Commander* (Ballantine, 1947)
2   Ibid.
3   Ibid.
4   Ibid.
5   Ibid.
6   Ibid.
7   H. Dupuy, *Lion in the Way* (Infantry Press, 1947)
8   *The Stars and Stripes* Jan. 1945
9   M. Brooks, *Playboy* 1982
10 C. Whiting, *Death of a Division* (Leo Cooper, 1975)
11 Ibid.
12 Ibid.
13 L. Atwell, *Private* (Dell Books , 1946)
14 Ibid.
15 *The GI War,* loc. cit.
16 *Company Commander,* op. cit.
17 *The GI War,* loc. cit.
18 *The Boy Scout's Handbook,* loc. cit.

Chapter 6

1   R. Wingfield, *The Only Way Out* (Hutchinson, 1956)
2   Ibid.
3   Ibid.
4   *Few Got Through,* loc. cit.
5   Ibid.
6   Ibid.
7   *The 51st Highland Division,* loc. cit.
8   Ibid.
9   Ibid.
10 Ibid.
11 *The Only Way Out,* op. cit.
12 Ibid.
13 Ibid.
14 Ibid.
15 Ibid.
16 Ibid.
17 R.W. Thompson, *Men Under Fire* (MacDonald, 1945)

18 Ibid.

Chapter 7

1 *Defeat into Victory,* loc. cit.
2 J. Masters, *Bugles and a Tiger* (Michael, Joseph , 1962)
3 Ibid.
4 *The Taste of Courage,* loc. cit.
5 Ibid.
6 The GI War, loc. cit.
7 Ibid.
8 Ibid.
9 Ibid.
10 G. Cox, *Road to Trieste* (Heineman, 1947)
11 Private communication to the author
12 *The GI War,* op. cit.
13 S. Terkel, *The Good War* (Hamilton, 1985)
14 Personal communication to the author
15 C. Whiting, *Finale at Flensburg* (Leo Cooper, 1973)
16 Ibid.
17 *Men Under Fire,* loc. cit.
18 Ibid.
19 *Taste of Courage,* op. cit.
20 *Naked Island,* loc. cit.
21 Private, loc. cit.

Envoi

1 *The Good War,* loc. cit.
2 *Boy Scout's Handbook,* loc. cit.
3 Private communication to the author
4 *Eclipse,* loc. cit.
5 *The Good War,* op. cit.
6 R. Woollcombe, *The Lion Rampant* (Leo Cooper, 1970)

Index